PRISMATIC THOUGHT

THEODOR W. ADORNO

Peter Uwe Hohendahl

University of Nebraska Press

Lincoln & London

⊗ The paper in this book meets the minimum
requirements of American National Standard for
Information Sciences – Permanence of Paper for
Printed Library Materials, ANSI z39.48-1984.

First paperback printing: 1997
Most recent printing indicated by the
first digit: 1 2 3 4 5 6 7 8 9 10

Library of Congress Cataloging
in Publication Data
Hohendahl, Peter Uwe. Prismatic thought:
Theodor W. Adorno / Peter Uwe Hohendahl.
p. cm. – (Modern German culture and literature)
Includes bibliographical references (p.) and index.
ISBN 0-8032-2378-1 (cloth: alkaline paper)
ISBN 0-8032-7305-3 (paperback: alkaline paper)
1. Adorno, Theodor W., 1903–1969. I. Title II. Series
B3199.A34H634 1995 193–dc20 95-3048 CIP

Parts of the present work appeared
in slightly different versions in the following works:
New German Critique 56 (1992); *Thesis
Eleven* 34 (1993); *Traditions of Experiment from the
Enlightenment to the Present*, ed.
Nancy Kaiser and David Wellbery, University of
Michigan Press, 1992; *Reason
and Its Other: Rationality in Modern German
Philosophy and Culture*, ed.
Dieter Freundlieb and Wayne Hudson,
Berg Publishers,
1993

Contents

Preface

✳

As more than one critic of Adorno has acknowledged, the presentation of his theory to an uninitiated audience, especially in the English-speaking world, borders on the impossible. Among serious readers of Adorno's work it has become a commonplace to argue that his style, the embeddedness of his thoughts in the language of German idealism, makes it exceedingly difficult to communicate his ideas in modern English prose, which demands simplicity, brevity, and clarity. While this is certainly true, it does not completely explain the unusual complexity of Adorno's work. Even if one recognizes the peculiar form of his writings and underscores the intricacy of his dialectic (especially in his late work), one has not yet fully accounted for the difficulty of Adorno's texts. There are two additional concerns which any critic has to address: the subjective character and the antisystematic, essayistic nature of Adorno's writings. Both aspects, however, need clarification to avoid misunderstanding. By subjective, I do not mean impressionistic or whimsical; rather, I want to point to the way Adorno makes use of the philosophical and intellectual tradition. As much as he is aware of and acknowledges the critical tradition in which his own writings are grounded, he does not see himself as someone who either continues or simply breaks away from this tradition. Instead, his work breaks up and displaces the elements of the philosophical tradition. Clearly, Adorno uses them in a highly personal and individualistic manner.

The same holds for the scope and organization of his work. It does not suffice to stress the multifaceted and interdisciplinary character of Adorno's oeuvre, the fact that he was equally at home in philosophy and music, in literature and sociology; one has to come to grips with Adorno's unique way of approaching the topics of his interest. His work ultimately resists the desire for systematic order, the search for a grand design that gives meaning to all the individual texts. Each piece, the small essay or the major study, follows its own internal logic, which cannot be schematically extended to other parts of Adorno's work. To put it differently, there is no obvious Archimedean point from which all parts can be read and understood. Thus the difference between center and margin becomes unstable. Even advanced readers of Adorno have found it difficult to deal with the consequences of this structure. On the one hand, it problematizes the preference for Adorno's more systematic studies, such as *Negative Dialectics* and *Aesthetic Theory,* as the supposed core of his writings; on the other, it encourages the reader to take seriously the reading of his essays and smaller pieces. The distinction between major works and minor pieces collapses; accordingly, Adorno ought to be explored from the margins. With this in mind, my introductory chapter examines, in more detail, the possibilities and limits of present Adorno criticism.

Involved in this process of rereading and reassessing is the person of Adorno himself, for the orthodox interpretation of his texts has gone hand in hand with certain assumptions about Adorno's biography and his position within the context of the Frankfurt School as well as in the larger historical constellation that motivated his work. Accordingly, part one continues with a reconsideration of two rather controversial aspects of Adorno's life: chapter 2 explores the significance of his years in American exile; chapter 3 examines his role in postwar Germany and the relevance of postfascist society there to his thought. In part two, chapters 4 and 5 deal with Adorno's essays on literature. Together with a reassessment of his controversial theory of mass culture in chapter 6 and in chapter 7, a reconsideration of his sociology of art, they raise methodological questions, which in the case of Adorno are closely related to questions of rhetoric and style. Part three addresses adjacent theoretical issues, beginning in chapter 8 with a more specific examination of Adorno's concept of art and the problems of grounding a philosophy of art. Chapter 9 turns to an issue that has not been sufficiently explored: Adorno's understanding of language, especially its function in philosophy. Finally, the epilogue summarizes his place in criticism today.

I do not attempt to offer a comprehensive analysis of Adorno's oeuvre; that would be a highly problematic endeavor. Instead, I mean to engage Adorno's texts from a number of different but overlapping perspectives, thereby searching for fresh insights. Although Adorno retained a concept of totality (as a strategically necessary means of understanding the concrete), his writings can hardly be subsumed under traditional philosophical or aesthetic categories. Accordingly, this study, responding to Adorno's strategy, proceeds by examining specific themes and problems to the point where they unfold their critical potential as well as their limitations.

Earlier versions of the first and second chapters appeared in *New German Critique*; part of the fourth chapter was first published in *Traditions of Experiment from the Enlightenment to the Present*, edited by Nancy Kaiser and David Wellbery; the fifth chapter, on Adorno and Heine, appeared in a slightly different version in *Reason and Its Other: Rationality in Modern German Philosophy and Culture*, edited by Dieter Freundlieb and Wayne Hudson; and an earlier version of the sixth chapter first appeared in the journal *Thesis Eleven*. I am grateful for the permission to make use of these essays.

This book benefited greatly from many friends and colleagues who read individual chapters or larger parts of the manuscript. Special thanks go to David Bathrick, Hal Foster, Martin Jay, Shierry Weber Nicholsen, and Anson Rabinbach for their critical comments and their encouragement. I owe gratitude to Adam Schnitzer and especially to Arthur Strum, who helped with the process of editing the manuscript. Arthur Strum's advice concerning the translation of Adorno quotations was invaluable. And last, but not least, I thank Gisela Podleski, who prepared the manuscript.

Finally, a word on citation. Whenever possible, I have used Adorno's *Gesammelte Schriften*, edited by Gretel Adorno and Rolf Tiedemann (Frankfurt am Main: Suhrkamp, 1973–); references to this edition are given within the text in parentheses, citing volume and page number (for example, GS 11:115). Where reliable English translations are available, I have consulted and used them as well, though sometimes with modifications; references to these translations are also given in parentheses (for instance, DE 87). Even when the translations are my own, as is uniformly the case for *Aesthetic Theory,* I have also given the reference to the existing English edition for those readers who are unfamiliar with German.

Abbreviations Used for Adorno's Works

AE   *Against Epistemology: A Metacritique.* Trans. Willis Domingo. Cambridge: MIT Press, 1983.

AT   *Aesthetic Theory.* Trans. C. Lenhardt. London: Routledge & Kegan Paul, 1984.

DE   With Max Horkheimer. *Dialectic of Enlightenment.* Trans. John Cumming. New York: Herder & Herder, 1972.

FW   'Fragmente über Wagner.' *Zeitschrift für Sozialforschung* 8 (1939–40): 1–49.

GS   *Gesammelte Schriften.* Ed. Rolf Tiedemann. Frankfurt am Main: Suhrkamp, 1973– (edition not yet complete).

ISM   *Introduction to the Sociology of Music.* Trans. E. B. Ashton. New York: Seabury Press, 1976.

ISW   *In Search of Wagner.* Trans. Rodney Livingstone. London: New Left Books, 1981.

MM   *Minima Moralia: Reflections from Damaged Life.* Trans. E. F. N. Jephcott. London: Verso, 1974.

ND   *Negative Dialectics.* Trans. E. B. Ashton. New York: Continuum, 1987.

NL   *Notes to Literature.* 2 vols. Trans. Shierry Weber Nicholsen. New York: Columbia University Press, 1991–92.

PR   *Prisms.* Trans. Samuel and Shierry Weber. Cambridge: MIT Press, 1981.

PART ONE: CONTEXTS

1. Approaches to Adorno: A Tentative Typology

ALTHOUGH the Marxist project has fallen on hard times since the collapse of the Communist bloc, the work of Theodor W. Adorno has received more attention in recent years than during the 1970s, when Western Marxism was the most significant oppositional theory in literary and cultural studies. The return of Adorno after years of relative neglect is particularly remarkable because it does not easily fit into any of the intellectual trends of the late 1980s and early 1990s. There is a growing awareness now that Adorno criticism cannot continue in its traditional form, for its grasp of Adorno's work was predicated on general assumptions that have since been challenged. First, it has become quite clear that the textual basis of American Adorno criticism has been shaky. Some of the existing translations are inadequate and have to be replaced – particularly *Aesthetic Theory,* but even *Dialectic of Enlightenment* has room for improvement.[1] The need for more accurate translations is closely related to the style of revisionist readings of Adorno's texts, since some make use of more radical forms of exegesis.[2] Although it would be difficult to link Adorno's theoretical efforts with postcolonial studies or feminist theory, it would not be impossible to develop a feminist position out of his oeuvre.

The most obvious explanation for the increasing interest in Adorno's work may be the poststructuralist connection: the supposed affinity between his project of negative dialectics and the antiessentialist and antimetaphysical turn in American criticism during the 1980s. More than one critic has suggested that Adorno may ultimately be closer to Jacques Derrida than to Georg Lukács or even Max Horkheimer. Yet the discovery of the 'poststructuralist' Adorno, as important as it has been for the revival of his reputation in the United States, certainly does not explain the intensity of the present debate and the outspoken hostility among some readers. His work has become the site of heated discussions and controversies because it has been claimed for different and conflicting intellectual agendas. In this respect, the present configuration in the United States differs significantly from that in Germany, where Adorno is mostly seen as part of a Marxist tradition that has been marginalized since the 1980s. In fact, one could argue that the somewhat marginal position of the Frankfurt School in this country encouraged interaction between Adorno's theory and other oppositional forces and that the interpretation of Adorno is, implicitly or explicitly, determined by conflicting modes of appropriation. For this reason, the historical approach that has dominated much of the recent work on Western Marxism seems to be less appropriate.[3]

The present debate is not chiefly about placing Adorno on a historical map, although forms of mapping may well be included in the various critical agendas. For instance, Fredric Jameson's radical claim that Adorno's work represents the legitimate form of Marxism for the 1990s implies a trajectory that leads from the Lukács of the 1920s, via the work of the Frankfurt School during the 1930s and 1940s, to Adorno's late writings, especially *Negative Dialectics* and *Aesthetic Theory*. Similarly, the contention that Adorno's postwar theory anticipates the poststructuralist turn of the 1970s reorganizes the historical map by taking Adorno out of the history of Marxism and claiming him for the history of the poststructuralist project. On this map he is obviously closer to Friedrich Nietzsche and Martin Heidegger than to Lukács, Antonio Gramsci, and Jürgen Habermas.

The following remarks are not intended to offer a survey of Adorno's American reception during the last twenty years or so.[4] Instead, they focus on the interface between reading and appropriation. The result might be termed a tentative typology of recent Adorno criticism in the United States. Accordingly, I emphasize common elements within a specific approach rather than nuances of reading and historical fluctuations within the work of individual critics. I distinguish the following positions: a strategy of (political) distancing, the poststructuralist rereading, the postmodernist critique, and a return to the 'authentic' Adorno. It goes without saying that in all instances the acts of reading, as well as

4

the construct of Adorno and his work that are the result of these readings, are politically informed; they clearly demarcate political positions within the American theoretical debate. Without this assumption the controversial nature of the present debate would be difficult to understand and to appreciate.

The political critique of Adorno has focused on his persona as well as on his writings, especially the late ones. This approach dominated much of German Adorno criticism during the 1970s when adherents of the New Left (many of them Adorno's disciples) tried to rewrite and utilize his work for their struggle against an increasingly repressive West German state. Adorno's reluctance to get involved in the political activities of the student movement and his resistance to emphatic notions of social praxis had resulted in a widening gap between the political position of the New Left (including Hans Magnus Enzensberger, Oskar Negt, Claus Offe, and Wolfgang Lefèvre), on the one hand, and that of the older generation of the Frankfurt School on the other (with Jürgen Habermas right in the middle). The New Left's critique focused on the lack of a political – that is, revolutionary – dimension in Adorno's work and his tendency to reestablish theory for its own sake (the regression to a Young Hegelian position). Similarly, the American New Left emphasized the difference between Adorno's position and the Marxist project as it was carried out, for instance, in the work of Herbert Marcuse. The search for revolutionary agents during the late 1960s and early 1970s disqualified much of Adorno's oeuvre, since it openly refused to offer an explicit political and revolutionary agenda.

From the point of view of the New Left, the evaluation of Adorno could either stress and condemn the distance between the political vanguard and the philosopher or underscore those elements in Adorno's writing that might, when used in a different context, be revitalized. The first strategy would tend to call for a more orthodox Marxist position (with a possible emphasis on the Feuerbach theses); the latter strategy would problematize the Marxist heritage in the work of Adorno and the Frankfurt School. Here the argument would point in the opposite direction: it would underscore the orthodox moments in Adorno's writing as the real reason for his shortcomings in the political arena. In this reading, the Frankfurt School failed not because its members abandoned the safe ground of Marxist theory but because they were impeded by the orthodox baggage they carried along. The call for a greater distance between the New Left and Adorno, in this instance, also stressed the need for a more critical approach to Critical Theory, the need for revisions that might safeguard the political project. This position is summarized succinctly in Paul Piccone's remark of 1977:

> In Adorno, especially, the dialectic becomes dehistoricized to cover the whole of Western civilization as the genesis of the domination of the concept. Consequently, critical theory does not even attempt to prefigure the future by elaborating the mediations necessary to bring it about, and becomes purely defensive; it ultimately retreats to defend particularity, autonomy and non-identity against an allegedly totally administered society where thinking itself disappears as a dispensable luxury.[5]

The point of the political critique is Adorno's pessimism and the lack of an emancipatory impulse in his writings beyond the moment of individual opposition. Similar concerns, although couched in a more academic style, can be found in Fredric Jameson's Adorno chapter of *Marxism and Form* (1971), which describes the late work, especially *Negative Dialectics*, as a 'massive failure' insofar as negative dialectics tries, against all odds, to save philosophy itself.[6] Jameson makes this attempt responsible for a lack of political commitment. Interestingly enough, however, he equally insists on the incomparable quality of Adorno's work as a model of the dialectical thought process, thereby balancing the lack of political commitment (generally abhorred by the New Left) with the sophistication of negative dialectics.

What Jameson alluded to in the early 1970s – namely, the complexity of Adorno's thought, especially of his conception of negative dialectics – became the focal point of the poststructuralist rereading of Adorno's writings during the 1980s. This reorientation followed a similar shift in the appropriation of Walter Benjamin's work by deconstructivist critics to whom the Marxist tradition and the Frankfurt School, as a part of this tradition, meant less (if anything at all) than Adorno's epistemological critique of phenomenology and the ontological project.[7] What characterizes the poststructuralist approach to Adorno is its deliberate attempt to distinguish his work from the body of Marxist theory and to underscore the difference between his thought and the conceptual apparatus of Marxist theory. This strategy can be directed either against other members of the Frankfurt School (such as Horkheimer or Marcuse) or at the post-Adornian turn of Critical Theory in the work of Jürgen Habermas and his students (for instance, Thomas McCarthy). In other words, the question of reason and rationality becomes the touchstone for the poststructuralist reading. Hence, the poststructuralist appropriation tends to deny the dogmatic unity of Critical Theory; it seeks to foreground epistemological problems and shows little interest in the question of social praxis and political relevance.

The obvious and most promising point of departure for this project is Adorno and Horkheimer's critique of the Western philosophical tradition in *Dialectic of Enlightenment*. Adorno's critique of the enlightenment project – with its emphasis on universal history, the autonomy of the subject, and the unity of reason and rationality through the transparency of language and communication – becomes the focus for poststructuralist readings. In this configuration Adorno is perceived as a rigorous antimetaphysical thinker who struggles against any form of (Hegelian) synthesis, someone who seeks out ruptures and breaks and consistently attacks the traditional epistemological preference for identity. Hence, the new context for the interpretation of Adorno is the work of Heidegger, Jacques Lacan, and Derrida. As Rainer Nägele notes: 'Given the eminent presence of Heidegger, especially in Derrida's and Lacan's thinking, a careful reading of this setting apart (*Auseinandersetzung*) might perhaps be the best beginning to trace the constellation of Critical Theory and Deconstruction.'[8]

As one might expect, this interpretation draws primarily on *Negative Dialectics* in order to sustain the proximity of Adorno to Derrida and Lacan. Adorno's rigorous and somewhat polemical critique of Heidegger in *Negative Dialectic* serves a special purpose: it underlines the parallel between Adorno and Derrida, each of whom developed his own version of negativity through a critique of Heidegger's ontology.[9] Whereas intellectual historians such as Martin Jay and Eugene Lunn emphasized the Hegelian tradition in the work of the Frankfurt School, and therefore also underscored the centrality of the concept of totality as the epistemological as well as historical horizon of their project,[10] the poststructuralist approach focuses on Adorno's critique of traditional logic, especially identity logic and its extension into the concept of the subject. This reading wants to subvert what Marxist theory had, by and large, taken for granted and therefore ascribed to the writings of Adorno: namely, a stable concept of subjectivity and agency (as opposed to the state of fragmentation and passivity found in advanced capitalism, for instance). The poststructuralist reading would emphasize Adorno's critique of subjectivity, a critique that does not merely focus (as does Lukács) on fragmentation under monopoly capitalism but rather calls the entire Western tradition – the very constitution of subjectivity and identity in Greek culture – into question.

The potential danger of this approach is its one-sided insistence on the subversion of the subject, since Adorno, unlike structuralist Marxists such as Louis Althusser, did not treat the subject as a moment of pure ideology. *Negative Dialectics* does not cancel the subject; rather, the text unfolds the dialectical tension between the principle of domination and the resistance to the social system. In a different dimension, this question resurfaces in Adorno's interpretation of Sigmund Freud. Is the integration of the Freudian corpus into Critical Theory based on ego psychology, or is it closer to Lacan's reading of Freud? Clearly, the poststructuralist reading prefers the latter. Quoting a passage from *Negative Dialectics*, Nägele argues that Adorno does not simply follow the traditional Freudian view that the Id should be replaced by the Ego; instead, as Nägele writes, 'both Adorno and Lacan undermine the traditional and dominant interpretation, according to which the I is supposed to appropriate "it" and replace "it." . . . Adorno and Lacan instead read the "where I [*sic*] was" as the constitutive

8

ground in which the I is rooted and founded.'[11] Nägele therefore insists that Adorno's understanding and use of Freud do not follow the lines of ego psychology and its emphasis on progressive development. Similarly, he submits that Adorno must not be understood as part of the Enlightenment project as it was redefined by Jürgen Habermas.

It is not surprising, therefore, that the poststructuralist approach emphatically validates what Habermas critiqued severely. Habermas's repeated interventions – first in *The Theory of Communicative Action* (1981) and later in *The Philosophical Discourse of Modernity* (1985) – against the loss of a rational grounding of Adorno and Horkheimer's project during the 1940s (beginning with *Dialectic of Enlightenment*) indeed demarcates the boundary between the poststructuralist celebration of the noncommunicative aspect of language and the subversion of rationality. Where the poststructuralist method underscores Adorno's interest in marginalized phenomena that have traditionally escaped the logic of the *grand récit* of history, Habermas invokes the possibility and indeed necessity of self-reflection in human relations. It goes without saying that this opposition has been played out with a great deal of acrimony on both sides, and both sides tend to claim Adorno (in the case of the Habermasians, of course, this claim is modified by their aversion toward the 'irrational' aspect of Adorno's work).

The poststructuralist insistence on Adorno's refusal to support the grand design of historical synthesis and teleology – his supposed refusal, in other words, to read the Marxist tradition through the lens of Hegel – deserves our special attention, since it contrasts sharply with the understanding of Adorno's work in the postmodernism debate and the recent discussion of mass culture. Here Adorno and Horkheimer play the role of heavies who have, without much respect for details, developed a totalizing theory of mass culture, based on questionable notions of the development of twentieth-century capitalism. Exclusively preoccupied with an outdated and outlandish conception of high culture, they fail to address the interaction between social groups and their (popular) cultures. In the oppositional logic, which divides modernism

from postmodernism, Adorno is perceived as a firm and sometimes rigid defender of the modernist position, especially in his
work on modern music and his late aesthetic theory. While the
postmodernist discourse has undermined the binary opposition
of high and low culture or, respectively, of advanced and regressive
art, Adorno's emphasis on the principle of aesthetic autonomy,
which cannot be overlooked, has encouraged his critics to see him
as a traditional modernist.

The postmodernist reading of Adorno's work has mostly focused on the culture industry chapter of *Dialectic of Enlightenment,* for this chapter seems to epitomize the tendency of the
Frankfurt School, and of Adorno in particular, to contrast nineteenth-century bourgeois high culture with twentieth-century
mass culture, linking this opposition closely to the transition from
liberal to monopoly capitalism. Adorno's failure, then, is seen as a
nostalgic normative appraisal of bourgeois culture as it was constituted in the bourgeois public sphere during the eighteenth and
early nineteenth centuries. Jim Collins, for instance, remarks,
'Rather than conceiving of the transition from the Enlightenment
to the Industrial Age as a shift from one public sphere to multiple
spheres, critics of mass culture from Matthew Arnold to Jean Bau-
drillard have characterized this transition as a profound fall from
grace, in which the twin evils of mechanization and commodification have eliminated any kind of cultural heterogeneity.'[12]

The emphasis of this critique is placed on the concept of heterogeneity and its application to modern mass culture. According to
Collins, who tries to summarize the postmodernist position vis-
à-vis mass culture, Adorno and Horkheimer's reading of mass
culture is characterized by three problematic tendencies: first, the
assumption of a center that defines the cultural essence of an era;
second, the presupposition that all cultural production is based
on a unitary master system; and third, the theoretical belief that
the evaluation of art has to distinguish between authentic art and
inauthentic, mass-produced pseudo-art. As a result, Adorno is
portrayed as a culture critic who sees himself as a defender of high
culture against the onslaught of mass culture.

The most troubling presupposition of the Adorno-Hork-heimer essay is the fundamental centrality and cohesiveness of all cultural activity supposedly produced by this cabal of executive authorities. This notion of culture czars in mas-ter control rooms orchestrating all forms of mass culture bears a striking resemblance to the visions of the State con-structed by Fritz Lang films of the twenties, especially *Me-tropolis* (1926), in which the State is conceived as one enor-mous circular Grand Hotel where the evil capitalist bosses reside at the top and the workers reside in the basement.[13]

What is most remarkable about this critique is its purely descrip-tive quality and its inability to define more clearly Horkheimer and Adorno's theoretical frame: namely, the conception of ad-vanced capitalism ('Fordism') and its fundamental restructuring of the relations of production. In other words, Collins's repression of the Marxist tradition and, especially, of the Lukácsian heritage in the work of the Frankfurt School (for example, its use of the concept of reification) results in a considerable flattening of the culture industry chapter. As a consequence, Adorno's critique of mass culture is never seen in its proper place as a reflection of the power of Western rationalism. In a strange reversal, for Collins, Adorno and Horkheimer become the defenders of the very en-lightenment that their own analysis challenged. Their further characterization as belated romantics underscores Collins's failure to understand the importance of European romanticism for the critique of the Enlightenment project.[14]

Of course, the radical rejection of Adorno's work, exemplified by the Collins book, defines merely one possible position within the postmodernist discourse. Tania Modleski's introduction to the essay volume *Studies in Entertainment: Critical Approaches to Mass Culture* (1986) offers a more carefully delineated and more balanced evaluation which, among other things, is quite con-scious of the importance of the Marxist tradition in the Frank-furt School. Still, there is a similar note in her assessment when she castigates the 'oversimplification' in Adorno's understanding of mass culture, especially in his theory of manipulation.[15] Again, behind her assessment of Adorno and Horkheimer lurks the assumption that as 'foreigners' on American soil they possibly misunderstood American mass culture (as if Adorno had been less critical of similar phenomena in Germany). Therefore, she stresses the need for a different approach by a new generation of American scholars, because the members of the Frankfurt School 'were too far outside the culture they examined.'[16] This claim is balanced, however, by the observation that the present generation appears to be too close to contemporary mass culture, which is definitely in need of a critical perspective, as the work of the Frankfurt School[17] maintained.

As we have seen, Adorno's place in the postmodernist discourse is highly contested; evaluations range from extreme rejection to critical acceptance. In either case, postmodernist readings (apart from their high degree of selectivity) bring to bear on Adorno's writings a paradigm with preconceived concepts quite different from the poststructuralist interest in Adorno. Whereas the poststructuralist approach embraces Adorno's work as fundamentally compatible with the writings of Derrida (although possibly less radical), the postmodernist discourse sets its own normative standards against which Adorno has to be read. The somewhat predictable result is a tendency of postmodernism to emphasize the distance between itself and Adorno. In Fredric Jameson's reassessment of contemporary mass culture in 1979, for instance, the work of the Frankfurt School serves as the foil for the constitution of a new postmodernist paradigm.[18] But Jameson, unlike Collins, not only fully recognizes the theoretical paradigm of the Frankfurt School (commodification and reification) but also uses it as a springboard for his own theory. His critique points to the centrality of modernism and the avant-garde in the work of Adorno: 'What is unsatisfactory about the Frankfurt School position is not the negative and critical apparatus, but rather the positive value on which the latter depends, namely the valorization of traditional modernist high art as the locus of some genuinely critical and subversive, "autonomous" aesthetic production.'[19]

Although the centrality of modernism can hardly be questioned in Adorno's writings, the claim that he celebrates modernism dogmatically and uncritically is more problematic. As Andreas Huyssen has pointed out in his reading of Adorno's writings on mass culture – a reading that can be seen as an answer to Jameson's position – modernism and mass culture cannot be separated in Adorno's work; they are, so to speak, opposite sides of the same coin.[20] Thus Jameson's claim that mass culture must be understood as the supplement of high culture turns out to be closer to Adorno than he wants us to believe.

For this reason, it is not entirely surprising that Jameson changed his position in his 1990 study: now he maintains that Adorno's version of Critical Theory, a dialectical version, 'which was no great help in the previous periods, may turn out to be just what we need today.'[21] In other words, the connection between Adorno's Marxism and postmodernism is no longer seen diachronically as different phases in history but rather synchronically as intertwined moments of a larger historical dialectic that must be unfolded in terms of an overarching Marxist theory. What has made *Late Marxism: Adorno or the Persistence of the Dialectic* so highly controversial is Jameson's twofold claim: first, his emphatic defense of Adorno as a Marxist philosopher; second, his attempt to close the gap between Adorno's aesthetic theory, which appears to be so firmly grounded in modernism, and a postmodernist problematic.[22] Jameson's reading of Adorno's late writings is predicated on the thesis that Adorno is first and foremost a theorist of late capitalism: that is, a social and cultural formation in which the traditional conceptual tools of Marxist theory (such as class and class conflict) seem to be less appropriate. Thus, the link between culture and society has to be reformulated. Jameson wants to insert Adorno's theory into the postmodern age by arguing that postmodernism is a later and more developed version of the positivism that Adorno attacked during the 1960s. In this context 'even his [Adorno's] archaic economics now seems apt and timely. . . . The utterly outmoded doctrine of monopoly capitalism may be just the image we need.'[23] Obviously, this reading is involved in a process of transcoding that reassembles the elements of Adorno's theory in unfamiliar ways – in itself a postmodernist approach that many of Jameson's critics have rejected as hermeneutically unsound.[24] In any case, however, Jameson should receive credit for asking a crucial question: what is the meaning and function of Adorno today? His answer stresses the local character of Adorno's theory: that is, its embeddedness in the First World as well as its limited but important function within this First World: namely, upholding dialectical thinking. Interestingly enough, this final and somewhat pessimistic note appears to exclude rather than include the moment of critical negativity as a form of social opposition and intervention.

The pressing question, then, can be formulated in the following way: what are the parameters for the return of Adorno? How should his writings be approached and used during the 1990s? Is the power of theory the major challenge for his new readers, or is theory's critical potential (through negativity) a viable moment in the process of appropriation? The reader of recent Adorno criticism in the United States may not find an immediate answer to these questions. The ongoing debate about Adorno's role in the late twentieth century is sometimes overshadowed by polemical infights between groups each claiming Adorno's work for its own purposes. The assertion that Critical Theory and Western Marxism must return to Adorno in order to regain their critical edge is frequently accompanied by attacks on other camps or individual theorists. The return of Adorno, then, is constructed as a narrative in which his persona and work have to be rescued from the clutches of false admirers or critics. For obvious reasons, both postmodernist theorists such as Fredric Jameson and post-Marxist theorists such as Jürgen Habermas come under attack, since they either explicitly or implicitly disagree with Adorno's position. One could also reverse this relationship and argue that the discussion about the fate of Critical Theory – that is, its change from a dialectical to a systematic social theory – together with the unresolved problems of the present cultural situation (postmodernism) have motivated and shaped the recent Adorno reception.

The defense of Adorno is frequently structured as a two-pronged attack against deconstruction or postmodernism, on the one hand, and the post-Marxist theory of Habermas, on the other. Strategically, this defense – which, incidentally, shares with Jameson an orientation toward the future (the 'true' Adorno has still to be discovered), although it does not recognize Jameson as a potential ally – describes and evaluates criticism of Adorno as intentional or unintentional misreadings caused by the particular biases of his critics. Insistence on the absolute truth value of his theory is particularly strong in some of the essays on Adorno published in *Telos*. In the 1970s the journal was sympathetic to the work of the Frankfurt School, though it kept a critical distance; in the more recent essays of Thomas Kuhn and Robert Hullot-Kentor this distance has disappeared.[25] For these members of a younger generation, the restitution of Adorno's work marks a decisive turningpoint in the American intellectual debate. Adorno's return signals the return of a dialectical and materialist theory that was lost during the 1980s in the writings of Jameson, Terry Eagleton, and Habermas.

The new agenda is not always easy to define, because it has to be separated from its polemical rhetoric, which tends to get bogged down in details of interpretation.[26] Still, certain features of this position emerge in various forms. Unlike the poststructuralists, Hullot-Kentor and Kuhn insist on and emphatically defend Adorno's dialectical reason as the essential core of Critical Theory. In other words, *Dialectic of Enlightenment* does not, as Habermas charged in *The Theory of Communicative Action* and *The Philosophical Discourse of Modernity*, chart the end of reason but unfolds its critique through the means of reason. In this defense both Immanuel Kant and G. W. F. Hegel, not to mention Friedrich von Schiller, can retain their rightful positions as part of the intellectual tradition on which Adorno drew, whereas Nietzsche – who is clearly of great importance for a poststructuralist reading, especially in the context of a radical critique of reason – does not figure prominently in this reconstruction of Adorno's project. Rather, it is Schiller's aesthetic theory that is given the important role of a precursor of Adorno's aesthetic theory. In Hullot-Kentor's view, in sharp contrast to Habermas's theory of social differentiation in modern society (where the aesthetic realm is indeed separate and independent from rationality), the utopian moment of the Enlightenment remains grounded in the aesthetic.[27] Hence, in Adorno's work, liberation cannot be thought without aesthetic reflection.[28] In this construction, which seems to show no awareness of the logic of Habermas's theory of modernity, art and reason remain entwined because reason is seen as critical philosophy rather than as instrumental reason or purposive rationality.

As the direction of Hullot-Kentor's argument makes quite clear, the ground on which the return of Adorno is conceived is first and foremost epistemological. The argument against Adorno's 'pessimism,' an argument that plays an important role in the defense of his politics, is derived from theoretical rather than immediate political or social considerations. Thus the question of his political commitment (or his lack of it) and the broader question of the theory/practice dialectic have again come into the foreground. Indeed, with Michael Sullivan and John Lysaker, one has to ask how these questions should be addressed.[29] Possibly, as they suggest, the questions need to be reformulated in the 1990s. Preconceived notions must be deconstructed: that is to say, theory is asked to question our ways of thinking about politics as well as of experiencing and practicing political participation or carrying out a political revolution.

At the same time, however, it is worth noting that this approach can possibly become an isolated, purely 'theoretical' procedure unless the deconstructive analysis simultaneously reflects upon its own embeddedness in social practices.[30] To put it differently, the New Left, in its search for a revolutionary solution of America's social and racial problems during the 1960s and 1970s, must fully understand its own involvement in the rather different social and political quandaries of the 1990s. The New Left's critique of the Frankfurt School, which contrasted Adorno and Horkheimer's critique of reason with Marx's definition of revolutionary class conflicts, may have already failed in this respect by not asking rigorously enough whether the late capitalist society of the 1960s could be theorized with the tools of classical Marxist dogma. The danger may be a repetition of this mistake, this time from the end of theory: the epistemological probe is seen as the ultimate and unquestionable frontier. Can one legitimately invoke Adorno's defense of theory against the power of conventional practice through *Negative Dialectics* without noting its specific function as a response to and critique of a presumably postideological society no longer in need of theory because technology has replaced philosophy? Also, we must not forget that Adorno's opposition to the conventional ideal of the unity of theory and practice is predicated on his concept of a totally administered society, which leaves its members with the futile choice between a revolution that would not change the structure of domination, on the one hand, and individual passivity, on the other.

Thus the epistemological problematic has to come to terms with the need for a deconstruction of traditional concepts through rational argument and reflection and a simultaneous questioning of theory's independence. It is Sullivan and Lysaker's thesis that Adorno's late work does fulfill this need. They disagree with Habermas, therefore, that Horkheimer and Adorno abandoned the rational grounding of critical reflection. What they try to demonstrate is that Adorno's epistemology can be reduced neither to subjective idealism (which can become pessimistic when the circumstances are not favorable for the subject) nor to objective materialism or positivism.

The interesting turn of this analysis, which goes over familiar ground (Adorno's critique of Kant especially), is its political application: that is, its defense of Adorno's political commitment. Here two aspects must not be conflated: first, the adequacy or failure of Adorno's position during the postwar period; second, the legitimacy of Adorno's work for the present. His conflict with the German New Left over political strategy during the late 1960s cannot be reduced to the opposition of abstract and thereby false political demands (that is, for revolutionary action) on the part of the students versus a correct theoretical position represented by Adorno. What has to be taken into account is that the student movement radicalized Critical Theory to the point that it transcended theoretical reflection and therefore raised questions of political strategy vis-à-vis the state, as well as problems of collective identity and collective organization.

A related but different issue concerns the appropriation of Adorno at the beginning of the 1990s in the United States, where not only the political constellation but also the social and cultural problematic have changed in ways that hardly fit the definition of Adorno's totally administered society. Discussion of that issue must come to terms not only with his postwar writings on modern society and social issues but also with his turn to aesthetic theory, which has sometimes been perceived by his critics as a renunciation of politics. Clearly, from the standpoint of Adorno's theory, a binary opposition of aesthetic theory and political practice is hardly a legitimate response. In *Aesthetic Theory* he repeatedly stresses the intertwinement of social and aesthetic aspects in the work of art. In this respect, the target of his criticism was precisely the bourgeois aesthetic and its attempt to separate once and for all, through a simplified version of a theory of autonomy, the political and aesthetic realms. Yet his necessary defense of the social and thereby political character of the artwork speaks more to the configuration of the early twentieth century. It would be hermeneutically implausible to ignore this distance and to treat Adorno's text and the nature of its intervention as direct responses to the postmodern condition of the late twentieth century.

For this reason, the unmediated application of Adorno's understanding of the emancipatory force contained in the advanced artwork cannot be taken for granted. Jameson, in underscoring the postmodernist transformation, questions the validity of Adorno's concept of negativity; other critics hold on to Adorno's claim and suggest that the collapse of modernism has not, *eo ipso,* undermined the truth claims of his aesthetic theory or his political project. For them, this project is primarily contained in the subject/object tension. This formalization of the political in terms of an epistemological problem that theory can solve allows them to bridge the gap between the historical moment of Adorno's text and the present.

The politics of the Frankfurt School, and of Adorno in particular, can be addressed in a number of ways: for instance, through a critical reassessment of the historical context,[31] or through an interface with strands of contemporary theory,[32] or, finally, through a confrontation with the present situation in its subjective as well as objective aspects – that is, both as lived experience and as structural configuration. For one thing, we must not forget that writing the history of the Frankfurt School and the biography of Adorno has been, and inevitably so, a political intervention. Works by Martin Jay, Rolf Wiggershaus, Helmut Dubiel, and others[33] have attempted either to underscore the lasting importance of Critical Theory or to question its political validity by differentiating between historical phases and contrasting American, European, and German culture. The assessment of the Frankfurt School's exile in the United States has been especially controversial with regard to its political implications. On the one hand, it has fostered the myth of Critical Theory's cultural elitism; on the other hand, it has encouraged a bias against American mass culture which has fueled the politics of the postmodernism debate. Clearly, the historical dimension cannot be separated from the theoretical and political. Any construction of the Frankfurt School's development depends, whether it is acknowledged or not, on the political as well as the theoretical position of the observer. This is clearly in evidence in Dubiel's and Habermas's work, where the difference between the early phase of Critical Theory (1932–38) and the later years plays a major role, as well as in the writings of their critics, who deny the significance of this development, especially in the case of Adorno.

While the phase model tends to emphasize the distance and thereby the impossibility of the immediate use of Adorno's theory, the insistence on the unity of Adorno's oeuvre tends to go hand in hand with a politics of resurrection. Here the historical embeddedness of all theoretical production (which the Frankfurt School took for granted) is either ignored in favor of theory as a primary agent or renegotiated in more complex forms of interfacing and imbrication. This moment of renegotiation, however, as Andrew Hewitt has pointed out, can no longer rely on a conventional construction of 'the reader' or even of contemporary American readers.[34] Instead, these renegotiations are particular events, motivated by particular interests and agendas. Hewitt argues that feminist appropriation, for example, has to come to terms with the tensions and performative contradictions between a forceful critique of patriarchy in *Dialectic of Enlightenment* and the (male)

19

philosophical discourse that structures this critique.[35] Hence, the interaction between Critical Theory and female readers, mediated through feminist theory, will produce readings that are not available through an immanent approach. Obviously, the difference between these readings leaves its traces in the political application of the theory as well.

As we have seen, then, the present debate remains controversial and inconclusive. The following chapters explore some of its aspects, beginning with the historical context and, specifically, Adorno's response to the United States and to postwar Germany.

2. The Philosopher in Exile

✳

I T would be difficult to describe Theodor W. Adorno's connection to America – which for him meant the United States – as a happy or successful relationship. In fact, most commentators have rightly stressed its highly problematic nature, either by pointing out how unable and unwilling Adorno was to adjust to the American way of life or by emphasizing how the United States failed to receive and integrate the persona and work of the German-Jewish philosopher. Charges of cultural elitism and arrogance, common among American as well as foreign contemporary observers, were later reiterated by critics of Adorno or intellectual historians dealing with the generation of German intellectuals exiled from Germany after 1933.[1] His defenders tend to foreground the incongruity between his European outlook and the intellectual atmosphere in the United States during the 1940s and early 1950s. By and large, foes and friends seem to agree that Adorno's complex and ambiguous attitude to America was rooted in his European and German *Weltanschauung* and his critical humanism, which motivated him to reject modern America: its political order, its economic system, and particularly its culture. Because of his education and his commitment to an (elitist) humanist tradition (steeped in classical literature), so the argument goes, he formulated a largely negative account of the United States. He even failed to acknowledge American democracy as the true antagonist of German fascism.

There is no denying that Adorno shared some of the typical prejudices of the cultured European against America, which not only influenced his behavior but also manifested themselves in his writings: his 1938 essay on jazz (GS 14:14–50) for instance, and his numerous remarks on the United States in *Minima Moralia*. There is no doubt that he never felt at home in America; he always remained – and self-consciously so – the exile waiting to be allowed to return home.

21

Although Adorno could never quite overcome the gulf between America and his German social and cultural formation, he was keenly aware of the potential dangers of his position. A dogmatic defense of high culture, so common among European émigrés of the 1930s and 1940s, would not do justice to the historical nature of the problems at hand. As Andreas Huyssen has persuasively argued, Adorno already understood in the 1930s, when he wrote his essay on Wagner (FW), that in the age of industrial capitalism high culture and mass culture are entwined and ultimately inseparable, because they are rooted in the same social conditions.[2] In other words, Adorno was aware of the problematic position of official high culture (as in the case of Richard Wagner) before he came to the United States and was therefore critical of a position that would identify 'bad' mass culture exclusively with America and 'good' high culture with Europe. This point has to be made; otherwise, an isolated reading of the famous chapter on the culture industry in *Dialectic of Enlightenment* may reinforce the image of Adorno as European elitist.

In the essay 'Cultural Criticism and Society,' written just before his return to Germany, Adorno once more clarified his understanding of *critique* by stressing that cultural criticism must not accept without suspicion the notion of culture (*Kultur*) as an unquestionable value (PR 17–34; GS 10 [1]: 11–30). What did distinguish America from Western Europe in his eyes was the more systematic transformation of literature and the arts under the impact of monopoly capitalism. As we will see, Adorno's writings tended to insist on the advanced character of American society – especially compared with that of prewar Germany. The fact that he spent his American years first in New York City and then in California, without ever seeing much of middle America, may have contributed to this conception.

Evidence for his negative view can be found in Adorno's letters as well as in *Minima Moralia,* where the New World seems to be portrayed in terms that recall Aldous Huxley's *Brave New World.* This conventional reconstruction of Adorno's view is not without problems, however. It fails to contextualize his American years, looking at them too exclusively from Adorno's point of view (or that of the Frankfurt School) without seriously interrogating the American experience of the 1940s. Although it is certainly true that Adorno's personal experience was limited in scope, his connections with the intellectual climate of the 1940s were, I believe, more complex than is commonly presumed. In many ways Adorno and Horkheimer, although hardly on close terms with the leading intellectual figures of that time, developed positions in their own work that were not as far removed from contemporary American thought as has typically been assumed. Their retreat from a Marxist-socialist position, for example, which occurred during the early 1940s, was paralleled by a significant shift within the American left from a socialist to a liberal position with strong nationalist overtones. When Horkheimer and Adorno returned to Germany after the war, they shared an explicitly anti-Communist bias with American intellectuals such as Sidney Hook and Irving Kristol, who, however, went much further to the right than the members of Frankfurt's Institut für Sozialforschung ever considered. In a curious way, they came back to Germany with an 'American' agenda, even though they clearly distanced themselves from American civilization as they had experienced it in California.

When Adorno entered the United States in 1938, the country had not yet fully overcome the economic depression, but its threat to the fabric of the American society was becoming less acute. By the same token, the enthusiasm for radical social reforms among American intellectuals was decreasing. There was a growing resistance to Communist solutions that would fundamentally change the American way of life and its legitimizing values. The suspicion of such solutions, which was not limited to one particular faction, was linked to major European events: on the one hand the Stalin trials, and on the other the rise of fascism in Germany. Especially after the outbreak of war in 1939 and Hitler's extraordinary military successes, the imminent threat of another world war forced all camps to reconsider their goals and allegiances. Indirectly, this situation helped Franklin Delano Roosevelt's nonsocialist New Deal to achieve a specifically democratic American response to the same economic and social problems that had led to fascism in Germany. The Moscow show trials had a similar effect on the

American left: Stalin's ruthless annihilation of his former comrades discredited Communism as a radical answer to social problems in the United States.[3] In the light of the impending war, the hostilities between progressive liberals and the radical left as well as the rivalries between the competing factions of the radical left were losing their former significance. As Richard Pells points out, the intellectual climate of the late 1930s can no longer be adequately described in terms of the socialist agenda that had defined the years following the crash of the stock market. In particular, the militancy of intellectuals' social commitment either weakened or shifted toward a new goal: the defense of American democracy.[4]

This assessment, strangely enough, applies equally to the Frankfurt School. By 1938, as Helmut Dubiel has shown, the core members of the Institute were beginning to distance themselves from the program of the early 1930s.[5] The rise of Stalin and the purges in the Soviet Union increasingly discouraged support of a Communist position. In other areas, however, this increasing distance vis-à-vis traditional Marxist positions did not coincide with the American configuration. Unlike Bertholt Brecht, the Frankfurt School did not give much support to the Popular Front, which became so important for the self-reflection of the American left. While the alliance of the Popular Front moved closer to Roosevelt's New Deal, thereby diminishing radical opposition, the Institute and Adorno began to work from a position that would implicitly critique the administration of the New Deal.

The fascist expansion in Europe after 1939 and the potential American involvement in the war transformed not only the agenda of the radical left but also the political position of the liberals. A common national concern became more important than the social issues that had dominated the debates of the 1930s, and the willingness of intellectuals to rally around Roosevelt certainly grew. Liberal intellectuals in particular began to emphasize the need for strong national leadership in a time of international crisis. During the 1940s Roosevelt's administration could count on considerably more support from both the moderate left and the liberals. Clearly, the fascist threat from the outside shifted the focus of the liberal project as much as that of the radicals.[6]

The *New Republic* in particular, with a growing circulation (28,000 in 1930; 41,000 in 1946), voiced the new political commitment of the liberals by affirming Roosevelt's representation of American democracy. The call for decisive action based on sober planning and management downplayed the role of the House of Representatives and the Senate. Both houses of Congress came in for scorn and anger because they failed to acknowledge the need for FDR's unrestricted leadership. 'By the early 1940s, the *New Republic* had come to speak within the intellectual community for a form of administrative liberalism that relied increasingly on the White House, the Cabinet, and government agencies staffed with ideologically sympathetic appointees for social reform at home and victory abroad.'[7] In other words, liberal intellectuals moved away from traditional liberal concerns with civil rights and individual freedom, toward a social democracy dependent on government agencies. In this respect they were not far removed from moderate socialist reformers, who accepted the existing economic system as the platform for social intervention.

Radicals such as C. Wright Mills and Dwight Macdonald, by contrast, warned against this potentially totalitarian combination of state power and corporate capitalism; Macdonald especially still relied on the notion that a revolutionary working class would ultimately overthrow the hegemonic bourgeoisie.[8] Indeed, one crucial issue of the debates of the 1940s was the question, could one assume that the American working class wanted a socialist economy and was prepared to fight for it? When Sidney Hook cautioned liberals and radicals against an alliance with the New Deal administration, arguing that the centralized power of the state would ultimately not benefit the working class,[9] he was more or less in agreement with the analysis of state capitalism articulated by the Frankfurt School. As we will see, however, Friedrich Pollock, Horkheimer, and Adorno were prepared to draw more radical conclusions than those of Hook or Macdonald.

Despite general agreement on the task of defeating fascist Germany and imperialist Japan, then, there was no consensus on the solution of America's internal social problems. Liberals such as

Bruce Brevan, George Soule, and Max Lerner argued in favor of a well-designed welfare state in which the working class would find a secure home; the radicals focused their attention on the political organizations of the working class.[10] A simultaneous critique of both positions would lead to the point of view articulated by Adorno and Horkheimer during the 1940s. The culture industry chapter of their *Dialectics of Enlightenment* presupposes the disintegration of the working class and its reconstitution as a mass, as well as the failure of a progressive conception of history in which the state can function as the primary agent of reason.

By 1944 Adorno and Horkheimer had come to the conclusion that the Second World War would probably result in the defeat of fascism but would not prepare a social revolution. Similarly, both American liberals and Marxists, who had perceived the war as 'revolutionary' and had predicted profound changes in Europe, began to realize that these expectations might not come true.[11] To American observers it became quite clear how much the war effort had helped to rebuild the American economy. Under Roosevelt's leadership the United States was expected to come out of the war not as a socialist but as a strong capitalist democracy facing the territorial expansion of the Soviet Union. The growing disappointment among liberal and radical intellectuals with the Democratic administration (especially after FDR's death) was increasingly overshadowed by the changes in the Soviet Union. Whereas the American left had perceived the Soviet Union as a socialist experiment during the 1930s, the emphasis of the war years was more on the national strength of Russia and the American-Russian alliance, which was praised by the liberal *New Republic* as well. By 1945, however, the notion of a common American-Russian agenda was no longer clear in the minds of the *New Republic*'s editors. The friction between those allies as soon as the enemy was defeated forced the left camp to reassess its own values and political priorities.

In this process (which began around 1944 and was more or less completed by 1948), the political discourse separated the concepts of democracy and socialism (Communism), turning them ultimately against each other. The defense of American democracy against the Eastern threat redefined the Soviet Union in such terms that it became similar to, if not identical with, Nazi Germany. It was Hannah Arendt, of course, who articulated this critical view, in her theory of the totalitarian state,[12] but it was by no means limited to her work; rather, the emergence of the Cold War was paralleled by a slow and sometimes painful realignment of the American left. The radical anti-Stalinist faction that gathered around such journals as *Commentary* and *Partisan Review*, disappointed in particular with Harry Truman's administration, had to struggle on two fronts: with the critiques of capitalism on the one hand, and the polemic against Stalinism on the other. As much as the contributors of *Partisan Review* attacked the former liberal supporters of the New Deal, their position on foreign politics after 1945 was primarily anti-Communist. The former distinction between anti-Stalinist and anti-Communist or anti-Marxist, which had defined the position of the radical left during the early 1940s, collapsed. Increasingly, the socialist project was conflated with the Soviet Union and thereby judged in terms of Stalin's oppressive use of the Party as well as his foreign politics, especially his expansionist moves during and after the war. In the context of the Cold War it became possible for the New York intellectuals to refer to Communism as 'Red Fascism.'[13] As Pells observed, 'For all their intellectual acrobatics, and their feelings of being newcomers dependent more on their wit than on their familial roots in America, the contributors to *Commentary* and *Partisan Review* evolved during the postwar years into articulate exponents of the new orthodoxy on foreign affairs.'[14]

This formulation would be equally appropriate for Horkheimer and Adorno. When they returned to Germany in 1949 and reopened the Institute, the spirit of the Cold War was part of their baggage. Furthermore, they shared with the younger generation of radical American intellectuals a skeptical, if not negative, attitude toward the socialist project of the 1930s. Their commitment to democracy no longer included an allegiance to a socialist revolution. Instead, they stressed the Western democratic tradition and focused their polemic on East European Communism. The parallel can be traced back to the early 1940s, when Adorno and Horkheimer had worked out the dialectic of instrumental reason that left no room for a socialist revolution.[15] It is important to remember that during the later 1940s the agenda of the *Partisan Review* radicals and Adorno's position were not far apart.

Adorno and Horkheimer took part also in the shift from an outright political critique to cultural criticism, a shift with significant political implications.[16] In fact, Adorno's work of the 1940s anticipated this change, since he was less involved in the American political discourse. Furthermore, since he did not participate in the war effort, his critique of America took the form of cultural criticism, beginning with his early essay on jazz, followed by *Minima Moralia* and *Dialectic of Enlightenment*. The concept of the culture industry was, at least in part, Adorno's critique of FDR's New Deal. Unlike American intellectuals of the 1930s and early 1940s, Adorno had no memory of the Great Depression in the United States; for him, as a refugee from Nazi Germany, the workers were not poor but docile. The position of Adorno and the Frankfurt School became viable in America only after the memory of the Depression had receded – that is, during the late 1940s and early 1950s. Looking back, the former radical Trotskyist Seymour Lipset summarized the new situation: 'Since domestic politics, even liberal and socialist politics, can no longer serve as the arena for serious criticism from the left, many intellectuals have turned from a basic concern with the political and economic systems to criticism of other sections of the basic culture of American society.'[17]

The new Pax Americana, the combination of democracy and advanced capitalism, called for a different approach. In the writings of Macdonald, Daniel Boorstin, Mary McCarthy, and David Riesman, the focus of criticism shifted from the political to the social and cultural. For the affluent society with its new suburban middle class, the traditional tools of liberal and Marxist theory appeared to be less effective than formerly. In particular, the impact of the new media (radio, film, television) resisted traditional analysis.[18] Radical left cultural criticism of the 1950s, articulated in the writings of Macdonald, Bell, Clement Greenberg, and Paul Goodman, paralleled the work of Adorno, particularly in its concern about traditional high culture and literature. As a result of this critique, their commitment to mass democracy became more ambivalent, since the undeniable greater political equality of the citizen was subverted by the emergence of 'mass man,' the consumer of cultural goods.

As we have seen, Adorno's intellectual position in the United States during the 1940s was less isolated than some scholars have assumed. In several respects his own development (within the Frankfurt School) and that of intellectuals of the American left show similarities – despite the fact that Adorno probably knew little about the United States when he arrived in 1938. He was unfamiliar with its history and not well informed about its political system. Initially, as a result, he found it difficult to follow and assess the ongoing political and social debates. The transformation of the presidency under FDR, for example, and the increased power of the central bureaucracy during the war years were not immediately visible to an observer for whom the fascist state was the immediate threat. Furthermore, we must keep in mind that Adorno, like fellow German émigrés such as Thomas Mann, Bertholt Brecht, and Lion Feuchtwanger, came with a Eurocentric view of a world in which North America was expected to play a supplementary role. What, then, did Adorno see of the United States? How could he incorporate his experience into his own philosophical 'system'? And how did he respond to this unfamiliar civilization for which numerous European stereotypes were available? Perhaps even more important, what did he *not* see? What remained beyond his horizon?

All the accounts we have of Adorno's experience in America, including his own testimony, point to a traumatic experience. He was, perhaps, psychologically even less prepared for exile than other members of the Frankfurt School. In his own account, written after his return to Germany, a sense of alienation is unmistakable. It ranges from the structure of research institutes to the formation of the American landscape, from greeting rituals to cultural entertainment. Adorno's own sense of not belonging clearly reinforced his perception of the reified nature of American society and the isolated status of the individual. To this marginalized observer, America appeared to be a country without tradition, a modern, completely rationalized society that aggressively celebrated its own modernity by rejecting its European past. Since Adorno spent most of his American years in southern California and never visited New England or the South, a notion of an older, *premodern* American tradition was not part of his personal experience. Moreover, his professional contacts in the East, where he was involved in a radio research project, and his links to Hollywood could only reinforce the image of a radically modern society dominated by the new mass media. For this reason, his analysis of the culture industry emphasized the 'American' nature of those phenomena, making Hollywood the center of the new cultural configuration. What mattered for Adorno was the contrast with traditional European high culture and the European avant-garde. In other words, his view of North America was strongly informed by a set of oppositions aligned in such a way that American mass culture, advanced capitalism, and technology stood against European high culture, a premodern social structure, and a traditional life-world. At least, this is the first impression one gets from Adorno's observations; a closer analysis will reveal how much more complex and involved his argument actually is.

What is striking in Adorno's writings of the 1940s, however, is his distance from the contemporary political configuration and American history. The numerous observations about North America in *Minima Moralia* do not examine the development of the United States or touch on political problems. From Adorno's writings it would be difficult to get a clear sense of racial problems or the social tensions of the 1930s to which Roosevelt's New Deal responded. Rural and small-town America too is almost invisible in Adorno's account; where it occasionally appears, it is represented as a strange and alienating landscape:

> The shortcoming of the American landscape is not so much, as romantic illusion would have it, the absence of historical memories, as that it bears no traces of the human hand. This

applies not only to the lack of arable land, the uncultivated woods often no higher than scrub, but above all to the roads. These are always inserted directly in the landscape, and the more impressively smooth and broad they are, the more unrelated and violent their gleaming track appears against its wild, overgrown surroundings. They are expressionless. Just as they know no marks of foot or wheel, no soft paths along their edges as a transition to the vegetation, no trails leading off into the valley, so they are without the mild, soothing, unangular quality of things that have felt the touch of hands or their immediate implements. It is as if no-one had ever passed their hand over the landscape's hair. It is uncomforted and comfortless. And it is perceived in a corresponding way. For what the hurrying eye has seen merely from the car it cannot retain, and the vanishing landscape leaves no more traces behind than it bears upon itself. (MM 48; GS 4:53–54)

Yet this negative verdict is contrasted with another comment that reveals Adorno's awe: 'Beauty of the American landscape: that even the smallest of its segments is inscribed, as its expression, with the immensity of the whole country' (MM 49; GS 4:54). In either case, the formulation articulates impressions and reflections. It is precisely this highly subjective element, the self-reflexive nature of the text, that gives Adorno's observations significance. The writer sees himself as an uprooted European intellectual who had to surrender his past when he was admitted to the United States. Not only are his observations fragmentary; his own subjectivity is fragmented, damaged. Accordingly, the force of his assessment of America in *Minima Moralia* results precisely from its lack of contextualization, its lack of 'understanding' the American way of life.

This comes out most clearly in Adorno's commentary on social situations and customs. His remarks tend to focus on particular moments, on incidents that the native American would treat as 'natural' and self-evident – rituals such as greeting another person, or the memo format instead of the formal letter in interoffice correspondence (MM 41; GS 4:45). Under Adorno's gaze the life-world of California crystallizes in the shape of allegories, strange habits and conventions that the outsider must learn to decipher. In the following example he remarks about the rules of the cocktail party that

> the taboo on talking shop and the inability to talk to each other are in reality the same thing. Because everything is business, the latter is unmentionable like rope in a hanged man's home. Behind the pseudo-democratic dismantling of ceremony, of old-fashioned courtesy, of the useless conversation suspected, not even unjustly, of being idle gossip, behind the seeming clarification and transparency of human relations that no longer admit anything undefined, naked brutality is ushered in. (MM 41–42; GS 4:46)

To this he adds:

> The direct statement without divagations, hesitations or reflections, that gives the other the facts full in the face, already has the form and timbre of the command issued under Fascism by the dumb to the silent. Matter-of-factness between people, doing away with all ideological ornamentation between them, has already itself become an ideology for treating people as things. (MM 42; GS 4:46)

In this reading, Adorno connects a seemingly harmless social convention in America with a general trend toward an 'objectivication' that ultimately results in fascism. Similarly, his observations about American hotels and motels, their cold but proper functionalism, quickly turns into a sharp critique of modern civilization – far beyond the immediate American context (MM 116–18; GS 4:130–31).

Whenever Adorno touches a detail, it becomes a frozen image, an emblem to be interrogated by the pondering mind. He sees an uninhabitable life-world where human beings have lost their individuality and derive their transitory happiness from filling out the role that society has assigned to them. Typical in this respect is his commentary on IQ tests as a quintessential reification of the mind: 'The socialization of mind keeps it boxed in, isolated in a glass case, as long as society is itself imprisoned. As thought earlier

internalized the duties exacted from without, today it has assimilated to itself its integration into the surrounding apparatus, and
is thus condemned even before the economic and political ver-
dicts on it come fully into force' (MM 197; GS 4:222). Adorno's gaze
focuses on the modern character of America, its preference for
technical solutions and its flair for social engineering. This perspective blends out history: for Adorno, even the American landscape lacks history; as unmediated nature it remains alien to the
observing critic.

One would expect this uncomfortable distance to reinforce his
European allegiance, provoke a positive stress on European high
culture. Although there are nostalgic moments in *Minima Moralia,* Adorno resists this attitude for the most part, emphasizing
instead the growing similarities between the continents. German
high culture, he argues, was not destroyed by the National Socialists in 1933; rather, its demise had occurred already during the
1920s. Consequently, he does not share the hope of many émigrés
that German culture can simply be rebuilt after the war. What he
expects is a configuration much closer to American mass culture
than to nineteenth-century European high culture, and these anticipated similarities distress him more than the life-style of Hollywood. The growing similarities frighten him even more in another respect: the warfare in Europe increasingly diminishes the
difference between the fighting parties. The mass destruction
of German cities caused by Allied air raids repeats the German
air raids on Rotterdam and Coventry. Again, Adorno's reflection
takes its cues from the isolated document, the newsreel, rather
than the contextualized, ideological version in the print media.
During the early 1940s he felt that the American defense of democracy did not coincide with an improvement of democracy;
hence, he was less inclined than Leo Lowenthal or Herbert Marcuse to support the war effort.

The representation of the United States in *Minima Moralia*
consists of many small, heterogeneous fragments that occasionally contradict one another; Adorno refrains from a synthetic
definition. Still, the particular details selected reflect a bias: they
are signifiers for the most advanced capitalist society. Adorno's

interest in North America, one might argue, was limited to what he perceived as relentless modernity bordering on self-destruction. It is important to note that like the other members of the Frankfurt School, he insisted on the link between capitalism, modernity, and the avant-garde. Hence, the more analytical approach to American society that we find in *Dialectic of Enlightenment* foregrounds this connection more than does *Minima Moralia*. The chapter on the culture industry, in particular, forcefully argues that American mass culture owes its existence as well as its function to organized capitalism. Adorno and Horkheimer were convinced that the transition from liberal to organized capitalism would result in a systematic reorganization of the cultural system, based on the principles of mass production. Just as Karl Marx had focused on England as the most economically advanced society of the nineteenth century, Adorno and Horkheimer decided to concentrate on the United States as the most advanced Western society of this century. Clearly, in *Dialectic of Enlightenment*, they are more concerned with structures than with particular moments, more with a general process (the dialectical history of reason) than with contrasts between Europe and America. When they do stress the contrast, it is usually within a temporal frame in which the United States marks the most advanced capitalist society. Yet even this scheme does not do justice to the complex configuration because, as we will see, fascist Germany appears in this context as the alternative version of modernity. For Adorno and Horkheimer, an analysis of the American society included, explicitly or implicitly, an analysis of modern Germany, since they saw both the political system of the National Socialists and the organization of culture in North America as aspects of the same historical dialectic of reason.

In fact, it was the rise of fascism in Germany that forced the members of the Frankfurt School to rethink received ideas about the development of modern industrial capitalism. Their early work during the 1930s remained more closely linked to the orthodox paradigm of Marxism, in which fascism had its place as the ultimate response of monopoly capitalism to severe economic crises, but during the early 1940s Franz Neumann, Otto Kirchheimer, Pollock, and Horkheimer advanced revised theories that could better account for the actual relationship between the fascist state and the capitalist economy. For Adorno, Pollock's theory of state capitalism was more important than Neumann's analysis in *Behemoth* or Kirchheimer's essays.[19] Adorno and Horkheimer followed Pollock's interpretation that state capitalism in Nazi Germany reversed the traditional causal connection between the political system and the economy. The priority of the economy vanishes. This means that the state has taken over the basic functions of capitalist enterprise. As Dubiel writes: 'The market, as an indirect instrument coordinating supply and demand, is replaced by a system of direct planning. This planning system rests in the hands of a powerful bureaucracy, itself the product of a fusion of state bureaucracy and top industrial management. The total economic process takes place within the framework of a general plan with guidelines for production, distribution, consumption, savings, and investments.'[20]

What made Pollock's theory significant for Adorno and Horkheimer was its drive toward a more general theory of advanced Western societies and its political applicability to, among other countries, the United States.[21] In *Dialectic of Enlightenment* Pollock has an unacknowledged presence, at least in the sense that his theory replaces more traditional Marxist notions about the structure of Nazi Germany, as well as that of the United States under the New Deal. The potentially common ground is the priority of politics over economics in the form of a governmental apparatus designed to centralize all efforts. Under the impact of Pollock's theory, traditional economic analysis becomes unnecessary.

The vantage point of Adorno and Horkheimer's analysis – namely, the concern with German fascism – explains the contrast between their understanding of the American society and the accounts of contemporary American historians and sociologists who tended to view their own society in terms of its internal development. This is not to say, however, that the Americans never came to similar conclusions. C. Wright Mills's assessment of the contemporary American middle class in *White Collar*, for example, describes the transition from the nineteenth-century middle class to the new society of the 1930s and 1940s in terms that are compatible with Adorno's critique. Yet his argument focuses almost exclusively on the United States, with no more than occasional references to the work of Arcadius Gurland, Kirchheimer, and Neumann. The parallels are not worked out in detail.[22]

Mills's emphasis was not motivated by patriotism; rather, it was determined by his focus on the political economy. The pioneering work of Robert and Helen Lynd has a different focus. In *Middletown* (1929) and *Middletown in Transition* (1937), they provide a detailed social map of a midwestern town from the 1890s to the 1930s. Their mostly descriptive approach avoids open political criticism, foregrounding instead the cultural matrix of the town. The Lynds share with Mills a preference for concrete details (basic empirical research) and a narrow focus, but the result is a picture with a different emphasis. Moreover, the American society of the 1920s, which the Lynds contrast with that of the late nineteenth century, seems far removed from the American society of the 1940s as it is represented in *Minima Moralia*. Even in *Middletown in Transition*, which deals with the Depression years, traditional social institutions appear to be in place. The reader hardly gets the impression of a radical qualitative change that would fundamentally question democracy in America.

Robert and Helen Lynd describe a modern, differentiated society but clearly not a mass society where the individual has become faceless and open to far-reaching manipulation. What the Lynds report is an attempt of the people in Middletown to cope with the problems of the Depression by reinforcing their traditional value system rather than by addressing the problems in a radical manner. Neither is the Lynds' own methodology radical; their 'thick description' affirms the self-understanding of the American society. It is noteworthy that for them the uprooting of American society, which Adorno took for granted in 1944, had hardly begun. The 1930s appear as a period of severe economic and social problems, but not as a period completely determined by alienation.

It is C. Wright Mills who, in *White Collar* (1951), redefines American modernity in Adornian terms: 'Estranged from community and society in a context of distrust and manipulation; alienated from work and, on the personality market, from self; expropriated of individual rationality, and politically apathetic – these are the new little people, the unwilling vanguard of modern society.'[23] By 1951, radical American sociology, using a model of class conflict, was reaching conclusions similar to those of Adorno and Horkheimer. For Mills the world of the small entrepreneur was a thing of the past, superseded by economic concentration and major transformation in property. His own narrative of American social history remains more concrete than Adorno's, though it is certainly less detailed than the Lynds' account. The difference is not just a matter of method and style; rather, particularly between Adorno and Mills, it is a difference in perception. Under Adorno's gaze the phenomena lose their particular context. The American society of the 1930s and 1940s appears to be decades ahead of itself. Rather than an analysis of the 1940s, Adorno's writings read more like a commentary on the 1960s and 1970s: that is, on the strains and the contradictions of the Pax Americana during the Vietnam War, when the convergence of organized capitalism and state power became much more problematic for American citizens. These were also, of course, the years of Critical Theory's greatest impact in the United States, although that impact occurred more through the work of Herbert Marcuse than through that of Adorno, who had become a rather marginal figure in America after his return to Germany.

Still, Critical Theory maintained a limited visibility in the United States during the 1950s. For anyone who had developed a highly critical assessment of contemporary America, as Mills had done, for instance, the question of mass culture could not be answered by celebrating the general access to culture as a democratic force. In the American debate on the politics of culture during the late 1940s and 1950s, Adorno had a (frequently unacknowledged) presence. In a prosperous postwar America, where traditional class struggles had become almost invisible, Adorno's analysis of mass-produced culture became more important than in 1944. As Richard Pells has argued, a significant shift in focus after the 1948 election brought the political implications of cul-

tural issues into the foreground: 'In a wealthy society, overt ideological and social quarrels rarely erupted; class antagonism remained muted; the real differences of life were minimized or
ignored in the electoral campaigns.'[24] Frustrations and unresolved
conflicts had to be addressed in a different way by writers such as
Dwight Macdonald, Daniel Bell, Paul Goodman, Mary McCarthy,
and David Riesman.[25] Now intellectuals dissatisfied with the status quo tended to articulate their opposition in terms of subversion rather than overt radicalism. The focus became the American dream that failed precisely because it had come true. In this
context the image of American society underwent an important
change. Clearly, the position of Bell and Mills and Macdonald and
Boorstin was much closer to Adorno's conception than to that of
Robert and Helen Lynd. For American critics the 'culture industry' became real, even if the term was not used.

Macdonald's influential essay 'Masscult & Midcult' (first published in *Politics* in 1944 under the title 'A Theory of Popular
Culture,' then rewritten and republished in 1953) explicitly refers
to Adorno's essay 'On Popular Music' without necessarily shar-
ing Adorno's theoretical foundations. What Macdonald did share
with Adorno was a strong sense of the danger of mass culture, a
threat not limited to artistic and aesthetic considerations. For
Macdonald, mass culture is defined by its impersonality and its
lack of standards.[26] Its products are the result of literary mass
production based on strictly regulated conventions. He answers
the obvious question as to why it exists in the first place by
referring to David Riesman's 'lonely crowd' and the concept of
'mass man,' the atomized individual. The parallel with Frankfurt
School thought is hard to overlook, yet by no means are either the
emphases or the theoretical positions identical. For one thing,
Macdonald maintains a much more positive view of traditional
high culture than Adorno ever did. When he offers a scathing
critique of mass culture, he does not question the legitimacy of
high culture, which appears to have transhistorical value. Hence,
his sharp attack on Edward Shils, the social scientist who defended
popular culture, concerns only the function of mass culture, leaving the function of high culture untouched. Macdonald's dis-

agreement with the defenders of popular culture comes out in his insistence on the manipulative character of mass culture, which, as a debased form of high culture, he sees as 'becoming an instrument of domination.'[27]

It was precisely this point that separated *Dialectic of Enlightenment* from traditional *Kulturkritik* (cultural criticism) and its emphasis on the literary canon. Macdonald extends his criticism to middlebrow culture – the slick but decent and polished version of high culture – without, however, working out the connection between 'mass cult' and 'midcult' systematically. As a result, he tends to revert to cultural criticism, showing a preference for a stable high culture, although he admits that this solution is less than democratic.[28] Looking at the wasteland of postwar American culture, he feels, as he states in the preface to *Against the American Grain*, 'that a people which loses contact with its past becomes culturally psychotic.'[29] In his view, the American cultural tradition rooted in the New England of the seventeenth and eighteenth centuries had been compromised by waves of immigrants from non-English-speaking countries who wanted easy access to the culture of their new homeland.[30]

In the heated debate of the 1950s over the value of modern mass culture in America, Adorno and the Frankfurt School did not play a central role; still, their arguments were picked up and utilized by the 'cultural' camp, while their opponents – mostly social scientists – branded the defense of high culture elitist and ultimately undemocratic. Both Edward Shils – whom Macdonald singled out as the Pangloss of the new enlightenment – and Seymour Lipset argued that mass culture was an inevitable and ultimately desirable feature of modern democracies, an important part of enlightenment and modernization. In their view, the expanded cultural market would not only proliferate 'bad' culture but also bring serious literature and music to a large segment of the population. Even Clement Greenberg, not known for his admiration of mass culture, felt that the media provided 'some sort of enlightenment' for the masses.'[31] From this perspective, the critique of mass culture smacked of conservatism, since it defended a cultural formation that excluded the majority of the population. Accordingly, intellectuals such as Paul Goodman, Daniel Boorstin, and Green-berg, who decried the corruption of high culture and the rise of the new media, seemed to misread the logic of modern history.

One aspect of Adorno's assessment of North America has to be stressed: his view that the tendency of modern mass societies is toward authoritarian and ultimately totalitarian structures. The definition of the mass as a passive body of manipulable people allows him to connect the fascist society in Germany and the consumer society in America. This link becomes especially ap-parent when he discusses American mass culture in *Dialectic of Enlightenment*. The chapter on the culture industry presents a two-pronged argument for Adorno's thesis that under advanced capitalism, mass democracies reorganize culture in such a way that older traditions of high culture and entertainment become completely integrated. On the one hand, he develops a psychoana-lytical theory of reception, focusing on the moment of regression in the mass reception of art. On the other hand, he advances economic and institutional arguments to demonstrate the deter-mination of mass culture by basic economic factors, such as its dependence on certain segments of the industry.

In *Dialectic of Enlightenment* this argument becomes part of the larger thesis that advanced monopoly capitalism has not only reorganized the workplace but also restructured leisure time in order to extend its grip over the working masses. In other words, for Adorno, mass culture in America is not simply a new phase of culture – for example, a more democratic version of culture – but, specifically, the result of a thorough restructuring of the cultural sphere by the industry that controls the newest media: radio and film. These media cannot have a liberating function, he argues, because their structure assumes complete control by the owner and a passive audience. Thus they are perfect instruments for fascist propaganda but, in Adorno's mind, unsuitable for democ-racy. For this reason, he disagrees with Walter Benjamin's position that the cinema might have a liberating function for the modern masses.

On the basis of the culture industry chapter, one might come to the conclusion that Adorno's response to America can be defined only in negative terms. It is important to note, however, that he does not regard the culture industry by any means as an exclusively American phenomenon. He attempts to explore the organization of culture in advanced industrial societies generally; for this reason, the German example is as significant for him as the American one. The transition from Weimar culture to fascist mass culture provides the focal point for his analysis. His concern is the defeat of the individual (of liberal societies) under the impact of monopoly capitalism: 'One has only to become aware of one's own nothingness, only to recognize defeat and one is one with it all. Society is full of desperate people and therefore a prey to rackets' (DE 153; GS 3:176). This insight applies not only to the Weimar entertainment industry but also to the highbrow novels of Alfred Döblin and Hans Fallada. For Adorno, Weimar culture was on the road to the fascist leader long before he actually entered the political arena; consequently, Adorno does not expect a restoration of German high culture after the defeat of the Nazis, since its existence before 1933 was largely an ideological construct. Adorno realizes that the opposition of Germany (as part of Europe) versus America is problematic, yet the analysis of the culture industry invokes this opposition as a means of contrasting the conception of culture in the nineteenth century with its reorganization under advanced capitalism. His cultural map is meant to signify the transition from the bourgeois individual to the fascist personality *or* the pseudo-individuality of the Hollywood star.

During the 1940s Adorno's perception of the United States emphasized the modern nature of its society, a social structure characterized by urban concentration and human alienation. Of course, he recognized the democratic nature of the political system, but, as can be gleaned from *Minima Moralia,* this knowledge did not play a major role in his evaluation of the country. Although he and Horkheimer certainly wished for the defeat of Nazi Germany, Adorno was not inclined to identify with the aims and strategies of the Allies. In this respect he was more isolated during the war years than those members of the Frankfurt School (Marcuse, Lowenthal) who served the American government. It was only after his return to Germany in 1949 that the matter of the

41

political system became more central to Adorno's view of America. His involvement with the project of German reeducation as a professor of philosophy at the University of Frankfurt significantly changed his evaluation of American democracy. To a certain degree this reorientation is reflected in the 1968 essay 'Scientific Experiences of a European Scholar in America,' which stresses, much more than one would expect from previous statements, his positive response to American civilization. Although he leaves no doubt about his European cultural allegiance and his unwillingness to develop an 'American' personality, he does point to a strand of American history with which he could identify – the Enlightenment tradition: 'The spirit of enlightenment also in relation to cultural problems, in the American intellectual climate a matter of course, had the greatest attraction for me.'[32] For Adorno, the American Enlightenment (unlike German culture) could manifest itself either as reified modern positivism (the strand that he critiqued in *Dialectic of Enlightenment*) or as a will to human emancipation through democratic forms – for example, through research projects involving groups of social scientists.

In this respect, the project on the 'authoritarian personality' in which Adorno participated during the 1940s, figures as a prominent example of politically committed social research within the American academy.[33] Confronting and analyzing racial prejudice, especially anti-Semitism, remained a crucial task for Adorno after he returned home. When he addressed this question in Germany, he frequently drew on the authoritarian personality project as a model of theory-oriented empirical research coming out of a specifically American cultural and intellectual climate. In 1968 he remarked: 'This kind of cooperation in a democratic spirit that does not get bogged down in formal political procedures and extends into all details of planning and execution, I found to be not only extremely enjoyable but also the most fruitful thing that I became acquainted with in America, in contrast to the academic tradition in Europe.'[34] A comparison with *Minima Moralia* makes it quite apparent that this statement articulates Adorno's reorientation during the 1950s and 1960s rather than his attitude during the 1940s. Looking at postwar Germany, where authoritarian and fascist patterns of thought had by no means automatically vanished in 1945, he now stresses the need for democratic reorganization of research and therefore favors an 'American' model.

The pro-American reorientation of Adorno and Horkheimer was, as we have seen, motivated by the confrontation with postwar Germany. There were both institutional and ideological reasons for this attitude. Horkheimer's desire to move the Institute back to Germany could be carried out only with the help of sympathetic forces in Frankfurt, especially at the university. But the university administration, as Rolf Wiggershaus has shown, was not particularly eager to reinstate the émigrés.[35] Under these circumstances, Horkheimer and Adorno decided to play the 'American' card, to use their United States citizenship along with their American connections. In particular, they shared the American assessment of the power relation between the two countries, an assessment in which the new Federal Republic was viewed as a 'colony' with little separate cultural and political identity. The power of the United States over West Germany, they thought, would help the Frankfurt School to reestablish itself in Frankfurt.

The American connection became important for Adorno's ideological position as well. The political division of Germany in 1949, resulting from the Cold War, raised the latent anti-Communist bias of the Western zones to the level of a state ideology. Under these circumstances, a pro-socialist position, not to mention a pro-Marxist point of view, could become a political liability. Hence, Adorno was very concerned about an essay by Max Bense in which the Frankfurt School was mentioned together with the work of Georg Lukács and Ernst Bloch; he tried to prevent its publication, arguing that the position of the Institute was clearly opposed to that of Lukács and Bloch, who were seen as ideologues of the East.[36] In 1949 this opposition was apparently more important for Adorno than the common theoretical heritage.[37] His 1958 polemical essay 'Reconciliation under Duress' (GS 11:251–80) extended his anti-Communist bias to the field of literary theory by attacking Lukácsian reflection theory.

This stance was probably motivated by two concerns: first, Adorno and Horkheimer had already distanced themselves from

43

their own orthodox socialist position of the early 1940s; second, the new West German society made anti-Communism almost a requirement for its citizens. The postwar definition of democracy included the stance against Communism; hence, a differentiated response to the 'threat' of Communism became difficult, to say the least. Although Adorno and Horkheimer continued to make use of core elements of Marxist theory, they now tended to avoid the rhetoric of dialectical materialism.[38] Needless to say, anti-Communism was also one of the effective ideological links between the United States and the Federal Republic of Germany. Although Adorno could not possibly support the presence of older right-wing ideologies in the Federal Republic, he and Horkheimer could and did participate in the new consensus. Their own theoretical development during the 1940s, which incidentally paralleled the development of many American intellectuals on the left, had prepared them for this position and moved them more to the center in the new West German system than they ever had been in the Weimar Republic. Still, although they shared certain political assumptions of the Konrad Adenauer era, they remained highly critical observers of the postwar years.

3. Education after the Holocaust

I N the third of his *Untimely Meditations* Nietzsche contrasts the essence of Schopenhauer's character and work with that of the average German scholar and professor of philosophy of his time. In this comparison Arthur Schopenhauer comes across as honest, thorough, and intellectually reliable, whereas Germany's academic philosophers are exposed as shallow and insincere because they have to present themselves in accordance with their official roles as state-appointed teachers.

> How completely this visible philosophical life is lacking in Germany! where the body is just beginning to liberate itself long after the spirit seems to have been liberated; yet it is only an illusion that a spirit can be free and independent if this achieved sovereignty over oneself – which is at bottom creative sovereignty over oneself – is not demonstrated anew from morning till night through every glance and every gesture.[1]

What characterizes Schopenhauer for the young Nietzsche is his decision to stand his own ground without compromises vis-à-vis the state and the public at large. This decision sets his teaching apart from the academic discourse of nineteenth-century German philosophy. For Nietzsche, Schopenhauer speaks to those who are truly concerned about intellectual and human self-formation, rather than those who merely want to acquire information and positive knowledge.

Nietzsche's scorn was directed at the *Gelehrte* and *Gebildete* (learned and educated men) who claimed to be distinguished from the crowd by their education, even though they did not grasp the deeper meaning of the concept of *Bildung* (self-formation). 'Where we discover talent devoid of that longing, in the world of scholars or that of the so-called cultivated, we are repelled and disgusted by it; for we sense that, with all their intellect, such people do not promote an evolving culture and the procreation of genius – which is the goal of all culture – but hinder it.'[2] For Nietzsche the German civilization of his time, although his contemporaries disagreed, was incompatible with the notion of individual culture and, for that reason, with the expansion of objective culture. Hence, Schopenhauer could not be a successful university teacher in his own era. A paragon among philosophers, he had to stand outside the sphere of officially acknowledged public learning and could become a spiritual guide only for those who were willing to listen and to read with care – and who would then be *gegen die Zeit erzogen*: that is, educated in opposition to their own time.[3]

The radical stance against the educational system of his own time, especially its claim to provide students with *Bildung* and critical knowledge, was certainly a leitmotif in Nietzsche's own early work. In very strong terms he emphasized the tension between the methods and goals of the school system of the state, and the original meaning of the term *Bildung* as it was used by German neohumanists around 1800. Nietzsche emphatically upheld the ideal of individual self-formation without the corresponding notion, however, that this ideal could be applied within the existing social and political conditions of his era.[4] Harmony between individual and society, precariously proclaimed by the neohumanists, struck Nietzsche as unattainable in late nineteenth-century Germany, where the concept of *Bildung* had become largely conflated with the concept of public education. Under these circumstances, the formation of the individual had become reified: the *Gebildete* was simply a person who had gone through a certain amount of formal schooling. Hence *Bildung* was increasingly measured in quantitative and objective terms; in the public discourse of the late nineteenth century a correlation between formal education and social status had become commonplace.[5] The term *die Gebildeten* referred to the aristocracy and the upper strata of the middle class: that is, to those who had attended a *Gymnasium* and were trained to understand and appreciate the classics and the German canon of great literature and music.[6] The *Bildungsbürgertum* (educated middle class) saw itself as the guardian of German high culture, charged with the task of disseminating and preserving the literary tradition.

As George Mosse has persuasively argued, Jewish emancipation in Germany during the nineteenth century was closely linked to a project of *Bildung,* which would enable the Jewish middle classes to assimilate themselves to German culture and to articulate their own emancipatory project through the great canon of German philosophy, literature, and music.[7] The classical tradition was perceived as promoting freedom, equality, and cosmopolitanism. *Bildung,* as Mosse underscores, would foster Jewish emancipation and make possible a shared German-Jewish culture. For the young Adorno, the son of an established German-Jewish wine merchant in Frankfurt, this tradition was of the greatest importance. Its musical aspects especially – embodied by such composers as Bach, Beethoven, and Mahler – determined his understanding of culture.[8]

While Theodor W. Adorno's social background leaves no doubt that he himself belonged to the educated German bourgeoisie,[9] he shared Nietzsche's scorn for the reification of the concept of culture. This pronounced distancing from the institutions of official high culture is already in evidence in his early writings. Still, Adorno did aspire to a university career; he did not plan to become a private scholar, although the economic status of his parents might have allowed him to do so. In order to receive the *venia legendi* (license to lecture) at the University of Frankfurt, he presented a thesis on Søren Kierkegaard's aesthetic theory, and after its formal acceptance he was admitted to the rank of university lecturer (*Privatdozent*) in 1931. The rise to power of the National Socialists in 1933 brought his brief academic career to an abrupt end, however; like many other Jewish and leftist faculty members, Adorno was stripped of his academic privileges and found himself unemployed. Neither during his stay at Oxford University between 1934 and 1938 nor during his years in the United States as a member of the Institute for Social Research (in exile) did he have an opportunity to teach. Thus the question of education and the wider concern for *Bildung* came up only after the war, when Max Horkheimer, director of the Institute, seriously considered returning to Frankfurt.

Cautiously, contacts with the University of Frankfurt, which in 1933 had cut its link with the Institute, were reestablished. It soon became clear that both sides were interested in bringing the Institute back to Frankfurt; the university even offered Horkheimer his old chair in the Faculty of Philosophy.[10] For Adorno, however, the return to Frankfurt and its university, which he wanted possibly even more than Horkheimer did, became a considerably more difficult process. Since Adorno had not yet held a chair in 1933, the university administration did not feel that it owed him a senior position. For a time he was considered for a chair in philosophy when Hans-Georg Gadamer left Frankfurt to accept a position at the University of Heidelberg, but the faculty voted against him because they were not eager to give Critical Theory too much influence. In the end, Adorno received a fairly modest appointment as *außerplanmäßiger außerordentlicher Professor*[11] of philosophy. It took him seven more years to reach the rank of full professor at the University of Frankfurt.

This slow rise typified the situation of the émigrés. Both Horkheimer and Adorno were aware of the mixed emotions of their German colleagues and the German government officials who were involved in their academic appointments: behind the facade of good will and eagerness to make up for injustice, there was an uneasy combination of guilt and resentment. Not uncommon among German academics was the feeling that the refugees had suffered less in their safe exile than had those who stayed in Germany.[12] *Wiedergutmachung* – compensation for losses of various kinds during the Third Reich – was not a popular concept. Moreover, Adorno and Horkheimer could by no means be certain whether the anti-Semitism that had played a major part in their removal from the university in 1933 had disappeared. In fact, during their negotiations with various German institutions they sensed that the old mentality was still alive.[13]

Although the return of the Institute for Social Research to Frankfurt was in most respects a success (primarily because of Horkheimer's extraordinary talents as a patient and persistent negotiator), it was not without problems. The rebuilding on German soil was largely achieved through the help of the American government, in particular its branches in the American occupation zone. Horkheimer and Adorno themselves returned to Germany as American citizens and realized that the American connection was essential for their plans, which came under the umbrella of German reeducation. Specifically, the Institute was expected to help with the rebuilding of the social sciences in West Germany.

But how could this task be achieved? How could Horkheimer and Adorno have an impact on the next generation of German academics? For Horkheimer, this became largely a matter of administration – not only in his position as the senior director of the Institute but also through his rank at the university. Within a short time he became, first, dean of the Faculty of Philosophy and then *Rektor* (president) of the University of Frankfurt.[14] At the same time, especially during the early 1950s, he was a highly successful teacher. For Adorno, the question of teaching was more difficult. As his essays from the 1960s make very clear, he felt that the role of the educator in postwar Germany had to be clarified. The project of *Bildung,* which had been at the center of Wilhelm von Humboldt's university reform during the early nineteenth century,[15] had to be reassessed in terms of both its goals and its pedagogical methods. In particular, the unproblematic acceptance of the concept of the subject could not be taken for granted.

Adorno's reflections in *Minima Moralia* (written during the 1940s) had already addressed this point. Under the conditions of advanced capitalism (either in its German fascist variety or in its American form as the culture industry), the ideal of *Bildung* – which contained the notions of a stable center and of biographical continuity, abstracted from the specific social and psychological configuration of the nineteenth century in which it had been embedded – had become an illusion. As Adorno pointed out, in his own time the individual was treated as an object available for manipulation, rather than as a subject who could be expected to pursue a process of *Bildung* in the traditional sense. His experience as a refugee in the United States had brought home to him what it meant to be taken out of one's traditional social and cultural context:

The past life of the émigrés is, as we know, annulled. Earlier it was the warrant of arrest, today it is intellectual experience, that is declared nontransferable and unnaturalizable. Anything that is not reified, cannot be counted and measured, ceases to exist. Not satisfied with this, however, reification spreads to its own opposite, the life that cannot be directly actualized; anything that lives on merely as thought and recollection. . . . To complete its violation, life is dragged along on the triumphal automobile of the united statisticians, and even the past is no longer safe from the present, whose remembrance of it consigns it a second time to oblivion. (MM 46–47; GS 4:52)

With professional résumés replacing autobiographical narratives, the subject is subdivided into useful but isolated features and elements whose interrelationship is no longer of interest to the prospective employer. For Adorno, this decomposition of the personality included the loss of personal experience (*Erfahrung*). For instance, those who participated in the war were exposed to the horror of destruction without gaining insights from the events themselves (MM 54; GS 4:60). According to Adorno, World War II went completely beyond the scope of individual experience, just as a machine differs from the responses of the body, which begins to act machinelike when it becomes ill. Adorno argued that modern warfare fractures continuity and thereby the conception of history as an epic narrative. Consequently, there is no continuous memory of the individual's involvement. Life turns into a series of shocks; between them, we find gaps of paralysis.

The terror of the war, which for Adorno reached its climax in the planned annihilation of the Jews, radically undermined the project of *Bildung*: a concept of *Bildung* that used the German cultural tradition to justify anti-Semitism was tainted by the mass murders. Nietzsche's scorn for Germany's educational system and the official high culture of the Second Empire had turned into the petrified distance of the isolated intellectual in exile, reduced to the role of a powerless observer. Unlike Nietzsche, however, Adorno, in distancing himself from the concept of *Bildung*, focused on the person of the potential educator and the damage done even to those who were not in the maelstrom of destruction. Could one reintroduce culture in Germany after the Holocaust? What was the moral position of the Jewish refugees who returned to Germany after the defeat of the Third Reich?

> To the question what is to be done with defeated Germany, I could say only two things in reply. Firstly: at no price, on no conditions, would I wish to be an executioner or to supply legitimations for executioners. Secondly: I should not wish, least of all with legal machinery, to stay the hand of anyone who was avenging past misdeeds. This is a thoroughly unsatisfactory, contradictory answer, one that makes a mockery of both principle and practice. But perhaps the fault lies in the question and not only in me. (MM 56; GS 4:62)

The possible alternative to this problematic and contradictory position was teaching: that is, influencing the next generation of Germans so that they would not repeat what their parents or grandparents had done.

For Adorno, the project of reeducation had to begin with an assessment of the mentality of the Germans after World War II; furthermore, it had to consider the educational approach itself, especially if one was convinced, as Adorno was, that the restoration of traditional German high culture was out of the question. The suggestion of the historian Friedrich Meinecke that Germany, after its defeat in 1945, set up many local Goethe Associations was precisely the kind of approach that Adorno had already discarded during the 1940s.[16] *Dialectic of Enlightenment* expressed as much an indictment of traditional German high culture as of American mass culture. At the same time, however, he was not prepared to write off the German tradition in philosophy, music, and literature simply as a failure; his commitment to the tradition of German and Austrian music from Bach to Arnold Schönberg and to the German philosophical tradition beginning with Kant remained as strong as ever.[17] During his tenure at the University of Frankfurt he regularly offered seminars on the German idealist tradition, especially on Hegel.

For Adorno, the German intellectual and cultural tradition was an indispensable means of carrying out the critical reassessment of the German postwar situation, but this tradition could not simply be invoked as if it were a mere neutral tool. It also had to be singled out as an object of study in order to reflect on its involvement in the course of German history that had resulted in National Socialism. Still, Adorno's own analysis of the German question drew heavily on this legacy, which for him contained the very elements necessary to address German history. In this respect he differed markedly from Georg Lukács, who in *The Destruction of Reason* (1953) simply divided the German intellectual tradition into a good strand leading into socialism and a bad one leading inevitably to fascism. For Adorno, by contrast, it was a matter of reading the tradition against the grain, of disarming enemies by robbing them of the instruments of destruction.

Of course, Adorno's assessment of German fascism began well before 1949, when he and Horkheimer returned to Frankfurt. Their work at the Institute for Social Research continued the research on the authoritarian personality which they had carried out as a group project during the mid-1940s in California.[18] Adorno in particular, while stressing the importance of social and economic elements, remained committed to a psychological approach to the analysis of National Socialism and anti-Semitism. This became clear with his involvement in the first empirical project undertaken by the Institute in postwar Germany in 1950. Its goal was an analysis of the political consciousness of the West German adult population.

In the critical literature on the Frankfurt School this study is rarely mentioned, possibly because it was not altogether successful.[19] It immediately met with severe criticism from experts because it had not entirely solved the crucial methodological problem of fusing quantitative and qualitative methods convincingly. Not without reason, however, Adorno sensed that the criticism derived in part from the subject matter itself. In his defense against the polemic of the Austrian psychologist Peter R. Hofstätter, [20] he pointed out that resistance to the results of the study was fundamentally motivated by an attempt to whitewash the Germans (GS 9 [2]: 378–94).

The question of method was of crucial concern to Adorno, not only because it possibly made the study vulnerable in the eyes of experts such as Hofstätter but, more important, because the very goal of the project could not be reached through a purely quantitative approach. In 1950 an analysis of public opinion in West Germany with respect to German war crimes had to take into account that conventional questionnaires would not necessarily expose the true attitudes of the respondents. It was the task of the study to differentiate between the layer of publicly acknowledged opinions and the deeper layer of more personal feelings and unacknowledged mentalities. In other words, Adorno and Horkheimer conceived public opinion as a complex construct that could not easily be assessed through traditional quantitative methods. Therefore, they devised a format of group discussions that would allow participants (who were not chosen at random but selected according to predetermined criteria of age, gender, and social status) to speak to the involvement of the German population in the war, especially in the annihilation of the Jews. These discussions, which were taped and transcribed, formed the text that became available for analysis. At the center of the project, then, was the hermeneutical task of reading the statements of the participants within the specific context of a recorded discussion, rather than analyzing statements that responded to isolated questions in a questionnaire. The evaluation of the discussions was designed to get at the hidden and buried aspects of the openly stated opinions, thereby providing the analyst with a depth that quantitative methods could not easily match.

The findings of the Institute, published in 1955, were anything but reassuring. The image of the Federal Republic as a stable democracy under the leadership of Konrad Adenauer and the Christian Democrats turned out to be less reliable than had commonly been assumed. With respect to the mentality of the adult population, 1945 had not been the radical turningpoint as which it was portrayed in the official West German narrative.[21] Rather, it became quite clear in the discussion groups that the past still had a grip on the population precisely because its meaning was frequently not acknowledged. Only a minority of the participants were ready to admit that they knew, at least in some form, about the Final Solution, though sometimes the statements contained facts or opinions suggesting to the analyst that the speaker knew more about the events at a half-conscious level than he or she was willing to concede.

Equally disturbing was the discovery that Nazi ideology had by no means completely disappeared in the minds of the subjects. For Adorno, such a radical change was not to be expected, as he stated at the opening of the section on the ideology of the National Socialists: 'During the twelve years of totalitarian information, propaganda, and education the indoctrination went so deep that it could not simply be erased by a (military) defeat; this defeat, while it destroyed delusions, insofar as the Reich was toppled from the dominant position in Europe, also gave birth to legends about its former glory' (GS 9 [2]: 263–64). Of course, the resistance to change rarely took the form of open affirmation of Nazi ideology; rather, in the discussions it was presented as a defense of the good or pure elements of this ideology compared with the corruption it underwent later in the Third Reich. Another way of defending the past was to emphasize the material benefits of the Third Reich, particularly during its early years, in contrast with the suffering of the population – or parts of it – during the Weimar period and again after World War II.

An example of Adorno's method of reading is his analysis of the statement of a master smith (GS 9 [2]: 269 ff), who made an open attempt to defend the ideological implications of the Third Reich with the (popular) argument that given the choice between left and right, the Nazis had been the better alternative.[22] He contended that they should not have been defeated, because they could have served as a weapon against the evil of Bolshevism. Adorno's commentary summarizes the typical elements in this position and argues that for this man nothing has changed. He does not experience a conflict between his Nazi past and the postwar situation; even the fact that the National Socialists ultimately lost the war does not fully register. Their defeat is perceived as an interlude in a larger project on which he still counts. His unrelenting fanaticism blocks any perception of change.

Important in this context is Adorno's insistence on the linguistic means of revealing the mentality of the speaker. Quite consciously, Adorno applies the methods of literary analysis to the recorded material in order to penetrate the mechanisms that block the retrieval of experience. At the heart of his critique we find the argument that the repeated invocation of fascist ideology makes the speaker's reflection on his or her own experience impossible. Reeducation would have to break through the ideological wall before the admission of guilt and responsibility could be achieved. The life of the perpetrator, Adorno suggests, is as damaged as that of the victim. In either case, a restoration of nineteenth-century humanism in the name of *Bildung* would be psychologically as well as socially inadequate. Adorno's later reflections on teaching and education make use of this insight.

The assessment of the political consciousness of the Germans in the early 1950s was an important link between the authoritarian personality study and Adorno's essays of the late 1950s and the 1960s. One can only speculate as to why he did not pursue the German question any further immediately after the publication of *Gruppenexperiment,* to which he contributed the part 'Schuld und Abwehr' (Guilt and defensiveness). He may have been disappointed that the study failed to have a major impact, or he may have decided that he and his collaborators had done all they could at the time. In any case, when Adorno returned to the topic at the end of that decade and in the next, the political atmosphere of the Federal Republic had already changed significantly. Now, he could speak to a new generation: that is, to those who had experienced the Third Reich as children or youths but had not been old enough to serve in the German army during World War II.[23]

Adorno addressed the German question in two essays: in 1959 he published 'Was bedeutet Aufarbeitung der Vergangenheit?' (What does coming to terms with the past mean? GS 10 [2]: 555–72), and in 1966 he wrote 'Erziehung nach Auschwitz' (Education after Auschwitz; GS 10 [2]: 674–90).[24] In both, much more strongly than in the group project of 1955, he foregrounded the personal nature of his reflections and more clearly marked the subject position of the author, although it never dominated the presentation. Less concrete, especially in the earlier essay, given as a lecture at the Christian Academy in 1959, is the profile of the recipient. Adorno avoided the rhetoric of admonition; his commitment and personal concern expressed themselves more through the presentation of the material than through direct moral intervention.

In its appraisal of the German past, the lecture harks back to the group study of 1955. Again, when addressing the problem of National Socialism, Adorno focuses almost exclusively on the annihilation of the Jews and the reasons for the inability of the German population to come to terms with its collective past; however, the speculative element of the Freudian model, which Adorno uses to explain the events, comes more clearly into the foreground. Once more he presents the thesis to his German audience that *Aufarbeitung* (a working-through) of the past failed because those who took part in it refused to acknowledge their involvement and consequently their responsibility. The failure to remember, Adorno argues, and therefore the failure to include the horror in one's own identity open up the possibility of the return of the repressed. For this reason, Adorno is not yet convinced that democracy in Germany has firm and lasting roots. Only the process of working through the guilt will enable the Germans to free themselves from the authoritarian and totalitarian elements of their mentality which Adorno still detects within German society.

For Adorno, the major problem was not the antidemocratic forces on the fringe, such as neo-Nazis and conservative radicals; instead, the true danger lay in the traces of the fascist mentality within the democratic political system. In his analysis of this danger he specifically uses Freud's theory of collective narcissism as an analytic tool, treating National Socialism as a severe case of collective narcissism. In 1933, national vanity exploded all boundaries. The narcissistic *Triebregelung* (instinctual order) that persisted in the individual, although the hardened contours of reality promised less and less gratification, found substitute gratification through the process of identification with the state. Adorno argues that although this collective narcissism was severely damaged by the breakdown of the Third Reich, the setback has occurred only in the realm of material facts – not in the mind of the Germans. Hence, the individual does not consciously realize the loss and cannot, therefore, overcome it (GS 10 [2]: 563).

Freudian theory plays an equally important role in the later essay. Again, referring to Freud's later cultural essays, Adorno focuses on the blind and therefore potentially violent identification of the individual with the collective, in which complete submission to the norms and values of the collective turns into hatred of those who are excluded. To avoid the danger of a return of fascism, Adorno argues, the most important measure is a defensive wall against the overwhelming power of all collectives, and resistance against these collectives should be strengthened by consciously focusing on the problematic nature of collective identity (GS 10 [2]: 681). This pedagogical strategy underscores Adorno's conviction that the critique of National Socialism must take the form of enlightenment, specifically of working through the psychological aspect of Nazism so that its unconscious elements can be brought into the open and made conscious. Although Adorno is aware of the limitations of this strategy and explicitly points to the material and social side of the complex, he considers it the only pedagogically viable path. In other words, he implicitly criticizes conservative pedagogical models, which regard the integration (*Einbindung*) of the individual into the community and its values as the instrument to overcome the danger of fascism. His critique is specifically based on the thesis that National Socialism was not merely the result of an older authoritarian structure but rather the effect of the decomposition of traditional authorities.

'Erziehung nach Auschwitz,' in short, contained a strong sociological and historical component that had been missing in the 1959 essay. When Adorno came back to the German question in 1966, he tried to combine the psychoanalytical approach with a sociological understanding by stressing the continuation after the war of those social forces that had been the preconditions for the rise of the Third Reich – not so much specific political or economic events as objective social structures in which the individual feels helplessly trapped and therefore responds with irrational behavior. This argument blends seamlessly with Adorno's assessment of postwar West Germany as a late capitalist society characterized by overwhelming administrative structures.

In 1966, Adorno placed more emphasis on the inevitable social reproduction of a reified consciousness among the masses than he had done in 1959. For this reason, the pedagogical project to which he was no less committed had to face the resistance of objective forces that could not be easily treated within the student-teacher relationship. Hence, Adorno's commitment contained a moment of pessimism and skepticism. Knowing well that political consciousness is both psychologically and socially mediated, he could only invoke the principle of human autonomy through reflection as a means of overcoming the fascist collective. 'The only true force against the principle of Auschwitz would be human autonomy, if I may use the Kantian term: that is, the force of reflection and of self-determination, the will to refuse participation' (GS 10 [2]: 670). It is not accidental that in the context of the Holocaust Adorno invokes the very principle of the enlightenment that he and Horkheimer had radically questioned in *Dialectic of Enlightenment*.

Adorno's pedagogical project emphasized the importance of individual teachers and students. Nowhere did he suggest that the educational system of the Federal Republic should be changed (for instance in its elitist stance vis-à-vis the working class).[25] Neither did he outline new curricula; his remarks about desirable subjects and classroom topics were brief and not offered as binding recommendations. What Adorno called the necessary *Entbarbarisierung* (debarbarization) of large segments of the German population in 1966 (for example the rural population)[26] was to be accomplished through intensive teaching rather than bureaucratic planning. The reason for this emphasis is not difficult to state: given the character of advanced industrial societies, any kind of planning would ultimately reinforce the reified consciousness it was supposed to subvert. That is why Adorno's emphatic claim concerning the need for education has a reverse side: an attitude of resignation with respect to the overwhelming power of the blind social forces within advanced Western societies.

Adorno's own pedagogical efforts were of course primarily located within the department of philosophy. One of his functions was that of an examiner of future high school teachers, who had to pass a general examination in philosophy (*Philosophicum*) before they were admitted to the general examinations in their field of specialization (*Staatsexamen*). In his capacity as an examiner for the state, Adorno had to deal with students who for the most part studied philosophy only in order to pass the *Philosophicum*. As he points out in his essay 'Philosophie und Lehrer' (Philosophy and teacher; GS 10 [2]: 474–94), these students usually showed no special interest in and little appreciation of philosophical discourse. For them, the examination was a nothing but a hurdle they had to overcome in order to receive their professional licenses. Adorno, on the other hand, thought the exam should prove that the candidate was able to understand and to discuss philosophical problems within a larger cultural context. He mentions the case of a student who chose to be examined about Henri Bergson but was completely unable to situate the texts she had selected, or to detect any link between Bergson and Impressionist painting. Adorno uses this example to demonstrate an approach to philosophy that altogether undercuts the purpose of the exam. By restricting her attention exclusively to the content, the candidate reified its meaning. Instead of relating to the text and its problems, she could at best reproduce the opinions of the philosopher. What Adorno's essay deplores more than the students' lack of extensive familiarity with the philosophical canon is their stubborn refusal to enter into philosophical dialogue with their teachers and examiners. For this reason, philosophy remains for them a mere object of study, not a mental exercise and intellectual experience. In other words, their attitude is that of specialists whose consciousness is largely ossified; they do not reach the level of active self-reflection (*lebendige Selbstbesinnung*).

Because Adorno wants the preliminary examination in philosophy to function as an intellectual exercise in which the candidate, through a dialogue with the examiner, demonstrates his or her grasp of the problems involved in the reading of the assigned text, he emphasizes the process of reflection rather than the factual result. The examination, he points out, is designed to find out whether the candidate, while reflecting on his or her special field, can move beyond the range of the prepared material. Adorno continues: 'To put it simply, the question is whether they are spiritual human beings [*geistige Menschen*], if the term "spiritual human beings" would not have certain arrogant connotations, reminding us of elitist desires to dominate, desires that prevent the academic teacher from achieving self-determination' (GS 10 [2]: 476 f.). Indeed, terms such as *geistiger Mensch* and *geistige Bildung* (spiritual self-formation) do have problematic connotations, invoking the kind of pre-war idealism that Adorno scorned. Nevertheless, he seems unable to do without them, since they refer to a project of *Bildung* of which philosophers such as Johann Fichte, Friedrich Schelling, and Wilhelm von Humboldt were representative. Thus it is not accidental that the essay contains an extensive quotation from Fichte's writings (GS 10 [2]: 477–78). The element of German idealism that Adorno wants to rescue is the moment of reflexivity: that is, self-understanding through the understanding of cultural texts. Though he can be highly critical of the absolute claims of idealism, in this instance he almost identifies with Fichte's definition of philosophical training as an antidote to the implicit positivist tendencies of his own time.

This strong pedagogical endorsement of the idealist tradition contains a political moment that deserves closer scrutiny. If the educational project is designed to make impossible the return of National Socialism, teachers must be trained in such a way that they can help with the eradication of fascist mentalities. For Adorno, the point of the examination is to find out whether the future teacher, who will be in part responsible for the intellectual as well as material development of Germany, is an intellectual or just a specialist (*Fachmensch*). Clearly, he has not completely abandoned the idea of self-formation, as it was articulated by German classicism and idealism; however, in Adorno's formulations it receives a more critical turn. His pedagogical essays stress that the political function of self-reflection (*Selbstbesinnung*) is largely negative, a scrutiny of mentalities that could lead back to political totalitarianism.

In this context the concept of *Urbanität* takes on a strong meaning. Ever since the 1950 group project Adorno had been particularly suspicious of the protofascist tendencies among the rural population in Germany; for instance, he noted that many concentration camp guards were the younger sons of peasants.[27] Their backwardness and lack of cultural schooling was perceived as a potential source of authoritarian attitudes. In the pedagogical essays Adorno argues that the persistent difference between the urban and the rural – especially the lack of cultural refinement outside the cities, resulting from centuries of neglect and depravation – is one of the reasons for the continued resistance to culture. In Adorno's mind, barbarism is in itself closely related to fascism, since for him the latter resulted from a regression to barbarism.

In a curious way, Adorno's program, if it can be called a program at all, points in two opposite directions. For him, literally and metaphorically, *Bildung* means *Urbanisierung*: that is, the process of transforming a premodern society into a modern industrial and urban society where the individual is exposed to culture and thus receives a higher degree of autonomy. But at the same time, Adorno warns against modern bureaucracy and its inclination toward total planning, which reduces the individual to a purely functional role. From this perspective, modern society comes across as the enemy of individual self-articulation. Modern man or woman is the expert (*Fachmensch*) who has lost the capacity of reflecting on the purpose of objective knowledge.

Adorno commented on education and pedagogical problems in occasional essays; he did not develop a systematic theory of education to deal with the foregoing contradiction. His essays must be seen as personal interventions bringing into the foreground precisely those elements that the professional discourse tended to repress. This is particularly true of his lecture 'Tabus über den Lehrerberuf' (Taboos of the teaching profession; GS 10 [2]: 656–73), first presented in 1965 at the Institut für Bildungsforschung (Institute for Pedagogical Research). There is no attempt at a systematic assessment of the social and cultural role of the teaching profession. The highly anecdotal lecture gains its intellectual momentum from Adorno's idiosyncratic reflections on personal experiences and works of literature, as well as sociological observations and cultural commentaries. To some extent the lecture can be seen as a supplement to the essay 'Philosophie und Lehrer.' The latter concentrates on the student; the former investigates the role and mentality of the teacher.

Adorno's observations focus exclusively on elementary and high school teachers, since in the German context university teachers represent, socially as well as culturally, a separate category. Because of this valid local distinction, Adorno does not talk about his own group and its position within the matrix of German society. In fact, the clearly marked division allows him, the prestigious university professor, to distance himself from the somewhat dubious position of the teacher. Still, one misses a significant aspect of the essay if one reads it exclusively as the psychological and sociological analysis of a professional group. What Adorno detects in the moral and intellectual physiognomy of the teacher also applies, at least indirectly, to those who teach at the university level – including Theodor W. Adorno.

For Adorno, teachers are professionals who have not made it, who – unlike lawyers and doctors – have never quite been accepted as a profession. In spite of their academic degrees and their status as tenured state employees, they are not part of Germany's social elite. Adorno perceives them as a relatively powerless and therefore potentially resentful social group that can all too easily displace social frustration by taking it out on the students. Although Adorno does not use the term in the essay, it is fairly apparent that in describing the teacher as a psychological type, the school tyrant, he is referring to the authoritarian personality. The use of physical violence in the school, certainly a common practice when Adorno was a student and possibly still tolerated in some places at the time of his lecture, marks the teacher as one who enforces necessary discipline through violence but is held in low esteem for doing so.

> Society delegates physical power to the teacher and at the same time disowns it in those to whom it has been delegated. The archetype [*Urbild*] (I am talking here about imaginary and unconsciously virulent ideas rather than empirical reality, or only to a very small extent), the archetype of these

images of the teacher is that of the jailer, possibly even that of the drill sergeant. (GS 10 [2]: 663)

The imaginary link between teaching and punishment, for which Adorno can cite powerful literary examples – both Heinrich Mann's novel *Professor Unrat* (1905) and Frank Wedekind's play *Frühlings Erwachen* (1891) deal with power relations between teachers and students – is a potentially explosive configuration that conventional empirical studies would necessarily miss. Teachers as the persons who enforce social discipline also become the mediators of social violence. But since their power is restricted to the classroom and the life-world of the students, they ultimately come across as impotent weaklings.

Adorno's analysis clearly touches on Germany's authoritarian past, an institutional tradition in which culture and political power had been so fused that culture and education were subservient to the political power elite. As Adorno knew from his own experience in 1933, this tradition was by no means limited to the level of the high school. German universities had actively participated in the expulsion of 'undesirable' faculty members, thereby demonstrating their own obedience to the new power elite. But Adorno's interest in the role of the teacher cannot be reduced to a specific historical situation. His attempt to offer, in a highly anecdotal manner, an archaeology of the teacher suggests that he perceives a larger problem. In order to define it, and possibly as an intertextual reference to Heinrich Mann's famous essay 'Geist und Macht' (1910), Adorno contrasts spirit (*Geist*) and power: 'Spirit is separated from physical power. Though it has always played a certain role in the steering mechanisms of society, it became suspect wherever the older preeminence of physical power survived the division of labor. This premodern element resurfaces again and again' (GS 10 [2]: 659).

In this version of the configuration, the weak position of intellectual work is not limited to the role of the teacher but applies to its various historical representations: shamans, priests, philosophers, and intellectuals. Although he does not explicitly include himself in this broader definition, Adorno has every reason to do so. His own precarious situation among colleagues at the Univer-

sity of Frankfurt who were frequently resentful of his rhetorical
brilliance, and vis-à-vis the larger public in West Germany who
admired his radio talks, public lectures, and essays but might also
disempower him again, reflected the very configuration he examines. Unlike Max Horkheimer, Adorno was never good at dealing
with political leaders or the business community. His strength was
that of the writer and intellectual.

Because of the ambivalent reputation of the teaching profession
in modern society, Adorno's pedagogical project does include
definite recommendations for the training of teachers. Hence, his
lecture ends on a practical note. He raises the question 'What is
to be done?' and recommends the public exploration of the repressed, the opening up of the problems that have haunted the
teaching profession. For Adorno, addressing the 'psychological
deformation' of the teachers is the only viable approach to changing the persistence of the authoritarian syndrome. What he envi-
sions is a sociological and psychoanalytical model of enlightenment: 'The psychological deformation of many teachers will
probably continue (if my observations as an examiner are not
misleading), though it has by and large lost its social basis. This deformation, apart from removing the still-existing control mechanisms, should be corrected through training' (GS 10 [2]: 671).

Here Adorno points to the well-known but mostly unacknowledged difference between the atmosphere at the university and the
practical training seminars for future teachers after they have
passed the state board: the institutional dulling of the mind
through the enforcement of strict intellectual discipline in post-
university training. He goes on to explain that future restructuring of post-university teacher training would have to question
the concept of 'educational necessity' (*schulische Notwendigkeit*)
which has repressed intellectual freedom and processes of self-
formation. Obviously, this kind of suggestion is made by someone
who has no institutional power: that is, by someone who speaks in
the precarious role of an intellectual and can only hope that his
rhetoric will influence his listeners.

Especially in the final paragraphs, where Adorno returns to
the consequences of the Holocaust, it becomes even clearer that

'Tabus über den Lehrerberuf' must be seen as a supplement to 'Philosophie und Lehrer.' Adorno's pedagogical project, with its emphatic invocation of the Enlightenment, underscores a critical confrontation with the aftermath of the Holocaust.

> My generation has experienced the relapse of humankind into barbarism, in a literal, unspeakable, and true sense. Barbarism is a state that defies all those formations [*Formungen*] that define education. As long as society produces barbarism from within, the school's resistance will remain minimal. However, since barbarism, the dreadful shadow falling on our existence, is the opposite of a process of self-formation [*Bildung*], the essential task will be to debarbarize the individual. (GS 10 [2]: 672)

This appeal to *Bildung* has a double edge: it simultaneously addresses the subjective and objective aspects of the problem, with the important difference, however, that for Adorno the objective side – that is, the social complex – is not as readily accessible to change as the subjective.

In his last years Adorno found himself confronting precisely this question: are the objective social and political conditions, as they determine the outlook and attitudes of the individual, open to change? Going back to the revolutionary writings of Marx and Engels (for instance, Marx's 'Theses on Feuerbach'), the student movement of the late 1960s challenged teachers by insisting on the nexus between theory and praxis.[28] In a short defense written in 1969 (translated as 'Resignation' in 1978), Adorno summarizes his own position. Although he underscores the dialectical principle of mediation between theory and praxis, he rejects the students' call for practice as mere activism without revolutionary legitimation. In Adorno's theory, since the time for revolutionary action has long since passed, those who favor political action through collectives undergo a process of regressive identification with the collective. Instead, theory itself must stand in for political practice, for 'the leap into praxis does not cure thought from resignation as long as this is paid for with the secret knowledge that this course is simply not the right one.'[29]

Adorno's outright rejection of the early student movement's emphasis on spontaneous action is based on the theory of advanced capitalist societies that he and Horkheimer developed during the mid-1940s. In 'Resignation' its main characteristics are merely hinted at: in a totally administered society, unmediated protest will ultimately affirm the status quo because it will necessarily copy the psychological patterns it wants to oppose. The individual activist, far from being an autonomous subject, has given up autonomy for membership in a collective that enables him or her to act. In other words, Freudian theory has to come to the rescue of Critical Theory in its defense of a purely critical stance that quite consciously retreats from a Marxian to a left-Hegelian position.

In Adorno's late social theory the social element becomes increasingly abstract and unavailable to empirical criticism.[30] Beginning with *Dialectic of Enlightenment,* social theory becomes subservient to the philosophy of history, more specifically to the thesis that the historical process has been largely determined by instrumental reason and the human drive to dominate nature. This overall design is supplemented by the argument that the twentieth century has witnessed the transition from liberal to state capitalism, either in its fascist or its corporate American (culture industry) version. For Adorno and Horkheimer, Friedrich Pollock's theory of state capitalism – developed during the early 1940s in competition with the theories of Franz Neumann and Otto Kirchheimer, who had stressed the private and primarily economically motivated character of the economy under National Socialism – becomes fundamental. In its more generalized version, as Horkheimer and Adorno apply it in their own writings, state capitalism refers to a mode of organization in which the competing interests of capitalists struggling for a share of the market have been replaced by a central administration ultimately controlled by the state.[31] In this configuration, the interests of large corporations and the state bureaucracy conflate in a form of technical rationality that relegates all social conflicts to a subordinate level. In Adorno's writings this position was first articulated in the 1942 essay 'Reflexionen zur Klassentheorie' (Reflection on the theory of class; GS 8:373–91) and stated once more, with minor modifications, in his famous late essay 'Spätkapitalismus oder Industriegesellschaft' (Late capitalism or industrial society; GS 8:354–70). What was originally meant to explain the relationship between state and economy under fascism served after the war as a universal theory of late capitalist societies such as West Germany.

Adorno's critique in 'Reflexionen' of the traditional Marxist class concept assumes that 'the total organization of society by big business and its everpresent technology . . . has so completely shaped reality and ideas that the thought that things could be in any way different has become an almost hopeless effort' (GS 8:376). Economic and social reproduction have been reorganized in such a way that traditional notions of conflict and antagonism have lost their significance. The older antagonistic model has been replaced by the concept of a total system that completely determines all its elements: 'In its blindness the system is dynamic and accumulates misery, but its own self-preservation, which is accomplished by this dynamic, terminates, even with regard to suffering, in that stasis which has always provided the background [*Orgelpunkt*] of the prehistorical dynamic' (GS 8:385). As a result, the individual has become a mere object of the monopolies and the state apparatus. 'This weakness,' Adorno argued in 1942, 'allows the carrying out of war in many countries' (GS 8:386).

After the war, his interest in reformulating the concept of class and class antagonism more or less disappeared. Instead, the power of the apparatus has moved to the center – a shift that necessarily underlined the passive and objectified nature of the individual human being. Adorno's definition of late capitalism as organized capitalism emphasizes its static dimension. He maintains that the social system of his time, however much it is characterized by dynamism and increased production, has more static elements as well. They are part of the relations of production. Relations of production are no longer conceived in terms of private property; rather, they are defined in terms of administrative processes, with the state as the ultimate administrator of the total system (GS 8: 363). Under these conditions the traditional distinction between masters and slaves has lost its force. More important, for Adorno, the dialectic of forces of production and relations of production has also come to an end. There is no hope for a revolution arising from their contradictions. Consequently, the fate of the human race is determined by the center. The essay 'Spätkapitalismus oder Industriegesellschaft' suggests that only the apparatus and its functionaries are empowered to ensure the maintenance of the system; the individual as well as traditional collectives are either powerless or completely manipulated.

It would have been difficult to provide empirical proof for this assessment of the social and economic system of the Federal Republic of Germany during the 1960s, but the force of Adorno's argument did not rest on empirical evidence; rather, his position was grounded in the philosophical perspective of a social theory developed by the Frankfurt School during the 1940s as a response to National Socialism. Its central category, state capitalism, implied a market paralyzed by the systematic and overwhelming intervention of the state. Adorno interpreted the emergence of the welfare state in America (the New Deal) and in postwar Germany as a continuation of World War II state capitalism.

Adorno's social diagnosis burdens his pedagogical project with a major problem: the thesis of a totally administered society in which the individual is conceived of as passive and manipulated leaves little room for individual self-formation. The immobile contemporary society that Adorno's theory insists on cannot, at least not in a systematic fashion, provide the space for transformations to take place; the fate of late capitalism is to reproduce identical patterns. Hence, Adorno's emphatic insistence on the possibility of human autonomy (reached through education) faces the objection that this process is objectively impossible. According to Adorno, late capitalist institutions cannot favor educational and cultural processes whose goals are defined in terms of human autonomy. For this reason, in his late essay 'Resignation' he rigorously rejects collective social action, for the collective – already determined by the administrative center – will necessarily rob the individual of his or her autonomy. At the same time, Adorno is rightly skeptical of traditional theories of *Bildung*, because they tend to separate individual and social structure and ignore the objective pressure of the social totality.

Adorno's response to this dilemma is a psychoanalytical model of enlightenment. Its advantage is its critical force on two levels: first, it can deal with the ideological and mental resistance to individual and collective education by analyzing and exposing the hidden causes of their failure; second, it can create a crucial link between individual and social processes. The individual process of working through one's biography is expected to have an impact on the collective, as much as collective learning processes will provide the individual with potential insights. Thus, the demand for enlightenment must not be confused with the rational strategies of the apparatus. The Freudian model is exempt from instrumental rationality precisely because it offers critical access to the structure of the individual.

For this reason, Adorno's position vis-à-vis Freudian theory has significant consequences for his pedagogical project. His critique of revisionism in his essay 'Die revidierte Psychoanalyse' (The revision of psychoanalysis; GS 8:20–41) underscores the importance he ascribes to Freud's interpretation of sexuality on the basis of his theory of drives (*Trieblehre*). What he rejects in the work of neo-Freudian revisionists such as Karen Horney is their 'castration' of Freud's theory in order to fit it into an affirmative social theory. While Adorno clearly disagrees with the neo-Freudian effort to redefine psychoanalysis in terms of a larger social theory, he equally resists the claim of the late Freud that sociology is no more than applied psychology.[32] For Adorno, the appropriate space of psychoanalysis is the intersection between the individual and the social – or, more precisely, the unmastered confrontation, the failure of rational interaction. 'On what is or used to be its homeground, psychoanalysis carries specific convictions; the further it removes itself from that sphere, the more its theses are threatened alternatively with shallowness or wild over-systematizations.'[33] Adorno goes on to argue that the proper realm of psychology is the relatively autonomous individual as the site of conflicts between instinctual desires and inhibition.

Yet this formulation, taken from the late essay 'Zum Verhältnis von Soziologie und Psychologie' (GS 8:42–85), translated as 'Sociology and Psychology,' cannot do complete justice to Adorno's interest in psychoanalysis or to its function in his social theory. Its clear-cut separation of the individual and the social, which seems to relegate psychology to the status of an auxiliary discipline, does not exactly correspond to Adorno's use of Freud's theory. As his critique of Talcott Parsons's attempt to treat the difference between sociology and psychology strictly as a question of methodology (finding the appropriate frame of reference) makes clear, for Adorno the central question remains the articulation of those areas within the social for which the model of rational market exchange, as defined by liberal theory, is insufficient. For him, the abstract act of exchange is the core around which the individual character crystallizes. Psychology, in its reified state, measures this individual with its own yardstick. The isolated individual – that is, the pure subject of self-preservation – embodies in its opposition to society the very principle of modern society.[34] In its sheer and abstract desire to survive, Adorno recognizes the individual's complete social determination, with which psychology has to come to terms.

In other words, for Adorno, Freud's theory is a social theory dealing with aspects of the individual; in particular, it must deal with the problematic formation of the ego. For this reason, Freud's model is not only indispensable for an analysis of historical configuration – for instance, for an examination of fascism that goes beyond basic economic facts – but also essential for Adorno's definition of his pedagogical project. Whereas the neo-humanist tradition defined the process of *Bildung* as a harmonious exchange between the subject and social reality, Adorno suggests that it must be redefined in psychoanalytical terms to foreground the actual suffering and deformation of the individual as it occurs in the material process of social integration. Social theory and psychoanalysis interface where the pressure of organizations and institutions have damaged the development of the individual. By tracing the damages inflicted on the ego and their consequences within the larger social realm, psychoanalysis restores the potential process of self-formation that has been arrested or gone wrong. Therefore, the Freudian model of psychology can serve as an answer to the problem of stasis in late

capitalism, for it offers, to use Adorno's terminology, an immanent critique of social deformation. Its admittedly one-sided concentration on the individual (at the expense of the social totality)
simultaneously breaks up the deadlock of social theory, which in
Adorno's eyes can only reformulate the overwhelming power of
the status quo. In other words, through psychoanalytical criticism different forms of moral and political consciousness can be
achieved, which in turn hold open at least the hope for social
change as well.

Strictly speaking, of course, psychoanalysis cannot solve Adorno's antinomy, unless one assumes with Freud that the process of
healing will have an impact on the construction of social relations
as well (sociology as applied psychology). But Adorno's diagnosis
of reification in late capitalist societies will not support such a
belief; hence, the tension cannot be permanently resolved one way
or the other. In fact, this tension creates the space for Adorno's
category of negative utopia. As he argues at the end of 'Resignation,' thought processes do not reproduce facts; as long as these
processes continue, they open up possibilities. Thus, through resistance to closure and to easy answers, one rejects the problematic wisdom of resignation. For Adorno, thinking includes a utopian moment, which, however, is not to be confused with the
elaboration of a utopian society.[35]

Does this formulation encourage a return to a humanistic program of *Bildung,* a celebration of the autonomous individual?
Such a reading would seriously violate a precarious and unstable balance that remains in place only because theory rigorously
questions itself. Yet Adorno does not deny the theoretical relevance of the neohumanist project of the early nineteenth century,
which reorganized education in the name of the autonomous
individual; in his writings it serves as a moment of historical
memory. What he cannot overlook almost two centuries later,
however, is the contradiction between the conception of an autonomous individual within a free society of equal human beings,
and the terms of their freedom as defined by the market – which,
following its own logic, would undermine the very autonomy it
was supposed to secure. For this reason, Adorno cannot conceive

the individual exclusively or even primarily in terms of its subjectivity. As we have seen, he again and again stresses its objectified, damaged, and problematic character. Yet he does not completely eliminate its subject position either. In his understanding, the Freudian model of critique and enlightenment offers the possibility of self-reflection as a means of working through the problematic ideological construction of subjectivity and social reality. In this sense, as a form of analytical probing, exposing, and healing, the concept of *Bildung* as self-formation remains a central concern in Adorno's work. Compared with the neohumanist tradition of the early nineteenth century, however, Adorno underscores the moment of decentering: that is, the impossibility of affirmative self-control.

PART TWO: CRITICISM AND METHOD

4. Interpretation as Critique: The Path to Literature

THEODOR W. Adorno is almost unknown in the English-speaking world as a literary critic. Although he wrote some fifty essays on literary topics – among them pieces on Goethe, Marcel Proust, Paul Valéry, Franz Kafka, Hugo von Hofmannsthal, and Honoré de Balzac – his reputation as a critic is largely based on his contributions to music criticism. Among American musicologists his work on Arnold Schönberg, Gustav Mahler, and Richard Wagner, for example, is well known. His music criticism has received an acclaim that has been denied to his literary essays, although these essays are by no means less important than his writing on music.[1] As far as the Frankfurt School is concerned, the literary criticism of Walter Benjamin has almost completely eclipsed the contributions of Adorno. The irony is that it was Adorno who launched Benjamin's rediscovery after World War II. Without the two-volume edition of his work that Adorno brought out in 1955 – which, incidentally, emphasized through its selection Benjamin's early criticism and deemphasized his Marxist phase – Benjamin would probably be a forgotten author today.

How do we explain the absence of attention to Adorno's literary criticism in the United States? The obvious but clearly insufficient answer is that most of his essays have been translated relatively recently. Yet although even his most complex work, *Aesthetic Theory*, was finally made available to the English-speaking reader in 1984 and has subsequently begun to make an impact, the resistance to his literary essays has not yet been overcome. This has in part to do with their character. They are hardly conventional academic articles dealing with acknowledged research topics in an accepted academic manner. Instead, they are almost without exception highly personal, subjective, critical interventions written in a very uncommon style. To appreciate them, one must pay attention to their form and manner of presentation as much as to their topics and arguments. Hence, they are very difficult to translate without losing significant elements – precisely those elements that are embedded in their language.

Any sensitive reader familiar with Adorno's original texts realizes that a translation relying primarily on the transfer of ideas and arguments – as important as they are – misses the meaning of Adorno's literary criticism. As Samuel Weber, the cotranslator of *Prisms*, pointed out: 'Adorno's thought is inseparable from its articulation.'[2] Indeed, the German language as used by Adorno is incompatible with standard English prose. Even some German critics, to be sure, have always argued that his style lacks clarity and balance. It is apparent, however, that traditional notions of clarity and balance fail to grasp the force and structure of Adorno's prose, for his language means to capture the dialectical unfolding of the argument rather than the result, thus preserving in its articulation the tension that conventional discursive language wants to eliminate. As a result, his critical prose is, as Weber rightly observes, untranslatable; indeed, 'the untranslatability of Adorno is his most profound and cruel truth.'[3] Hence, any attempt to communicate the ideas of his literary essays must necessarily result in allegorical readings.

These observations pertain also to Adorno's writing on music – perhaps less to his commentary on sociological topics in his *Introduction to the Sociology of Music*, but certainly with similar force to his exploration of the structure of modern music. Still, Adorno's writing on modern composers is much better known in English than his pieces on literature. This discrepancy cannot be explained from within; rather, it appears to be the result of Adorno's peculiar reception in the English-speaking world. His multifaceted oeuvre, which he himself considered unified, was separated and channeled into three fields when it arrived in England and the United States. Adorno's importance was recognized by philosophers (at least by those familiar with the continental tradition), by social scientists, and by musicologists. In these fields Adorno has had a measurable impact on scholarship. His literary criticism, on the other hand, however influential within the boundaries of German culture, has been without a clearly defined Anglophone audience, a group of professional readers to appropriate its ideas and disseminate its method.

Even in Germany it is not easy to determine his impact on academic criticism. The second generation of the Frankfurt School was certainly familiar with Adorno's essays and occasionally tried to imitate their style; on the whole, however, they did not model their own work on his, for Adorno's prose could not be applied within academic criticism proper. His essays were rooted in a literary culture that emerged in the late nineteenth century, was then hailed by the young Georg Lukács in *Soul and Form*,[4] and later practiced by critics such as Ernst Bloch, Siegfried Kracauer, and Walter Benjamin and writers such as Thomas Mann and Robert Musil. Their artistic form makes Adorno's essays incompatible with and suspect to the project of academic criticism, which is based on the idea of research and scientific argument.

Adorno was, of course, conscious of this problem. The channels of reception mentioned above reflect precisely the reification of twentieth-century culture that he and Horkheimer analyzed in *Dialectic of Enlightenment.* The culture industry, with its desire to differentiate and categorize the cultural sphere in terms of consumer groups, tends to marginalize forms of criticism that cannot be legitimized through identifiable groups of producers and consumers. Adorno's literary criticism, however, insists on its public function. Its proper space is the public sphere, its task that of critique as it was defined by the Enlightenment. Although Adorno was certainly more distant from the Enlightenment than his student and successor Jürgen Habermas, he shared with the eighteenth century the understanding of criticism as *Kritik,* as critical intervention. Hence, he also emphasized the implied political dimension of literary criticism. Yet he viewed the aspect of professionalism – the foregrounding of the critic's expert status – with reservations. Although critics are clearly expected to be experts in their subject matter, they should not be constrained by professional boundaries. For Adorno, the expert status of professional critics (whether academics or journalists) can be redeemed only through the radical and subversive nature of their writing.

It is characteristic of the late Adorno that in an essay published in 1969, clearly responding to the radical political demands of students, he insisted on the democratic dimension of the concept of *Kritik* – 'Critique is essential to the institution of democracy' (GS 10 [2]: 785) – thereby stressing the political aspect as well as the direction of his project. Reading literature, where it is more than facile consumption, is neither mere appreciation nor mere explication, although both elements are, as Adorno emphasized in *Aesthetic Theory,* indispensable for criticism. Critical reading implies a critique of the artwork, of its technique, its formal structure, and most of all its *Wahrheitsgehalt* (truth content). This probing of the text, as we will see, is historical through and through – with respect to the situation of the critic as well as to the genesis of the work of art. For Adorno there is no reading outside of history – yet it would be misleading to call him a historicist. What distinguishes his method from the method of historicism is precisely the element of *Kritik,* the resistance to the act of historical empathy or the attempt at factual reconstruction. Adorno's literary essays consistently articulate their awareness of the historical force field but rarely provide background information on the particular historical circumstances. This absence of 'research' is in part due to the essay form – that is to say, it is a generic characteristic that Adorno took very seriously – yet it also applies to much of his music criticism, even in book-length works, where formal constraints could not be the cause.

Criticism entails the element of critique; historically, as Adorno pointed out in 1969, it emerged together with the formation of a public sphere in the eighteenth century where an unrestricted exchange of opinions became a reality, at least in Western Europe. This was a lesson that the young Adorno learned in the early 1930s from his friend and mentor Benjamin, who had already established himself as a professional critic and wrote reviews regularly for major newspapers and magazines. Benjamin stressed the negative force of criticism, its very lack of empathy and appreciation. Characteristically, he compared the critic to a cannibal: the critic approaches the text with the same feelings as those of the cannibal who is preparing the body of a baby for the feast. Adorno never had quite the stomach for this cannibalistic attitude; it took either a strong ideological provocation (as in the case of the late Georg Lukács)[5] or personal dislike (as in the case of Brecht)[6] to turn his critique into full-fledged polemic. But when we compare Adorno and Benjamin in this respect, we have to bear in mind that Adorno was never a freelance journalist who had to turn out reviews under time pressure to make a living. Especially once he had received a position at the University of Frankfurt after his return to Germany in 1949, he could afford to be selective and write exclusively on topics that interested him. Hence, his essays on literature reflect his personal preoccupations more directly than Benjamin's reviews reflect the preferences of their author. In Benjamin's case, we have to distinguish between his reviews, which were written to earn money, and his essays, which articulated his literary and political concerns.[7]

Nevertheless, Adorno's literary criticism is clearly indebted to the work of Benjamin in more than one respect. It was from Benjamin that the young Adorno appropriated the concept of negative dialectics,[8] and the impact of the *Trauerspiel* book can hardly be overestimated. At the same time, Adorno's reading of Benjamin's work was always selective and biased; relative to Benjamin's project, his appropriation can be called a productive misreading, as their exchange of letters on the *Passagen* project in 1936 makes abundantly clear.[9] Yet even though Adorno's version of negative dialectics turned out to differ significantly from Benjamin's materialism, this basic epistemological disagreement is not our concern. Benjamin's influence on Adorno in literary matters is first and foremost reflected in the latter's choices of authors and texts: that is, the literary horizon of Adorno is largely identical with that of Benjamin. Adorno's music criticism, although it stays fairly close to the canon, explores a terrain that he discovered for himself, whereas his literary criticism, which emerged only after Benjamin's death in 1940, tends to follow the lead of the older friend. There are exceptions of course, among them essays on Thomas Mann, Ernst Bloch, and younger writers such as Samuel Beckett and Rolf Hochhuth.

The scope of Adorno's literary criticism is considerable, ranging from Goethe and Friedrich Hölderlin to major writers of the twentieth century such as Proust, Valéry, Kafka, Thomas Mann, and Benjamin. His contributions to nineteenth-century criticism focus on such authors as Joseph von Eichendorff, Heinrich Heine, Balzac, and (in a rare excursion into English literature) Charles Dickens. To these we have to add his major theoretical and methodological essays, among them 'Reconciliation under Duress' and 'Commitment,' as well as his famous 'On Lyric Poetry and Society' (NL 1:37–54; GS 11:48–68), which argues for an intrinsic sociology of literature. The center of Adorno's literary criticism is clearly the early twentieth century: his favorite authors are the modernists, and his most pressing theoretical concern relates to modernism and the avant-garde.

It is in this area that he particularly overlaps with and also – as one sees in looking more closely – disagrees with Benjamin. His piece on surrealism[10] and his essay on Brecht, among others, can be seen as responses to Benjamin's work: they are critical rereadings whose thrust remains concealed unless the reader remembers Benjamin's position. The essence of Adorno's rereading is typically a critique of his friend's arguments. The most obvious case is their different attitudes toward the theorist and playwright Brecht. Adorno's polemic was at least partly motivated by the central role that Brecht's oeuvre occupied in Benjamin's definition of modernism, and it is here that their most fundamental disagreement comes into the foreground. Whereas Benjamin insisted on a break with high culture and therefore, especially during the early 1930s, searched for a post-auratic model of art,[11] Adorno consistently rejected this project as a dangerous regression to the level of pre-autonomous art. His concept of modernism was, as we will see, firmly based on the idea that art is an end in itself and must not be defined (as Benjamin had defined it) in operationalist terms.

This interest in and concern with the autonomous status of art is reflected also in the horizon of Adorno's literary criticism. It emphasizes the nineteenth and twentieth centuries, avoiding for the most part any contact with premodern – that is, pre-autonomous – literature. Unlike Benjamin, Adorno took no interest in the sixteenth or the seventeenth century. It might be added that his attitude toward baroque music is equally ambivalent, and he never shared the postwar nostalgia for premodern music. Even his rigorous defense of Bach is directed primarily against the admirers of baroque music, stressing the modern character of Bach's compositions and arguing that they are structurally related to the rise of industrial capitalism in the early eighteenth century.[12] Similarly, his essay 'On Lyric Poetry and Society' concentrates on the German tradition from Goethe to Stefan George, excluding the medieval period with the argument that our understanding of poetry is not really applicable to medieval literature.

To these historical boundaries we have to add the geographical borders of Adorno's criticism. For him, literature is European – particularly West European – literature. Outside the German tradition, he is primarily drawn to French authors. Excursions into English literature are rare (Dickens, Beckett), and there is no indication that he was ever interested in American literature, even though he lived in the United States for more than a decade. That he never wrote on major Russian or Spanish authors is possibly due to the fact that he did not feel comfortable with texts he could not read in the original language. Clearly, Adorno's panorama of literature has blind spots, the most noticeable being the absence of South American, Asian, and African literature, but even within European literature his preferences are unmistakable: it is obvious that English writers are marginal to his definition of literature. The same is, of course, true for Walter Benjamin, whose preference for the French tradition was even more outspoken. Yet Benjamin also showed a deep interest in Russian literature, a concern that Adorno did not share. No doubt it was Adorno's point of view, which was largely determined by his fundamental theoretical assumptions about the autonomous status of art, that resulted in a selection of texts and authors both unique and – relative to the European canon – fairly orthodox.

Adorno's literary essays articulate his moral and aesthetic concerns and, taken together, offer an important contribution to the definition of modernism. By and large, he stayed fairly close to the pantheon of great figures and masterpieces. There is no attempt to discover and come to terms with marginal traditions such as proletarian literature or that of ethnic groups. These blind spots come out most clearly in his understanding of the German tradition, which is – at least by today's standards – closer to the mainstream than one might expect from a radical theorist like Adorno. With very few exceptions (Hölderlin, Heine, Wedekind) the radical tradition is missing. There is no equivalent to Benjamin's essays on Carl Gustav Jochmann. Such authors as Georg Forster, Andreas Friedrich von Rebmann, Heinrich von Kleist, Ludwig Börne, Georg Büchner, and Heinrich Mann are not present. We would look in vain even for Friedrich Schlegel and Novalis.

The discovery of unfamiliar writers or unknown parts of the literary tradition was not Adorno's strength. In this respect his critical writings resemble those of Lukács: the energy of both critics went mostly into the rereading of well-known works. For Lukács, this approach was politically motivated: he wanted to rescue the German literary tradition from inclusion in the literary pantheon of the National Socialists. For Adorno, the insistence on canonical texts was in part determined by the conservative bias of postwar Germany; his readings struggled with the limited cultural vision of the Adenauer years. In some instances, however, a more ideological motif played a role: a rather strident anti-Communist bias directed against East Germany and the Soviet Union. Apart from the political thrust of an anti-Stalinist position, Adorno's hostility toward the East was connected with a promodernist stance that would necessarily clash with any defense of reflection theory and realism.

The celebration of modernism is indeed the key to Adorno's literary criticism, particularly in his essays on Kafka, Proust, and Valéry. But even a relatively light essay on Thomas Mann written in 1962 – a portrait of the author, rather than a close reading of his work – speaks to this concern.[13] Adorno's defense of Mann against unfavorable criticism suggests that Mann's German critics, who had accused the novelist of arrogance and a lack of human commitment, misunderstood Mann's complete devotion to his oeuvre. Especially, they failed to grasp the difference between Mann's private life and his work, and they did not understand his use of masks to shield his artistic intentions from social obligations.

'Masks can be switched,' writes Adorno, 'and the many-sided Mann had more than one. The best known is that of the Hanseatic, the cool and reserved senator's son from Lübeck.' Hiding behind a social mask is a strategy, Adorno suggests, that Mann shared with Kafka, who played 'the run-of-the-mill insurance company employee,' and Proust, who presented himself as 'the dandy of the operetta, in top hat and cane' (NL 2:14 [trans. modified]; GS 11:337 f.). These comparisons direct us to Adorno's interest in Mann: the fate of the modern artist who can no longer bring life and work together because the rigor of the aesthetic task leaves no space for the unfolding of the traditional subject. The romantic cult of the genius, which seemed to ground the work of art in the person of the author, had become a cliché. Adorno wants to separate the work from the writer because he wants to warn his readers against the intentional fallacy. The aesthetic truth of Mann's novels, he suggests, transcends the strategies and skills of the author. Thus, in critiquing the original ending of Mann's *Doctor Faustus,* he refers to 'the force of concrete negation as the only legitimate chiffre of the other' (NL 2:18 [trans. modified]; GS 11:3–11). To put it differently, the modern work of art is not allowed to be affirmative. Reconciliation is denied because any harmonious ending would be tantamount to untruth.

What is only suggested in the Mann essay, the two essays on Valéry treat more rigorously: the nature of postromantic literature.[14] For Adorno as for Benjamin, Valéry is the quintessential modern artist, the very opposite of the romantic genius. As the intellectual, completely conscious of his situation as well as his artistic means, Valéry appears to be fully in control. This could be read as a praise of classicism, but Adorno makes it quite clear that Valéry's oeuvre does not serve as a model for timeless beauty and perfection.

> I want to demonstrate that insisting on the formal immanence of the work of art need not have anything to do with praising ideas that are inalienable but damaged, and that a deeper knowledge of historical changes of essence is revealed in this kind of art and the thought that feeds on and resembles it than in utterances so adroitly aimed at changing the

83

world that the burdensome weight of the world threatens to
slip away from them. (NL 1:99; GS 11:115)

Following Valéry's notes on Degas, Adorno – in a reading of a
reading – exposes his radically historical concept of modernism.
According to Adorno, modernist art responded to social as well as
psychological reification. In this context he quotes Valéry's text –
Degas 'was and wished to be a specialist, of a kind that can rise to
a sort of universality' – and adds the following commentary:
'According to Valéry, this kind of intensification of specialization
to the point of universality, the congealed intensification of production organized in terms of the division of labor, may contain
the potential to counteract the deterioration of human capaci-
ties' (NL 1:102; GS 11:119). This reading clearly historicizes Valéry's
thoughts. On the one hand, it underlines deterioration (*Zerfall*);
on the other, it stresses the possibility of *Gegenwirkung*: that is,
of resistance and countermoves against a situation of reification.

Adorno embraces the modernist credo that art stands outside
social practice and follows, exclusively, its own immanent laws.
Consequently, he distances himself from any notion of engaged
literature, arguing that a theory demanding immediate social application from the artwork overlooks its autonomous status and
thereby indirectly supports precisely the general reification that is
relentlessly reproduced in a social system based on market exchange. The language of modern art and literature can be truthful
only by refusing to cooperate with the expectations of the social
system, for the theory of commitment 'degrades word and form
to a mere means, to an element in the context of the work's effect,
to psychological manipulation; and it erodes the work's coherence
and logic, which are no longer to develop in accordance with the
law of their own truth but are to follow the line of least resistance
in the consumer' (NL 1:103; GS 11:120).

Valéry's superior aestheticism, asserts Adorno – and this is a
very typical move in his criticism – is the opposite of what it
appears to be. Whereas the aestheticist position of the modernist
seems to express a lack of social responsibility, it in fact articulates
through the artwork the very social criticism that an unmediated
polemic or engagement ultimately fails to do. Closely connected

84

with this critique of immediate expression and personal responsibility of the artist in the age of advanced capitalism is Adorno's insistence that the authentic work of art always transcends its author, that its critical force does not depend on the author's intention but flows out of the formal structure. Valéry, Adorno argues, knows 'that in actuality the process of artistic production, and with it the unfolding of the truth contained in the work of art, has the strict form of a lawfulness wrested from the subject matter, and that the much invoked creative freedom of the artist is of little consequence in comparison' (NL 1:104; GS 11:122). The modern artist serves the work; the only task is to unfold and bring out the truth content. Yet this truth content speaks primarily through the form rather than through themes or opinions. The utopian dimension that Adorno ascribes to Valéry's work – and thereby indirectly to the modern literary text – is its foreshadowing of what is repressed in modern social systems. Thus Adorno, referring to Valéry's theory, stresses the closure of artworks that is supposed to shield us from the contingent element of modern life.

This plea for closure (*Geschlossenheit*) has to be seen, however, in the context of a specific argument; it articulates the moment of truth in Valéry's modernist position without fully articulating Adorno's own theory. It is important to note that his defense of modernism is not dogmatic but contains a critical edge directed against the blindness of the work, its supposed self-sufficiency. What distinguishes Adorno's criticism from mainstream celebrations of modernism is his dialectical understanding of postromantic art – its legitimacy as well as its culpability. Although he never consistently differentiates modernism from the avant-garde, his understanding of modern art includes rather than excludes the avant-garde, at least as long as the avant-garde artist does not call for the elimination of art altogether. Adorno's ambivalent attitude toward French surrealism has to do with his fear of regression to a state of pre-autonomous art, not with an animus against the avant-garde.

Although Adorno's criticism is never far from the canon of masterpieces, his choices are usually not motivated by a desire to celebrate famous writers. Rather, he means to subvert – either by denouncing established reputations or by focusing on forgotten aspects. His resistance to confirmed opinions is apparent in his essay on Kafka.[15] Its agenda is to scorn the existentialist appropriation of his work that made the novelist popular in the 1950s. Kafka, Adorno writes, 'is assimilated into an established trend of thought while little attention is paid to those aspects of his works which resist such assimilation and which, precisely for this reason, require interpretation' (PR 245; GS 10 [1]: 254). What Adorno dislikes in the popular reading is first and foremost its reductionist tendency, which equates the meaning of Kafka's stories and novels with a philosophical doctrine; and second, the specific nature of this doctrine, its subjectivist interpretation of history. Adorno, following Benjamin, draws attention instead to Kafka's narratives and points out that they cannot be read through Goethe's concept of the symbol. Kafka's texts are concrete representations, yet they force the reader into the search for meaning: 'Each sentence is literal and each signifies. The two moments are not merged, as the symbol would have it, but yawn apart and out of the abyss between them blinds the glaring ray of fascination' (PR 246; GS 10 [1]: 255). This need for significance has led the critics astray; it has encouraged them, as Adorno observes, to superimpose metaphysical ideas instead of carefully reading the text. To subvert this tendency, Adorno redirects the reader's attention, suggesting a 'literal' reading that does not succumb to the lure of symbolizing. Kafka can be understood only by paying attention to the details.

The modern work of art, argues Adorno – and this comes close to a definition – defies conventional interpretation; there is no reliable mediation between its language and the language of philosophical discourse. Thus, interpretation is required, but no reading can do justice to the text. In the Kafka essay Adorno uses the term 'windowless monad' for the modern work of art: 'The windowless monad preserves itself as the magic lantern, mother of all the images as in Proust and Joyce' (PR 252; GS 10 [1]: 263). The term *monad* strongly suggests that it is impossible to deduce the artwork from first principles but at the same time underlines that the work is connected with the outside. It is important to note that modernism for Adorno is not merely the latest and most advanced phase in art and literature; the works of Kafka, Joyce, and Proust are intrinsically related to general history as well. Our understanding of Kafka's 'Penal Colony' is connected with 'bird's eye photos of bombed out cities' (PR 254; GS 10 [1]: 266). Yet Adorno steadfastly refuses to explain this relationship in causal terms. The common ground for art and history is the extreme: modern works of art articulate, more poignantly than do historical narratives or philosophical systems (such as existentialism), the horrors of the twentieth century. Only through their extreme formal construction do the works of Kafka or Joyce and Beckett become legitimate witnesses to this horror – reflections on the failure of historical progress.

Adorno's sometimes stubborn resistance to authors and movements that do not recognize or even attack the principle of aesthetic autonomy is ultimately rooted in this understanding of the artwork as a historical witness. Thus the hermetic character of Kafka's oeuvre is for Adorno an argument not against but for history. 'What is enclosed in Kafka's glass ball is even more monotonous, more coherent and hence more horrible than the system outside' (PR 261; GS 10 [1]: 275). The principle of hermetic closure that Adorno finds in Kafka's narratives does not imply, however, that the text is constructed as a rounded or even harmonious unity. The opposite is true: the advanced text subverts the very notion of the classical and its insistence on formal balance. 'The fragmentary quality of [Kafka's] three large novels, works which, moreover, are hardly covered any more by the concept of the novel, is determined by their inner form' (PR 265; GS 10 [1]: 27).

The fragmentary nature of the modern work is at the heart of Adorno's concept of modernism. Although he shares with traditional criticism an emphasis on the autonomy of literature and therefore also a bias toward high culture, he stands out by ultimately subverting any comfortable notion of high culture. Adorno's aversion to sanitized versions of modernity reveals itself in his literary criticism at various points, for instance in his disregard for Rainer Maria Rilke and *Jugendstil*. In fact, it would not be unthinkable to see Adorno in the camp of Thomas Mann's foes, since Mann in many ways represented the cultural establishment and the conservative side of modernism in Germany. Accordingly, there ought to be essays on Alfred Döblin's *Berlin Alexanderplatz* and Hermann Broch's *Sleepwalkers,* works that even more radically than Mann's *Doctor Faustus* question the novel form. Their absence is one of the inexplicable blind spots in Adorno's criticism.

Adorno's map of European modernism is broad, including expressionism, surrealism, and radical movements such as dadaism; still, it is not without boundaries. His short essay on surrealism tells us something about the limitations of his vision. As with Kafka, Adorno is out to undermine conventional interpretations, which approached surrealism with the help of André Breton's manifestos, highlighting the dream and the unconscious. Adorno refuses to valorize this psychoanalytical reading of surrealist texts. Instead, he offers a historical reading that leads to a fairly rigorous critique of surrealism and also of Benjamin's assessment of its importance for the European avant-garde.

Adorno defines surrealism as montage: 'One could easily show that even genuine Surrealist painting works with its motifs and that the discontinuous juxtaposition of images in Surrealist lyric poetry is montage-like' (NL 1:87 f.; GS 11:103). For Adorno, the impact of this technique is restricted to shock value. Surrealism, he argues, has become obsolete 'because human beings are now denying themselves the consciousness of denial that was captured in the photographic negative that was Surrealism' (NL 1:90; GS 11: 105). What Adorno does not explicitly argue, although he suggests it in his readings of surrealist texts, is that unlike the works of Kafka or Joyce they cannot claim authenticity. Or, to put it differently, their authenticity is only that of inauthenticity. 'The dialectical images of Surrealism are images of a dialectic of subjective freedom in a situation of objective unfreedom' (NL 1:88; GS 11: 104). Adorno calls these images fetishes (in the Marxist sense): instances of complete reification, but not monads containing their own inner form. In short, Adorno's criticism insists on the formal nature of the text. It may be open, fragmented, subversive, but it must not be just material in the configuration of a montage. It was precisely this break with the concept of the work of art and its aura that Benjamin in his 1929 essay on surrealism had valorized as the radical feature of the French movement. The surrealists' poems, Benjamin maintained, were demonstrations and watchwords 'but at any rate not literature.'[16] In 1929 Benjamin was quite prepared to sacrifice culture and side with the surrealist attack on the aesthetic sphere – a move that Adorno resisted and never approved of in his friend's criticism.

The attempt of the European avant-garde to break away from literature and art, its desire to reach a realm of utopian social practice, marks the boundaries of Adorno's criticism. His skeptical position is largely grounded in his understanding of modern mass culture: that is, the culture industry. As early as in his essay on the regression of listening (1938), he had rejected Benjamin's idea of a post-auratic popular culture.[17] The chapter on the culture industry in *Dialectic of Enlightenment* merely developed the idea that the ultimate threat was the leveling of cultural difference, which would rob the work of art of its critical power. For Adorno (and Horkheimer, of course), institutionalized modern mass culture not only reified the contemporary production and reception of art and literature but also undermined the cultural tradition by reorganizing it. It was this concern about the inauthentic appropriation of the literary past that motivated and shaped Adorno's essays on the German literary tradition. His criticism had to be double-edged: it had to scrutinize and undercut the comfortable notion of a 'cultural heritage' which guides most of academic criticism; at the same time, it had to rescue the literature of the past from the maelstrom of inauthentic appropriation by the culture industry. In other words, neither the academic nor the popular reception could be trusted. The concept of a literary canon could be acknowledged only in order to be questioned. Adorno's radical gesture had to turn upon itself, however, because he had an equally strong desire to protect the tradition against misuse by the agents of the culture industry. Hence, reading the classics meant to brush the text against the grain, stripping it of layers of false appropriations and bringing out its authentic meaning.

The opening of Adorno's essay 'On the Classicism of Goethe's *Iphigenie*' (NL 2:153–70; GS 11:495–514) makes this intention quite clear: 'The still prevailing understanding subsumes Goethe's development under the cliché of a process of maturation.' The close reading of a classic will necessarily encounter clichés, the sediment of previous interpretations. Goethe himself, as Adorno shrewdly observes, helped to establish his own canonization as a classic – not only transcending his own time but also becoming a cultural as well as literary model for future generations. The aim of Adorno's essay is to undercut the notion of Goethe's classical maturity and serene harmony. This agenda could be carried out in different ways. One could emphasize Goethe's early work – for instance, the poems of the Sesenheim period, *Werther* and *Goetz von Berlichingen* – thereby shunning the mature work as a self-imposed regression to premodern classicism. Or one might stress the importance of the late work, such as *Faust II*, *Märchen*, and *Wilhelm Meisters Wanderjahre*, thereby arguing that Goethe's classical period (1795–1805) was only a passing phase. Adorno chooses neither strategy. Instead, he deconstructs the notion of Goethe's classicism by focusing on the very drama that traditional criticism has viewed as its purest example.

Adorno's reading of Goethe's *Iphigenie* pushes aside its German nineteenth-century reception with its insistence on *Bildung* through the Greek-German symbiosis. The concept of humanism (*das Humane*), unless it is critically reconsidered, becomes a stifling blanket that hides the real contours of the play:

> Invoking Goethe's own words and the contemporaneous ones of Schiller, it is customary to call that content *Humanität* or *das Humane*, in accordance with the unmistakable intention of elevating respect for human freedom, for the self-determination of every individual, to a status of a universal standing above particularistic customs and nationalistic narrowmindedness. As unequivocally as *Iphigenie* opts for the humane, however, its substance is not exhausted in that *pladoyer*; humanity is the content of the play rather than its substance. (NL 2:157; GS 11:499)

Adorno's distinction between *Inhalt* (content) and *Gehalt* (substance) is strategically significant indeed, for it allows the critic to reject the conventional reading of the drama without losing an important category for his or her own interpretation. The concept of humanism becomes part of the material on which the play is based, just as the Greek myth of Iphigenia's sacrifice is a material element of the drama.

Adorno's reading owes its force to his concept of history or, more specifically, to his understanding of the process of civilization. Its dialectic is reflected in Goethe's play in such a way, Adorno argues, that the antinomies of this process are split between two peoples: Greeks and barbarians. Yet this opposition – and this is precisely the moment that the conventional interpretation overlooks – cannot be adequately resolved by the victory of civilization (and humanism) over barbarism, since Iphigenie and the Greeks themselves are implicated in the process of guilt and retribution from which they want to distance themselves. 'Civilization, the stage of the mature subject, outflanks mythic immaturity, thereby incurring guilt in relation to it and becoming entangled in the mythic context of culpability' (NL 2:158 [trans. modified]; GS 11:500). It is Hegel's philosophy of history with which Adorno confronts Goethe's text, without, however, basing his reading dogmatically on Hegel's doctrine. Much more than Hegel ever did, Adorno places the emphasis on the price humanity has to pay for its own 'progress': the European center's displacement of its own problems on the 'underdeveloped' countries: 'The imperialism of the later nineteenth century, which transposed the class struggle into a struggle between nations or blocs, down to the current opposition between highly industrialized and underdeveloped peoples, making it invisible, is vaguely anticipated here' (NL 2:164; GS 11:507).

In this context Iphigenie's humanism – her insistence on freedom and self-determination – appears, Adorno suggests, in a more problematic light. Ultimately, the text subverts itself. As much as Goethe strengthens Iphigenie's position vis-à-vis King Thoas, it is Thoas who is expected to show good will and generosity when Iphigenie and her friends are leaving him: 'To use one of Goethe's turns of phrase, he [Thoas] is not permitted to participate in the highest *Humanität* but is condemned to remain its object, while in fact he acts as its subject. The inadequacy of the resolution, which achieves only a fraudulent reconciliation, manifests itself aesthetically. . . . The masterpiece creaks, and by doing so indicts the concept of a masterpiece' (NL 2:168; GS 11:509). The play's message, its official humanism, Adorno argues, fails; thus its most authentic figure is not Iphigenie but her brother Orest, whose utopian vision of *Versöhnung,* of peace and love, is at the same time the vision of a madman. He is still in the process of freeing himself from the realm of myth with its eternal chain of guilt and punishment, and this very desire makes him, according to Adorno, a modern hero. Goethe's Orest 'comes to the stage as a mature person' (NL 2:168; GS 11:511). To put it differently, his thoughts and actions are the result of and reflect the ongoing process of enlightenment.

Adorno's essay effectively turns the traditional interpretation of Goethe's drama inside out. Where the conventional reading saw the solution (in Iphigenie's position), Adorno discovers a problem; where the traditional reading recognized the problem (Orest's guilt and madness), Adorno finds at least the promise of a solution, since Orest overcomes the greatest danger: namely, the relapse into the configuration of mythic thought. Not surprisingly, then, Adorno's verdict is that Goethe is not a classicist whose oeuvre is far removed from today's concerns. Referring to the work of the 'mature' Goethe, he writes: 'It is only this Goethe who embodies the protest against classicism which, as though it should not exist, ultimately takes the side of myth nevertheless' (NL 2:170; GS 11:514). This sentence is nothing less than a radical indictment of the entire construct of German literature, as it was developed by the first generation of German literary historians during the early nineteenth century. This construct was based on the concept of classicism (*Klassik*), in which Goethe was ascribed a central position. To maintain, as Adorno does, that this classicism ultimately sustains myth rather than enlightenment casts doubts on the entire construct of a German tradition. If there is an authentic tradition at all, it must be one that can be rediscovered only through subversive readings.

Two examples may give us a more concrete understanding of

the gains and limits of Adorno's counterreadings: the first is his attempt to rescue Eichendorff's poetry from its conservative admirers; the second is his exploration of Heinrich Heine's importance to the German tradition. The basic structure of 'In Memory of Eichendorff' (NL 1:55–79; GS 11:69–94) is similar to that of the Goethe essay: the critic argues against a conventional appropriation of the romantic poet. Unlike Novalis or Hölderlin, Eichendorff has been a truly popular poet in Germany, his broad reception due largely to the fact that many of his poems have been set to music by major German composers; thus his poetry has become part of a major German as well as European music tradition. Its national popularity, Adorno observes, confirmed a conservative agenda; Eichendorff scholarship has by and large reflected the conservative catholic bias of its authors. He has seldom found admirers on the left; Lukács, for instance, gave Eichendorff no more than a cursory glance in his *Deutsche Realisten,* dismissing him as a minor figure within the reactionary romantic tradition.[18] This split creates a complex situation for Adorno: 'Rescuing Eichendorff from both friends and foes by understanding him is the opposite of a stubborn apologetic' (NL 1:57; GS 11:71). Reading Eichendorff critically has to begin with a critique of conventional receptions. The ease and seeming triviality of his poems turn out to be the stumbling block. They can collapse, as Adorno admits, when they are reduced to an affirmative message; their authenticity depends on their language and what Adorno liked to call 'metaphysical tact [*metaphysischer Takt*]' (NL 1:59; GS 11:73), a special sensitivity to the historical feasibility of words.

Adorno's dialectical defense of Eichendorff is not without its problems when applied to his critical prose. The attempt, for example, to read Eichendorff's 'Der Adel und die Revolution' as a progressive document has to discard most of the text and cling with vigor and determination to the passages about the problems of the *ancien régime.*[19] It is difficult, however, to read Eichendorff's concept of freedom as a supplement to the Hegel-Marx tradition, as Adorno wants us to believe it is. Eichendorff's political writings made it quite clear that he favored a hierarchical society under the leadership of a strong nobility. Although he did not participate in the wave of post-Napoleonic German chauvinism, neither did he champion liberal democracy. It would be difficult indeed to rescue Eichendorff's political essays or his literary criticism from a conservative appropriation. Thus, Adorno can succeed only by separating the author's life and opinions from his poems. Because Eichendorff's poetry owes its force and authenticity to its negative impulse, to its rejection of the security of conservative ideology, Adorno calls Eichendorff an 'unreliable conservative.' His poems tend to subvert his own system of beliefs in celebrating vagrants, soldiers, and outcasts who stand outside the social order that conservative doctrine typically supports. Through these marginal figures Eichendorff approaches the utopian, a realm of *Erfüllung* (realization). Suddenly, the ambivalent conservative romantic appears in a very different light: 'Without realizing it, Eichendorff's unchained Romanticism leads to the threshold of modernism' (NL 1:64; GS 11:78). Eichendorff's poetry is closer to Charles Baudelaire's *Fleurs du mal* than to Goethe's Sesenheim poems.

Again, Adorno's defense of the tradition ends up as an indictment of the tradition, an attempt to revise the conventional order of history in which Eichendorff has had his place as a member of the second romantic generation. From a modernist perspective, however, Eichendorff's place is closer to European symbolism (Baudelaire and Arthur Rimbaud). This postromantic character of Eichendorff's poems is not, Adorno argues, a matter of a new consciousness or attitude; rather, it is reflected in the poetic language itself. Language 'as something autonomous, is the divining rod. The subject's self-extinction is in the service of language' (NL 1:68; GS 11:83). Similar things could be said about Georg Büchner, who opposed the conservative position that Eichendorff adopted. Accordingly, Adorno tries to find a more suitable literary context for Eichendorff. To do so, he makes two suggestions that are not entirely compatible: on the one hand, he brings Eichendorff, as we have seen, closer to European symbolism; on the other hand, he wants to place him within the anticlassicist German tradition that begins with the young Goethe and then includes authors such as Büchner, Gerhart Hauptmann, Wedekind, and Brecht (NL 1:65; GS 11:79). But what about Novalis, Hölderlin, and Kleist? This typol-

94

ogy undermines the essay's more important distinction between romantic and modern writers. Ultimately, Adorno does not argue rigorously in favor of either solution, because he remains skeptical of any schematic principle. He rejects conventional notions of the tradition and literary history in general – yet his criticism cannot quite do without these concepts as long as he is seriously involved in historical readings. Hence he mocks the concept of periodization as inadequate for the language of Eichendorff and at the same time invokes the 'break with tradition' in order to capture Eichendorff's historical situation (NL 1:72; GS 11:87).

Adorno's essay, searching for the authentic aesthetic moment, cannot do without the idea of a tradition as a negative element, the convention that blocks access to the hidden meaning of the text. When Adorno reflects on the category of tradition in his essay 'On Tradition' (GS 10 [1]: 310–20), he is quite aware of the problematic nature of the concept for the analysis of modern history, because tradition as a premodern category is hardly compatible with a social system based on a market economy. Thus modern art and literature respond to the loss of tradition (that is, accepted cultural practices). This historical approach explains Adorno's ambivalence. Insofar as modern societies become rational and functional, they destroy cultural traditions. Under these circumstances these traditions stand in opposition to the reification caused by modern rationalism. Thus, for Adorno, cultural traditions can also assume a critical role. The element of convention that is constitutive of traditions tends to confirm the status quo, however, and therefore to undercut the critical force that society needs. Tradition becomes false in two respects: first, as a remnant from the past it is an inadequate guide for the future in a permanently changing social system; second, as a conceptual construct typical of a modern society it is false and inauthentic. 'The false tradition, which arose almost simultaneously with the consolidation of civil society, wallows in false riches' (GS 10 [1]: 313). The concept of tradition developed in a capitalist society is subsumed under the concepts of property and exchange value. What they try to comprehend freezes, turning into inauthentic images. Consequently, Adorno calls for a Kantian approach to the problem of tradition.

95

'Not to forget tradition and yet to conform to it means to confront it with the state of consciousness that has been reached – at its most progressive – and to ask what is upheld and what is not' (GS 10 [1]: 315).

Yet this solution, I think, does not quite do justice to the contradiction involved in the category of tradition. Adorno's approach remains a balancing act that relies mostly on the tact of the individual critic. It avoids the radical question as to whether the concept is fruitful for the interpretation of modern literature, particularly its intertextual and contextual aspects. The reason Adorno did not eliminate the term, despite its problematic character, was probably his fear of a complete collapse of high culture. Brecht's vision of the literary past as a heap of building material could not entice Adorno, because it clearly degraded the works of the past to the status of mere material, robbing them of their truth content. Adorno therefore encourages a tradition of negation, which defines intertextuality as a historical dynamic that forbids the repetition of the same techniques. The Adornian touchstone for this process is the concept of the authentic work of art: 'Poetry redeems its truth content only when it rejects tradition at precisely those points where it comes into closest contact with it' (GS 10 [1]: 320).

Ironically, this concept of the tradition ultimately favors conservative rather than radical or liberal-progressive authors. Heinrich Heine is a case in point. It is difficult to overlook the fact that Adorno becomes rather uncomfortable when he addresses the work of this author, a German-Jewish liberal, and his place in the German literary tradition (NL 1:80–85; GS 11:95–100). Although Adorno clearly sympathizes with Heine's political stance, particularly his unmitigated defense of the Enlightenment tradition, he cannot fully acknowledge Heine's poetry as part of the German canon. Obviously, his reservations go back to Karl Kraus's indictment of Heine as the spoiler of the German language; he explicitly invokes Kraus's authority when he turns to the problem of Heine's poetic language. Still, the fact that Adorno's generation was very much under the spell of Karl Kraus's radical rhetoric does not adequately explain this hesitation. Adorno's doubts about the value of Heine's poems lead us to the center of his idea of the tradition. He suggests that Heine's poetry – despite its formal accomplishments – ultimately fails because of its language. In a crucial passage Adorno connects Heine's distance from the German language with his style: 'Only someone who is actually not inside language can manipulate it like an instrument. If the language were really his own, he would allow the dialectic between his own words and words that are pregiven to take place, and the smooth linguistic structure would disintegrate' (NL 1:82 f.; GS 11:98).

The dialectic between a received poetic language and his own style was indeed Heine's problem. As a member of the second romantic generation (born in 1797), he was faced with the poetry of Novalis, Clemens Brentano, and Ludwig Tieck – not to mention Goethe and Schiller, of course. Any German poet who started out in the 1820s, as Heine did, had to respond to and deal with an established poetic language. Young writers found themselves in the position of epigones, as the nineteenth-century novelist Karl Immermann (1796–1840) put it.[20] Adorno, however, suggests that Heine's problem was a special one; his failure was due to the fact that he lacked 'being at home in language' [*heimatliche Geborgenheit in der Sprache*] (NL 1:82; GS 11:98). Coming from a Jewish background with Yiddish as his mother tongue, Heine supposedly had to learn the German language almost like a foreigner. His mastery of German, which Adorno does not dispute, is therefore a 'borrowed fluency' (NL 11:83; GS 11:98), unsuitable for the writing of poetry because it is already reified language.

So far, Adorno's argument can hardly be distinguished from a conservative celebration of *Heimat* (home). Authenticity of language is rooted in the mother tongue (Heine's mother, Adorno tells us, could never quite master German); hence, the basis of the literary tradition is the existence of an authentic poetic language that can – as in the case of Goethe and Eichendorff – both inspire and absorb the subject of the poet. This position gets dangerously close to an essentialist definition of tradition as the continuity of literature based on authentic language as its source. But Adorno gives this argument an interesting turn: in the final paragraph of the essay he revalorizes Heine's poetry by suggesting that it was the poet's very lack of an authentic language that allowed him to succeed. Heine turned the deficit into an advantage: 'If all expression is the trace left by suffering, then Heine was able to recast his own inadequacy, the muteness of his language, as an expression of rupture' (NL 1:83; GS 11:98).

We find similar remarks in the Eichendorff essay and the passages on George in 'On Lyric Poetry and Society.' The authentic tradition turns out to be an illusion; fortunately, Adorno is willing to say so. After the Holocaust there is no *Heimat* left, and there is no undamaged language (NL 1:85; GS 11:100). Strangely enough, because he is so much concerned with Heine's Jewish identity, Adorno fails to see Heine's modernity. He wants to rescue Eichendorff's poetry from the conventional label 'late romantic' and stresses its vicinity to the poems of Baudelaire, but he does not grasp Heine's far greater importance for European modernity – a failure he shares, incidentally, with his mentor and friend Walter Benjamin.

Adorno's essays point to a German literary tradition – in fact, to several traditions – yet never attempt to offer a complete account of the history of German literature. They remain fragmentary and suggestive rather than systematic; an academic reader might be inclined to reproach them for their lack of interpretive rigor. It would be too easy, however, to assume that a critic as highly self-conscious as Adorno was not aware of this lack. More than once, the text of his essays reflects on its own procedure by problematizing the task of reading literature. In his essay on Hans G. Helms, an avant-garde author almost unknown outside Germany, he confronts the question of understanding head on.[21] The hermetic text of the avant-garde, he notes, resists easy understanding. 'Essential to such text is the shock with which it forcibly interrupts communication. The harsh light of unintelligibility that such work turns toward the reader renders the usual intelligibility suspect as being shallow, habitual – in short, preartistic' (NL 2:95; GS 11:431). In this passage, Adorno suggests first and foremost that the modern advanced work of art is so complex and strange that it is not readily accessible. In this respect, he comes across as a typical modernist, a position that was still radical in 1960 but would hardly offend mainstream criticism today. Furthermore, he obliquely introduces a distinction between the language of communication and poetic language: the former facilitates understanding (exchange of meaning); the latter does not – it requires careful reading procedures.

In the Helms essay, which deals more with the idea of an avant-garde text than with Helms's work, Adorno conflates these two aspects. Modern literature calls conventional methods of understanding into question because it has destroyed the illusion of a definite and closed context of meaning, which allowed the reader to situate the text. Yet this conflation is problematic: it is by no means certain that older literature is by definition more accessible than modern works. And ultimately, this opinion does not reflect Adorno's own position, for he consistently rejects, as we have seen, conventional readings of classical texts. Thus Adorno later returns to his second distinction: the difference between communication and art, between 'normal understanding' and reading literature.

As soon as we raise the question of what we mean by understanding a literary text, Adorno argues, we realize that understanding cannot be equated with capturing the meaning (*das Gemeinte*): 'One does not understand works of art the way one understands a foreign language, or the way one understands concepts, judgments, and conclusions in one's own' (NL 2:96; GS 11:432). Adorno refers to the understanding of concepts and arguments as rational *Verstehen* (comprehension) because it deals with discursive matters. Literature, however, stands outside this realm; understanding a literary text can be accomplished only through a process of mediation, 'in that the substance grasped through the completed experience is reflected and named in its relationship to the material of the work and the language of its forms' (NL 2:97; GS 11:433). Understanding, in other words, is based on experience (*Erfahrung*), yet it cannot stop there: it is incomplete without reflection on the material of the artwork and its relationship to form (*Formensprache*).

Adorno's definition of understanding literature, then, is wedged between two approaches that he rejects. Understanding can be neither a purely rational conceptual translation nor a merely intuitive (irrational) process of empathy. For Adorno, the irrational approach fails as much as the rational, since the work is never fully accessible to immediate experience. Its element of self-reflection, an element that is independent of the intentions of the author, calls for a philosophy of art that will, by means of its conceptual work, overcome the blindness of the text. Hence, criticism is always more than reading a text, and the critic cannot pretend to be just a 'reader.' For Adorno, criticism participates in but is not identical with the philosophy of art.

What, then, is the difference? Why is literary criticism not simply applied philosophy of art? Traditional philosophy of art (*Ästhetik*), Adorno argues in his introduction to *Aesthetic Theory*, is at home in the realm of abstract categories and arguments, which can be derived from ultimate principles. Both Kant and Hegel keep their distance from the individual work of art. Criticism, on the other hand, begins its work within the text, quite consciously using the concrete experience of the reader or listener as a springboard for a close reading and the subsequent reflection that leads the critic back to the realm of philosophical discourse. What Adorno shares with formalist and poststructuralist approaches is his insistence on an intrinsic method. In 'On Lyric Poetry and Society,' for instance, in which he outlines the principles for a sociology of literature, he argues that the deciphering of the social meaning has to begin with a close reading of the poem. Whatever the problems of this method may be, it foregrounds Adorno's concern with form and structure rather than content (themes and topics).

Yet although considerations of theory and method obviously play a major role in Adorno's literary criticism, it would be misleading and ultimately false to appropriate his essays purely in terms of their philosophical rigor. Their formal structure is of equal importance. They are written as essays rather than *Abhandlungen* or articles: that is to say, they are not meant to be scholarly and scientific (*wissenschaftlich*). It is not accidental, therefore, that the first essay of *Notes to Literature*, titled 'The Essay as Form,' reflects on the formal problem of criticism. Adorno sees his own contribution in the tradition of a literary genre that was defined and also practiced by the young Lukács. His conception of the essay form explicitly refers to Lukács's *Soul and Form* (1911) and systematically responds to Lukács's theory. As Adorno suggests, an essay 'starts not with Adam and Eve but with what it wants to talk about; it says what occurs to it in that context and stops when it feels finished rather than when there is nothing to say. Hence it is classified a trivial endeavor' (NL 1:4; GS 11:10). The essay wants to remain nonsystematic, playful, unbound by rules of rigor. For Adorno the essay is the very form that allows the critic to explore the margins. Its strategies are suggestions and associations but not, as Adorno observes, fiction and *ästhetischer Schein* (aesthetic semblance) (NL 1:5; GS 11:11). The essay is informed by theory, but it does not develop concepts and doctrines. In this configuration, therefore, reading and understanding take on a new meaning.

Occasionally, critics of Adorno have suggested that his method of reading lacks rigor, that he never works completely through a text. This observation is correct, especially for his essays on literature: they refrain from systematic readings and prefer a tangential method of allusions and cross-references that successfully avoids the heavy pedagogical turn of the *explication de texte*. Adorno's essays rarely present a straightforward argument using standard discursive prose. His style, highly mannered in its syntax and choice of words, complements the structure of the essay. Its success depends on the tension between an individual, sometimes playful approach and the significance of the subject matter. Significance in this context, however, should not be confused with high seriousness. Adorno liked to write on marginal topics such as punctuation and *Fremdwörter*, and his essays on Balzac and Proust would hardly meet with academic approval as serious contributions to Balzac and Proust scholarship. Quite consciously, Adorno called his collection of literary essays *Notes to Literature*, hinting at their marginal character, which would both accept and subvert the central position of academic criticism. His essays are supposed to remind their readers of the public function of criticism; they insist on the Kantian element of critique, which is rooted in but not limited to the literary text.

When Adorno's popularity was at its peak in the late 1960s, this method of reading was termed *Ideologiekritik* (ideology critique). It became fashionable to take apart and dismiss authors and texts on the basis of their implicit ideology. But unlike some of his students, Adorno never applied his critical method of reading mechanically. In fact, it would be difficult to define his method in terms of academic schools and traditions. His concept of dialectical criticism, which, in principle, subverts overt meanings, owes its force to Hegel and Marx, without accepting their doctrines as fixed norms.

As for his German contemporaries, the most interesting comparison is perhaps with Hans-Georg Gadamer and the hermeneutic tradition. It goes without saying that Adorno had little sympathy for traditional hermeneutics, and his scorn for *Einfühlung* (empathy) reminds us of Benjamin's frontal attack on the German *Geistesgeschichte* that regularly invoked Wilhelm Dilthey for its own legitimation. What distinguishes Adorno from this tradition is his polemical stance against the desire to objectify meaning and history. In this regard he approaches Gadamer's critique of objectivity in *Truth and Method,* yet the directions taken by their critiques are hardly compatible. This is particularly true for their concepts of tradition. Whereas Gadamer, wanting to remind his readers that critique is not possible without prejudice, stresses the priority of tradition over reason, Adorno consistently criticizes the conservative idea of tradition and continuity. His essays, as we have seen, quite deliberately subvert the notion of an unquestioned cultural tradition that gives us transhistorical values. If there is any truth in a work of art, it cannot be handed down through institutional channels. In fact, in dealing with classical texts, the unfolding of the truth content (*Wahrheitsgehalt*) has to begin with the removal of previous readings that have conventionalized the artwork.

Truth in a literary work of art, apart from the fact that it cannot be spelled out simply in terms of concepts and ideas, escapes any attempt to pin it down and fix its meaning. Truth, Adorno maintains, becomes visible only in the moment of reflection on concrete experience – which, to be sure, is determined in history. Working out a method in terms of prescribed procedures – beyond the obvious requirement of reading – would disturb Adorno, since such a method would necessarily reify the two essential elements of criticism: experience and reflection.

5. Language, Poetry, and Race: The Example of Heinrich Heine

✳

THE preceding chapter attempted to explore the contours of Adorno's literary criticism; this one examines a single essay: namely, Adorno's lecture on Heinrich Heine – its rhetoric, the ideological implications of Adorno's position, and specifically the link between language and race.

When Adorno presented this lecture in 1956 – the occasion was the one hundredth anniversary of the poet's death – Heine's status within the German tradition was anything but secure. East German criticism had begun to include him among the canonical authors of German literature, but the West German attitude was characterized by a curious strategy of resistance that subconsciously continued the fascist repression of 1933 to 1945.[1] Of course, it had become quite legitimate to write about Heine, yet the emphasis of criticism in the new Federal Republic was on Weimar classicism rather than Heinrich Heine and the Young Germans. Hence Adorno was justified to title his lecture (later published in the journal *Texte und Zeichen*) 'Die Wunde Heine' (GS 11:95–100; 'Heine the Wound,' NL 1:80–90).

Talking about Heine in 1956 meant talking about a Jewish author, about an author who had committed himself to the German language as his medium (even when he resided in Paris after 1830), and, finally, a writer who, unlike most of his contemporaries, openly criticized the political repression in post-Napoleonic Germany. Adorno was very much aware that he was dealing with an author who did not fit the profile of the *German poet*. Heine was not Eichendorff – notwithstanding the fact that their poems were equally used by major German composers of *Lieder*.

Adorno's defense of Heine must be understood as a response to a situation where the anomaly of Heine's repression was still treated as normal, a defense that wants to face the problem by lifting the bandages that covered the wound. Yet in a curious way this attempt to restore the status of Heine in Germany shares some of the problems it wants to address. Adorno's essay vindicates some aspects of Heine's oeuvre, leaving others in doubt. Among the problematic aspects are Heine's Jewish background and, more specifically, Heine's use of the German language. When it comes to Heine's poetry, Adorno cannot conceal that he has reservations.

How do we account for Adorno's reluctance to acknowledge the force and quality of Heine's poetry? After all, Adorno, a Jewish-German author himself, was far removed from the chauvinistic cultural milieu in which Jewish authors were automatically excluded from the realm of German culture. In fact, after his return to Germany in 1949, Adorno considered it one of his major tasks to advance the discussion about German anti-Semitism. He was clearly involved in the struggle to unearth and analyze the roots of anti-Semitism. Thus his reservations must not be confused with the indifference of conservative intellectuals or the hostility of unreconstructed nationalists.

Adorno's essay does not deal with crude forms of anti-Semitism, the polemics of Adolf Bartels and similar cultural chauvinists; rather, at the very beginning it refers to the criticism of the George circle and of Karl Kraus. Though Adorno is willing to dismiss the resistance of the George circle as motivated by German nationalism, he takes seriously Kraus's negative verdict that Heine's use of the German language undermined its purity, that he commercialized the language of Goethe by introducing the feuilleton style into German literature.[2] The corruption of the German language is a threatening notion for Adorno as well – although for different reasons. In his analysis of German fascism, linguistic aspects played an important role; hence, the Krausian argument directed against Heine and the feuilleton touched on Adorno's own experience of the fate of the German language under fascism. For him, the idea of an authentic poetic language remains crucial – particularly after the Holocaust.[3]

Adorno leaves no doubt that he holds Heine's critical prose in high esteem. He praises not only the polemical power of Heine's critical interventions but also the refinement of his prose: 'This prose is not limited to Heine's capacity for conscious pointed linguistic formulation, a polemical power extremely rare in Germany and in no way inhibited by servility' (NL 1:80–81; GS 11:95). A decade before young academic critics in West Germany began to discover its importance, Adorno is insisting on the Enlightenment tradition in Heine's prose work and stressing its subversive nature, which resisted facile categorization. It is Heine's poetry that troubles Adorno: 'The wound, however, is Heine's lyric poetry. . . . Heine's poems were ready mediators between art and everyday life bereft of meaning. For them as for the feuilletonist, the experiences they processed secretly became raw materials that one could write about' (NL 1:81; GS 11:96). Adorno calls Heine's language *präpariert* (GS 11:97): that is, ready-made and functional. This critique leaves no doubt about the historical context: Adorno sees Heine's poetry as an example of poetic reification caused by the rise of capitalism in Europe. It has come under the law of the market: 'In Heine commodity and exchange seized control of sound and tone' (NL 1:82; GS 11:97). It is not the historical situation that Adorno holds against Heine; rather, it is Heine's supposed lack of resistance that Adorno deplores, his seeming willingness to work with the linguistic material of the romantics. Unlike Baudelaire, Adorno's paradigm for modernism, Heine failed to transform the loss of tradition into *Traum und Bild* (dream and image); he reproduced reified language instead of breaking it down.

So far, Adorno's criticism uses the arguments already developed in *Dialectic of Enlightenment* (1947); hence, Heine could be called a precursor of the culture industry. Yet Adorno's argument is considerably more complex. Heine, he insists, is both a belated romantic whose poetry relied on the autonomy of modern art, and an enlightener who openly foregrounded the commodified character of art and literature. Insofar as Heine's poetry is self-conscious, it imitates and mocks romantic poetry at the same time, in a mode of self-criticism that enraged Heine's German foes, including Karl Kraus. Adorno suggests that the 'rage' displaces the reader's feeling of *Erniedrigung* (degradation) –something caused by social reality – onto the poems' author.

Here we have reached the center of Adorno's argument. Heine's poetry makes its reader uneasy because it points to the failure of human emancipation, since the process of modernization cannot preserve authentic language. Yet this is the very language it would need to articulate true emancipation. Heine's lack of authentic poetic language, his proximity to communicative language, exposes him to anti-Semitic polemic. Heine simply made use of the material he borrowed from the previous generation. The result is, in Adorno's words, 'the smooth linguistic structure,' a symptom of reification: 'The excessive mimetic zeal [is that] of the person who is excluded' (NL 1:83; GS 11:98). Reification, Jewish marginality, and anti-Semitic polemic are closely linked in Adorno's argument. Heine's poetry is singled out by German anti-Semites because it brings into the foreground the power of modernization that they fear but steadfastly deny. Instead of confronting the power of the modern state, they displace their anger onto the marginal group. According to Adorno, the moment of truth in their polemic is the inauthenticity of Heine's language, yet this lack of authenticity becomes the very reason why Heine's poetry can succeed after all. It prevails by making use of its own deficiency, by pointing to its own *Bruch* (rupture) (NL 1:83; GS 11:98).

This somewhat surprising argument is more complex than it appears. On one level, Adorno suggests that Heine's text becomes self-conscious and thereby self-critical, yet there is more at stake. What Adorno wants to bring out is a radically changed situation of the reader. The post–World War II reader perceives the poem 'Mein Herz, mein Herz ist traurig'[4] in the context of the Holocaust.

> Mein Herz, mein Herz ist traurig,
> Doch lustig leuchtet der Mai;
> Ich stehe, gelehnt an der Linde,
> Hoch auf der alten Bastei.
>
> Da drunten fließt der blaue
> Stadtgraben in stiller Ruh;
> Ein Knabe fährt im Kahne,
> Und angelt und pfeift dazu.
>
> Jenseits erheben sich freundlich,
> In winziger, bunter Gestalt,
> Lusthäuser, und Gärten, und Menschen,
> Und Ochsen, und Wiesen, und Wald.

Die Mägde bleichen Wäsche,
Und springen im Gras herum:
Das Mühlrad stäubt Diamanten,
Ich höre sein fernes Gesumm.

Am alten grauen Turme
Ein Schilderhäuschen steht;
Ein rotgeröckter Bursche
Dort auf und nieder geht.

Er spielt mit seiner Flinte,
Die funkelt im Sonnenrot,
Er präsentiert und schultert -
Ich wollt, er schösse mich tot.

(My heart, my heart is heavy
Though May shines bright on all;
I stand and lean on the linden
High on the bastion wall.

Below me the moat is flowing
In the still afternoon;
A boy is rowing a boat and
Fishing and whistling a tune.

Beyond in colored patches
So tiny below one sees
Villas and gardens and people
And oxen and meadows and trees.

The girls bleach clothes on the meadow
And merrily go and come;
The mill wheel scatters diamonds –
I hear its distant hum.

On top of the old gray tower
A sentry looks over the town;
A young red-coated lad there
Is marching up and down.

He handles his shining rifle,
It gleams in the sunlight's red;

He shoulders arms, presents arms –
I wish he would shoot me dead.)[5]

Thus its intertextual reference might be Paul Celan's *Todesfuge* rather than Eichendorff's poetry. The radically new meaning of Heine's poem lies in its post-Holocaust reception, which was tentatively anticipated in Mahler's musical setting of this poem. The stigma of reified language becomes the *signature* of complete alienation that goes far beyond the poem's thematic concern. Adorno's radical reading cancels *Heimat*, the realm of being at home, which the poem invokes as the absent space: 'Now that the destiny that Heine sensed has been fulfilled literally, . . . the homelessness has also become everyone's homelessness; all human beings have been as badly injured in their beings and their language as Heine the outcast was' (NL 1:85; GS 11:100) – a veiled reference to the Second World War and the Holocaust.

Grudgingly, as we have seen – so to speak, through the back door – Adorno admits Heine to the canon of German literature and assigns him a place next to Goethe, Eichendorff, Eduard Mörike, Nietzsche, and George. His reservations are grounded in his idea of an authentic poetic language based on Goethe's poetry and that of the romantics. In his essay 'On Lyric Poetry and Society' (1957), written almost at the same time as the essay on Heine, Adorno makes it quite clear that his concept of poetry is confined to modernity and does not include medieval poems, such as those of Walter von der Vogelweide. Referring to Goethe's 'Wanderers Nachtlied,' Adorno defines the completion (success) of a poem as subjectivity that is completely sublated in its language, which occurs only 'when the subject reaches an accord with language itself, with the inherent tendency of language' (NL 1:43; GS 11:56). For Adorno, poetic language is anything but a vehicle; rather, it is a configuration in which communicative language transcends its pragmatic function in order to articulate the tension between the subject and the objectified world.

Adorno can apply this concept of poetic language successfully to Mörike and George but hardly to Heine, whose texts respond to the trivialization of romantic poetry, the incompatibility of a con-

ventionalized poetic language, and the emergence of a modern society in Germany. Adorno was by no means blind to this change.
In the case of Baudelaire, for instance, he suggests that the modern
poet is a cross between Jean Baptiste Racine and a journalist. He
argues: 'In industrial society the lyric idea of a self-restoring immediacy becomes – where it does not impotently evoke a romantic past – more and more something that flashes out abruptly,
something in which what is possible transcends its own impossibility' (NL 1:50; GS 11:63–64). Strangely enough, however, Adorno
is unwilling or unable to apply this insight to Heine's poetry. He
fails to grasp Heine's modernity (which is also connected with his
Jewish identity) because he emphasizes the romantic character of
the poems without much attention to the way in which Heine
refunctions this element. Thus the rupture, Heine's self-conscious
distance, becomes nearly invisible. Adorno's resistance to Heine's
modernity is particularly remarkable, given his argument in another essay that Eichendorff's poetry is postromantic, closer to
Baudelaire than to Novalis or Brentano. Hence, we have to ask,
what is the distinctive element in Eichendorff that is supposedly
missing in Heine? Adorno suggests that Eichendorff's poetry
tends to cancel the subject; he speaks of 'the self-effacement of the
subject' (NL 1:68; GS 11:83). Eichendorff responds to reified romanticism in a unique way: through self-cancellation the poetic
subject transcends the thematic and linguistic conventions and
reaches 'reconciliation with things through language' (NL 1:70;
GS 11:84).

Clearly, Heine's response to the conventional language of romanticism was very different. Instead of the *Selbstpreisgabe* (giving oneself up) of the subject, there is reinforcement of the subject. Heine openly points to the rupture that, according to
Adorno, is the constitutive moment of posttraditional poetry.
Although Adorno admires Heine's unwillingness to give up his
intellectual independence, he seems to be troubled by the unveiled
appearance of a poetic idiom that is no longer grounded in unquestioned collective language. This is the moment when Heine's
Jewish identity becomes important. In Adorno's mind the lack of
an authentic language, modernity, and Jewish identity are closely

connected and determine Heine's poetry. They bring about a highly problematic configuration that anticipates the catastrophe of the German-Jewish symbiosis.[6]

Obviously, the essay's few remarks about Heine's Jewish background – for example, those about his mother and her deficient knowledge of German – tell us little about Adorno's familiarity with Heine's biography or the importance of the Jewish question in the poet's life and work.[7] I conclude that he was primarily interested in two aspects: in Heine's social marginality, and in the relationship between Yiddish and German.[8] The religious question, on the other hand – for instance, Heine's decision to convert to Christianity and his later 'return' to the Jewish faith, whatever that may have entailed – leaves no trace in the essay. Adorno, not a religious person, does not foreground the question of Heine's faith. Heine's complex relationship to the Jewish tradition – his affinity as well as his resistance – comes into view only as an absent space from which he moved into the realm of German culture. As much as Adorno questioned the notion of German culture as an affirmative value, he did not question Jewish emancipation and, with it, the breaking down of traditional Jewish culture. In that respect Adorno is very close to Hannah Arendt's thesis that for Heine an unimpaired concept of freedom was the center of his life and work.[9] Where they differ is in their assessments of Heine's appropriation of the German language: Arendt celebrates Heine's symbiosis of German, Yiddish, and Hebrew as an enrichment of the German language; Adorno, holding on to a notion of purity taken over from Karl Kraus, rejects the idea of a mélange.

What Adorno seems to overlook is the fact that Heine himself was very conscious of the problem of language. Precisely because he was an outsider, socially and legally, he was particularly sensitive about his status within German literature and the possibility of including elements of the Jewish tradition.[10] Not only did Heine realize that Goethean classicism had become unattainable; he also clearly understood the *historical* character of the German language. His understanding of the history of the German language from Luther to Goethe and the romantics stresses the moment of production, the force that can intervene and change reality. It is clearly not a model predicated on the dichotomy of purity and contamination; rather, it is a model in which the poet and writer are encouraged to draw on various linguistic traditions. In this respect, Heine was a conscious and determined anticlassicist. The moment of dissemination and communication not only is essential for his critical prose but also influences his conception of poetry. He uses irony and parody to subvert the institutionalized aesthetic autonomy, particularly in his late poetry such as 'Hebräische Melodien.' Heine's attempt to capture the oriental world of the Old Testament and the Middle Ages, to make it accessible to his German and European readers, remains highly ambivalent; it both integrates and distances the Jewish tradition with a playful seriousness that always borders on blasphemy. It is not accidental that the *Romanzero* was censured by the Austrian and Prussian governments soon after its publication because of its *unsittlicher Inhalt* (unethical content).[11] The poems deliberately undercut the expectations of a self-enclosed religious world by combining levels of style that were considered incompatible. The seemingly conventional form of these poems is deceptive; its ease is unreliable. Heine's language in 'Hebräische Melodien' deliberately subverts notions of poetic purity, for in this context purity would entail a relapse to premodern dogma. Certainly Heine was not simply *in der Sprache* (inside language), as, according to Adorno, he should have been.

Yet the notion of a tradition that could serve as *Heimat* is problematic. In his discussions of Goethe and Eichendorff, Adorno was certainly aware of the dialectic of tradition. The very modernity he postulates and holds against Heine's poetry cancels tradition as a premodern category. In fact, Heine's use of the past, of its cultural monuments, reflects his conscious resistance to naive forms of appropriation. But it is also quite clear that Adorno does not appreciate Heine's way of dealing with the cultural tradition. Consequently, he reduces the poet to the status of a second-generation romantic who is not quite at the critical edge in his use of poetic language. Unlike Mörike or George, to bring in two examples from Adorno's 'On Lyric Poetry and Society,' Heine does not show the tact of avoidance that Adorno demands; rather, he insists on demonstrating his own modernity and that of his readers by both invoking and distancing the cultural past through ironic ruptures. Hence, the *glatte Fügung* (smooth linguistic structure) in Heine's poems, which Adorno seems to dislike and reject (as a symptom of Heine's reification), is deceptive; it must not be taken at face value.

It would be too easy, however, to conclude that Adorno simply failed to understand the nature of Heine's poetry, possibly because his own reading was too much influenced by a nineteenth-century reception that saw Heine as the embodiment of German romantic profundity. The surprising turn at the end of his essay, when Adorno connects Heine's poetry with the Second World War and the Holocaust, points to another level of reception. Here Heine's fate as an outsider and his failure to go beyond the romantic idiom becomes the touchstone for a general condition of *Heimatlosigkeit,* and Heine becomes *the* representative modern figure.

The argument that the fate of the Jew is representative of the fate of mankind had begun to emerge in Adorno's writings as early as 1944, when he and Horkheimer reflected on German fascism and anti-Semitism.[12] *Dialectic of Enlightenment* placed the emphasis, of course, on the 'dialectical link between enlightenment and domination' (DE 163), which the liberal Jews, relying on the project of assimilation, failed to grasp. Furthermore, *Dialectic of Enlightenment* links modern anti-Semitism to capitalism and defines it as a search for scapegoats. The blame for the inevitable exploitation under capitalism is shifted to the Jews because they are highly visible in the sphere of circulation. When Adorno came back to the problem of German fascism and its anti-Semitism in 1955, the parameter of the public debate had changed. After the discovery of the death camps in 1945, anti-Semitism as well as fascism had become a German question, a problem of German history and German culture that was largely ignored and repressed during the phase of West German reconstruction. His essay 'Was bedeutet Aufarbeitung der Vergangenheit?'[13] not only refers to the quasi-official German terms but also raises the question of why the Holocaust was repressed in postwar Germany. Adorno presents once more both the psychological and the economic arguments that the Frankfurt School had developed during World War II.

Adorno's reeducation program of 1955 invokes the idea of *Aufklärung*: that is, the changing of consciousness through theoretical work, especially sociological and psychoanalytical theory. Adorno stresses at the same time that the failure of reeducation in Germany was not merely or even primarily a matter of insufficient consciousness-raising. He points to the continuation of the objective social conditions that made fascism possible and keep its potential alive: 'Fascism lives on because the objective social presuppositions that call it forth still obtain' (GS 10 [2]: 566). This argument by no means refers only to the economic system; in fact, the target of Adorno's theory is the culture industry and its ability to neutralize the efforts of the individual in Germany to carry out *die schmerzliche Anstrengung der Erkenntnis* (the painful effort of cognition) because he or she is again under pressure to conform (GS 10:567). The real impotence of the individual, Adorno fears, will necessarily undermine the process of critical reflection.

Anti-Semitism, Adorno rightly argues, has little to do with Jews; its mechanisms do not depend on but rather exclude real experience with its victims. At the same time, however, Adorno suggests that there is a link between Heine's Jewishness and his lack of an authentic language, that there is a real difference after all between a German poet and a Jewish-German writer. Obviously, these arguments are not quite compatible. The psychological model of racism as a mechanism in which the victim is replaceable presupposes that there can be no essentially Jewish character, that the 'Jewish' character – its otherness – is the invention of the racist. Yet Heine's linguistic deficit, his not being quite at home in the German language, appears to be real – a specifically Jewish deficiency that can be recuperated only when it has become a universal human condition: that is, after the Second World War and the Holocaust.

In writing about Heine, Adorno becomes caught up in conflicting discourses that he is unable to control. The claim for an authentic poetic language that provides the poet with his or her material invites the opposite term and, by extension, the critical argument that a poet's language can be inauthentic and therefore less valuable. Typically, Adorno uses this construct to stress the need for historical change, since a conventional poetic idiom signals reification and untruth. In the Heine essay, however, where the critique of a borrowed language is also concerned with the difference between German and Yiddish, the meaning of the argument shifts – although not completely. Nowhere does Adorno suggest that Yiddish, Heine's mother tongue, is bad; what he does suggest is that someone who comes from that background will find it more difficult, if not impossible, to become fully at home in the German language.

This notion of a 'natural' access to German is dubious for two reasons, historical and philosophical. Historically, it is untenable. In the German case, particularly during the eighteenth and early nineteenth centuries, *Hochdeutsch* was an almost artificial language, not spoken at home but learned outside.[14] Poets would acquire it only through schooling, and this was no less true for Hölderlin and Eichendorff than for Heine. Each started out with a regional language similar but not identical to the language of German literature. Since Adorno fails to recognize the historicity of literary German, he overestimates Heine's difference. Philosophically, the assumption of a 'natural' access to authentic German relies on the questionable premise that pure poetic expression is grounded in the essence of the native speaker, who is by definition 'at home' in his or her language, while nonnative speakers or those who use dialects and regional languages remain outside.

Adorno's emphasis on authenticity leads him down a dangerous road. It is not the argument that Heine's language is secondhand and borrowed that I find problematic in principle; it is the link between Heine's way of writing and his Jewish background that leaves me with doubts. When Adorno addresses the phenomenon of anti-Semitism, he makes it quite clear that he does not believe in Jewish characteristics per se; hence, there is no Jewish language. In his treatment of Heine, however, he seems to deviate from this path. The question is, why? It turns out that Adorno is somewhat ambivalent about the nature of authentic

German. His own prose style – involved, complex, and saturated with foreign words (frequently French) – was anything but the simple straightforward German that nationalists obsessed with the purity of the language were recommending.[15] In fact, his prose might well have served as an example of the 'Frenchified' German typical of Jewish intellectuals. Adorno was, no doubt, familiar with this discourse and, hence, aware of his own position. His small essay 'Words from Abroad' (NL 1:185–95; GS 11:216–32) can be read as an acknowledgment of his own vulnerability in writing un-German Jewish German. Yet his definition of authentic poetic German is meant to transcend the sophistication of prose – that of Heinrich Heine as well as his own.

Unlike Heine, Adorno did not attempt to write poetry; thus he did not directly face Heine's problem of mediating between Yiddish and German, 'compromised' and 'poetic' language. It is interesting to note in this context that Adorno rejects Lukács's claim that the essay is an art form. Instead, he stresses its rhetorical nature: situated between the rigorous argument of philosophy and the pure expression of poetry, it is a problematic form that can easily collapse under the impact of the culture industry. Hence, the modern essay is never far removed from the feuilleton, a mode of journalism frequently associated with Jewish intellectuals such as Heine. Nevertheless, the essay is for Adorno the critical form par excellence, precisely because it is 'impure' and relies on rhetoric rather than logic.

As we can see, Adorno, when he discusses Heine's language, is more implicated than he may at first appear. The initial distinction between commercialized and authentic poetry, compromised and pure language, finally collapses when Adorno concludes that Heine could succeed only through the open presentation of rupture: 'Failure, reversing itself, is transformed into success' (NL 1:83). Yet this applies to the essay form as well, since its truth is mediated through its untruth (NL 1:17; GS 11:25): that is, through its lack of solidity, its protean character. Thus the ending of the Heine essay points to a dilemma as well as a solution, one that involves Adorno the essayist, the refugee, and the survivor of the Holocaust.

6. Reading Mass Culture

In the recent critical debate on popular or mass culture, Adorno and Horkheimer's concept of the culture industry and their theory of culture in the age of advanced capitalism have received less than favorable treatment. In fact, the position of the Frankfurt School, or what is supposed to be the approach of Critical Theory, has served as the 'old' paradigm, which more advanced criticism is expected to overcome. Jim Collins has taken this position most vigorously, developing a classic binary opposition in which Adorno and Horkheimer's *Dialectic of Enlightenment* turns out to represent an outmoded approach, ill-suited to the analysis of mass culture in the 1980s.[1]

In certain respects this hostility refurbishes the arguments of the 1950s, when Adorno especially was attacked as an irresponsible cultural elitist who failed to grasp the advantage of American democracy. His insistence on the autonomy of art and its dialectical process in the avant-garde was perceived as a fundamental flaw, an attitude demonstrating his aversion to the notion of a broadly based popular culture.[2] Much of the heated discussion of the 1950s and early 1960s was carried out as a battle between the populist, democratic camp and the defenders of high culture, who annexed Adorno's writings for their own purposes, thereby pressing his theory into a dichotomy that did not make proper use of its structure.

Some of the old problems have resurfaced, among them the notion of Adorno's cultural elitism, which is now labeled not so much undemocratic as traditional. Collins, for instance, portrays Adorno (and Horkheimer) as a tenant of the Grand Hotel Culture, someone unaware of the variety and difference of cultural practices below the level of high art. In this perspective, which relies primarily on spatial metaphors, Adorno becomes indistinguishable from a traditional champion of serious high culture, someone who is unable as well as unwilling to do justice to the complexity of mass culture and its changing relationship to modernism and the avant-garde.

To some extent, this critique can use the chapter on the culture industry in *Dialectic of Enlightenment* as evidence. Quotations that can be lifted from the text appear to confirm the suspicion of Adorno's critics. He and Horkheimer obviously do not mind using sweeping generalizations to define the nature of the culture industry, thereby attracting the criticism that their inadequate concept of cultural totality encourages them to divide modern culture into two separate, hierarchically organized spheres. Again, this assessment is not completely off the mark. Undoubtedly, Adorno did consider the culture industry the embodiment of untruth: that is, an articulation of false human needs and interests.

Still, his verdict – to which I will have to come back – is by no means limited to mass or popular culture; it extends in equal measure to the sphere of traditional high culture (for instance, opera). In other words, Adorno's theory does not easily respond to the conventional dichotomy of high and low culture. Its double-edged character has frequently been misunderstood, not only in America but also in Germany, where the discourse on mass culture was heavily influenced by the Frankfurt School. While metaphysical kitsch theories, following Hermann Broch, insisted on isolating 'true art' from trivial literature or entertainment art,[3] critics such as Hans Magnus Enzensberger emphasized the crucial importance of the avant-garde; that is, they underscored the historical aspect.[4] For these critics the distinction between high and low culture was rooted in the process of modernity, a specific phenomenon of the nineteenth and twentieth centuries. Their approach certainly encouraged, at least indirectly, a closer scrutiny of popular literature and mass culture as the Other, but it did retain, though frequently unacknowledged, the binary opposition that marked older metaphysical kitsch theories. While the increasing influence of Critical Theory during the 1960s opened up a space for the analysis of mass culture in the German academy, its use still included a hierarchical concept of culture in which the modernist tradition was seen as the dominant line, and the study of trivial literature had the function of uncovering false consciousness in novels and plays geared toward a broad audience. Such a method, present in the early work of Christa Bürger,[5] for instance, stresses the discrepancy between the explicit message of the text and its hierarchical ideology, which circumvents the recognition of social conflicts. Although Peter Bürger's *Theory of the Avant-Garde* (1974), clearly an extension of Adornian thought, did not deal with mass culture, its overriding concern with the development of the avant-garde in nineteenth- and early twentieth-century Europe also privileged high art and the avant-garde as dominant factors.[6] By comparison, popular literature and mass culture received, of necessity, the status of derivative art.

The various strands of the German debate concurred in one important aspect: the assumption (in most cases not made explicit) that there was a clearly defined center (for instance, the modern tradition) against which mass culture had to be read. Therefore, the study of popular literature within literature departments was generally perceived as a supplement to the study of canonical texts. As much as structuralist and reception-oriented approaches disagreed about theoretical frame and method, they shared a hierarchical conception of the literary system in which popular literature, as interesting as it might be, would ultimately appear as inferior, less innovative, or structurally less complex.[7]

This unacknowledged bias marked the boundaries of the German debate; only a radically nonelitist position (such as that of Helmut Kreuzer)[8] could break down the traditional distinctions between high and low by arguing that these divisions were mere reflections of social distinctions. Yet this position did not find many followers, because it was bound to end up in aesthetic relativism. Another solution appeared more viable: a closer scrutiny of the dichotomy not as an abstract philosophical problem but as a concrete historical one. By focusing on the discourse of literary criticism between 1800 and 1900 – which strongly emphasized the distinction between art and non-art (*Unterhaltungsliteratur, Modeliteratur*) as the excluded Other – rather than on the material aspects of mass production and mass consumption, the debate took a crucial turn in the early 1980s. Even this new effort did not completely break away from the traditional binary opposition, however, since it still assumed that the discourse reflected actual material literary processes. Unshaken was the belief that the constructs of nineteenth-century critics could serve as a map for the increasing differentiation that took place between the late eighteenth century and the emergence of the avant-garde. To put it differently, German critics such as Peter and Christa Bürger remained close enough to the aesthetic theory of German classicism and romanticism to conflate these historical constructs with the historical structure of eighteenth-century German literature. In this respect, the German debate of the 1970s and early 1980s still used basic categories of modernism (aesthetic autonomy, innovation, formal complexity) as criteria for vertical distinctions.[9]

It is not accidental, therefore, that the renewed discussion of mass culture in recent criticism has followed the break with the modernist tradition. The perception of the present as a transition to a postmodern age had a strong impact on the theoretical articulation of mass culture. Although this chapter is certainly not the place to reassess the postmodernism debate, I want to foreground one key element: namely, the undercutting of the traditional high-low culture distinction. Typical of the new attitude is Umberto Eco's *Travels in Hyperreality* (1983). The very type of phenomenon that Horkheimer and Adorno described as the essence of the culture industry – namely, show business – takes on a new meaning for Eco. Culture and entertainment are, so his argument goes, no longer contradictory opposites. Rather, since the 1970s they have tended to merge in a new kind of event, the collective happening, which is by no means limited to trivial entertainment.[10]

Eco's point is that cultural communication has changed its media to such an extent that our traditional perception of high culture and its legitimate concerns no longer corresponds to our social realities. There is no longer a bunker mentality among the users of high culture; similarly, the masses have incorporated traditional forms of high culture into the 'happening' format. Hence, the older understanding of high culture, still in place until the late 1960s – especially within the social order – has collapsed, according to Eco, inviting new and different interpretations.

It is in this configuration that Adorno's theory of mass culture has come under attack for its elitist binary opposition. Some theorists in this constellation attempt to redeem the critical dimension of Frankfurt School theory, at the same time censuring a purportedly uncritical valorization of high culture. Tania Modleski's introduction to *Studies in Entertainment* (1986) uses the work of the Frankfurt School to demonstrate a mode of criticism that is no longer viable, since it relies on a utopian potential in high culture that seems no longer available. By contrast, she underscores the genuine interest of the new generation of analysts who are not impeded by the fixation on high culture that she sees in the Frankfurt School. Yet unlike Jim Collins, she does not discard the critical aspects of the Frankfurt School in toto; rather, she calls for a balance: 'While working to retain the critical edge of the Frankfurt School's Critical Theory, these analysts reject what they regard as the oversimplifications of the Frankfurt School, especially the emphasis on the way mass culture "manipulates" its consumers, imposing on them "false needs" and "false desires" and preventing them from coming to understand their own best interests.'[11]

The question is, however, whether one *can* retain Critical Theory's critical edge while rejecting the aesthetic and social theory in which it was honed. Since the critical edge cannot be reduced (as some American critics like to suggest) to a European attitude toward culture that is foreign to the American mind, the question points to a systemic problem, which at one level turns into the question of compatibility: can a contemporary postmodern analysis of mass culture – for instance, of television or fashion – rely on the categories developed by the Frankfurt School?

Most emphatically, Jim Collins has rejected this path by arguing that the categories of the Frankfurt School are both too narrow and too inflexible to cope with today's mass culture. Specifically, he criticizes Horkheimer and Adorno's adoption of a concept of high culture that necessarily marginalizes differences among cultural practices. According to Collins, the Frankfurt School's analysis relies on 'a unitary master system' that controls all cultural production. This master plan divides cultural production into authentic art and inauthentic mass culture produced by 'machines and corporations.' Moreover, Horkheimer and Adorno extend this binary opposition to the concept of the audience: the recipients of authentic art are described as 'diverse because they are enlightened'; the audience of mass culture is perceived as uniform and manipulated. Collins concludes: 'The most troubling presupposition of the Adorno-Horkheimer essay is the fundamental central cohesiveness of all cultural activity supposedly produced by this cabal of executive authorities.'[12] Collins's analysis of the culture industry chapter raises a number of important questions but ultimately fails to produce more than an out-of-hand rejection. Blinded by his bias against the supposed cultural elitism of Frankfurt School theory, Collins fails to bring into the foreground the deep structure of Adorno and Horkheimer's text.

Whether Adorno was a cultural elitist or not is less relevant than the grounding of his theory. For him, certainly, mass culture is not merely a sign system that has to be decoded. This does not mean, however, that he does not pay attention to matters of style; rather, his approach is guided by the larger question of the dialectic of enlightenment and, more specifically, by the process of modernization under capitalism. The theory of the culture industry extends the Lukácsian concept of reification under advanced capitalism to the cultural sphere. Its Marxian core, the concept of commodity fetishism, is rather faithfully retained, although the argument of the culture industry chapter is by no means limited to the verdict of commodification.[13] Crucial to the argument is the distinction between liberal nineteenth-century capitalism and postwar Taylorism (or, to use the more recent term, Fordism). The most important insights of Adorno and Horkheimer, as well as their limitations, depend on the conceptual apparatus of the Marxist tradition. Adorno underscores the fundamental shift in the relationship between mode of production and the cultural sphere. Just as Lukács argued in *History and Class Consciousness* that commodity fetishism within the economic sphere turned into general reification, *Dialectic of Enlightenment* argues that the mode of production of advanced capitalism extends into the cultural sphere, which was not controlled in the same way during the nineteenth century.

One can maintain (with Fredric Jameson)[14] that Adorno did not mean to write a theory of mass culture, yet this argument must not lead us to the conclusion that Adorno is exclusively concerned with the aspect of industrial mass production. Instead, the theory of the culture industry perceives the cultural sphere as imprinted by the economic system. Whereas cultural institutions in the age of liberal capitalism were allowed to keep a certain distance from the market, the linkage has become tight and direct. Hence, the rules and norms of industrial organization can be applied to the cultural sphere – first and foremost to the new media, film and radio, but also, as Adorno points out in various essays, to traditional high culture. The reproduction and consumption of classical music, for instance, follows the same principles as the production and distribution of popular music; for the record industry, the only difference is between specific consumer groups whose needs and interests have to be met. It is not, as Collins and others claim, the high/low opposition that defines Adorno's approach but the temporal distinction between liberal and organized capitalism. In fact, under the conditions of organized capitalism, the traditional division of high and popular culture breaks down; instead, we find the streamlined version of culture for which Adorno and Horkheimer coined the term 'culture industry.' It is the extraordinary integrative force of the new system that *Dialectic of Enlightenment* emphasizes, its character of 'ruthless unity.' As the authors argue: 'Something is provided for all so that none may escape; the distinctions are emphasized and extended. The public is catered for with a hierarchical range of mass-produced products of varying quality, thus advancing the rule of complete quantification' (DE 123; GS 3:144). In a postliberal market both production and consumption are planned and controlled through large organizations, which are interlinked to such an extent that the traditional hierarchy of culture is reproduced by market strategies.

For obvious reasons, Hollywood became the model for this configuration because the studio system of the 1930s and 1940s, which Adorno could observe closely, had all the features contained in the concept of the culture industry. The 'ruthless unity' was carried further here than anywhere else. Indeed, film production and distribution were dominated by a small number of companies that tightly controlled not only stars, directors, scriptwriters, and authors but – more important – film distribution through their links with cinema chains.[15] Not unlike Detroit, Hollywood operated according to the principle of mass production: the films it produced were made up of interchangeable elements, put together by a process that relied on formulas. Horkheimer and Adorno describe distribution and reception in similar terms: 'The culture industry as a whole has molded men as a type unfailingly reproduced in every product' (DE 127; GS 3:148); hence, cultural difference based on class or ethnic difference is reduced to a minimum.

The assessment made in *Dialectic of Enlightenment* reminds the reader of Huxley's *Brave New World*; the dystopian elements are hard to overlook.[16] For Adorno, the culture industry articulates a utopia that went wrong, a world without cultural privileges, it is true, but one in which the democratization of culture has harmed the masses that were expected to benefit from the wealth. It is the authors' view of this discrepancy that explains the strong polemical tone of the essay, its hyperbolic formulation, and its tendency to construct the whole system from extreme elements. At all points, the critical intention influences the analysis. Without a counterfactual idea of authentic human progress and genuine happiness, the analysis could have taken a very different turn. It would have been possible to argue that the conditions of advanced capitalism necessarily change the status and the form of culture, that the rise of industrial mass culture was the price the age had to pay for democratization – in short, that traditional high culture was not compatible with mass participation. This was precisely the argument Adorno's critics used in the United States and Germany after the war, and I will come back to this point. For the time being, I want to focus on the economic aspect of the argument: that is, Adorno's interpretation of the link between economy and culture in advanced Western societies.

Characteristic of the treatment of mass culture are such categories as system, apparatus, industrial production, series – concepts more familiar in sociological studies than in cultural criticism. Their application has, as we have seen, recently come under attack – but, I think, for the wrong reasons. Contemporary critics have rightly noted that these categories are not generally applicable to the formation of mass culture since the 1970s. Yet they seem to overlook the historical frame: that is, the structural change of capitalism itself. The postmodern resistance to total systems and centralized cultural organization corresponds with a new mode of production that favors decentralization and flexibility over structure and control.

Given the Marxist approach of the authors of *Dialectic of Enlightenment* and the prevalence of the Fordist system during the 1930s and 1940s, the direction of their analysis does not come as a surprise, especially when one keeps in mind the impact of *History and Class Consciousness* on the Frankfurt School. The Weberian element in Lukács's analysis of reification clearly underscored the all-pervasive nature of reification in modern industrial societies. Hence, Adorno and Horkheimer perceive the culture industry as a part of a larger system of capitalist corporations: 'Culture monopolies are weak and dependent in comparison. . . . The dependence of the most powerful broadcasting company on the electrical industry, or of the motion picture industry on the banks is characteristic of the whole sphere, whose individual branches are themselves economically interwoven' (DE 122–23; GS 3:143–44). Although this dependence is never demonstrated in empirical terms, the notion of a coherent hierarchical system certainly shaped Adorno's reading of the new media. The necessary technological apparatus, he suggests, favors centralized planning and control. The radio, to take an example, structures communication as nondialogical, turning the listener into a passive recipient. In this instance, Adorno conflates the (political) use of the medium (propaganda) with the structure of the apparatus and the organization of capitalist enterprises.

From a late twentieth-century point of view, such a conflation appears less plausible than it did fifty years ago, when the structure of capitalism supported Adorno's views. Fordism – the scientific-technological organization of a capitalist economy – implied more than a specific approach to the problem of growth and stability. Ultimately, as David Harvey points out, it contained a way of life: 'Mass production meant standardization of product as well as mass consumption; and that meant a whole new aesthetic and the commodification of culture that many neo-conservatives, such as Daniel Bell, were later to see as detrimental to the preservation of the work ethic and other supposed capitalist virtues.'[17] Clearly, this aspect is crucial for Adorno's analysis, but it is the principles of Fordist capitalism itself – its scientific approach to the use of labor (Taylorism), its style of management, and its organization of production – that form the background of *Dialectic of Enlightenment*.[18] In particular, North American capitalism after 1900, the model for the theory of the culture industry, was characterized by a strong centralization of capital that went hand in hand with an emphasis on technological change to improve mass production: 'Scientific management of all facets of corporate activity (not only production, but also personnel relations, on-the-job training, marketing, product design, pricing strategies, planned obsolescence of equipment and product) became the hallmark of bureaucratic corporate rationality.'[19] Hence the most important decisions about mass production were made at the headquarters where entrepreneurial authority was concentrated.

In this organizational structure the working class had a dual function: on the one hand, workers had to carry out production in highly mechanized plants and, on the other, they had to become the consumers of their own products. Their dual function entailed a dual strategy on the part of management: while it continued the traditional task of disciplining and taming the work force, it also had to enable the workers to consume, since only the participation of the working class in mass consumption would make large-scale mass production viable. Therefore, a certain affluence of both blue- and white-collar workers was a precondition for the successful extension of mass production. In order to achieve this balance, capitalists needed to curb the activism of radical unions, which demanded a fundamentally different mode of production. In the United States the Wagner Act of 1933 balanced its recognition of the legitimacy of the unions' power in the market (collective bargaining rights) by strengthening management's position in the realm of production. The Taft-Hartley Act of 1952 continued the strategy of taming the working class through strict legal control of the unions. Their legitimate status as bargaining agencies both empowered the unions and controlled their goals. By and large, the unions became collaborative forces whose antagonistic role with respect to the system was severely limited, while it enhanced the economic efficiency that Fordism needed for mass consumption. Accordingly, in the social theory of the Frankfurt School, the disciplined work force of advanced capitalism becomes the apolitical fragmented masses, the willing victims of the culture industry.

Before I can return to Adorno's analysis, however, I have to consider another important feature of its historical context. Under Fordist capitalism the traditional role of the state as guardian of the political and social system (as guarantor of property) had to be strengthened, especially under conditions of extreme political strain. The stabilization of capitalism demanded the intervention of the state, either in the form of authoritarian or totalitarian political systems or in the form of (Keynesian) fiscal policies designed to stimulate the economy. Harvey points out that 'the problem of the proper configuration and deployment of state power was resolved only after 1945.'[20] Still, the New Deal in the United States and the fascist state in Germany, which the members of the Frankfurt School observed during the 1930s and early 1940s, provided models for alternative solutions.[21] In both cases the intervention of the state altered the relationship between the work force and capital, but only the American model, a mass democracy, developed an adequate balance between mass production and mass consumption in which mass culture could thrive.

By and large, the older generation of the Frankfurt School based its cultural analyses on the Fordist model. During the 1950s and 1960s Adorno, as well as Herbert Marcuse, defined advanced capitalism as an overarching system of total control in which the fragmented individual finds itself weak and isolated. Marcuse's *One-Dimensional Man* (1964), with its strong emphasis on a unified, administrated society, presupposes the existence of a closed, hierarchical economic system. Similarly, Adorno's social criticism after his return to Germany in 1949 emphasizes the inevitability of a totally administered society where negativity is the only form of viable resistance.

When Adorno returned to the problem of the culture industry in the 1960s, he felt that in view of more recent developments some modifications had to be made, but he did not attempt to problematize his previous assessment of advanced capitalism. Hence, his reappraisal offers a description of the culture industry that clearly harks back to the earlier definition: 'The culture industry fuses the old and familiar into a new quality. In all its branches, products which are tailored for consumption by masses, and which to a great extent determine the nature of that consumption, are manufactured more or less according to plan.'[22] Again, Adorno underscores the systemic character of modern mass culture, its *Lükkenlosigkeit* (seamlessness). In a way, the reappraisal stresses the economic moment even more than the earlier account did. For the late Adorno, the culture industry transfers capitalism's primary interest in profit to the cultural realm, leaving no distinction between art and refrigerators. In other respects, however, Adorno modifies or, at least, clarifies his position. For example, he points out that the term 'culture *industry*' must not be taken literally, for cultural mass production is only partly comparable with industrial material production. Now, he emphasizes the organization of the distribution system and the mode of reception: individual reception of the autonomous artwork contrasts with mechanical, pseudo-individual mass reception.

Ultimately, Adorno's reassessment in 'Culture Industry Reconsidered' defends his critical assessment of mass culture, especially against the charge of elitism that came from social scientists. Adorno uses a dual strategy to undercut this charge: first, he points to the affirmative stance of those who insist on the need for mass culture; second, he insists on the truth claim involved in aesthetic discussions. In other words, he stresses the truth value of autonomous art in order to criticize the culture industry. What made this defense viable in the 1960s was the fact that by and large his opponents did not seriously challenge the validity of aesthetic truth. Adorno argues that the products of the culture industry contain untruth; they are ideological in both their communicative aspect and their content. Of course, in order to provide critical distinctions, this concept of ideology must presuppose a firm ground. For the late Adorno, this ground is supplied by the concept of the autonomous work of art.[23]

Furthermore, we have to note that for Adorno the aesthetic position is also the socially critical position. His unrelenting attack on the culture industry implies a strong social critique, a polemic against an authoritarian society: 'The consensus which it propagates strengthens blind, opaque authority.'[24] Adorno's postmodernist critics would probably see this critique as confirming an unresolved dualism in which art and mass culture face each other in rigid opposition, but such a reading does not do justice to the complexity of his writings. Although his position vis-à-vis the culture industry remained a fairly stable negation, his treatment of the phenomenon cannot be summarized so succinctly. The best-known 'deviation' occurs in his late essay 'Transparencies on Film' of 1966.[25] As Miriam Hansen has pointed out, this essay breaks away from the conceptual framework of Adorno's previous writings on the culture industry.[26] More specifically, he retreats from his earlier treatment of the cinema, where his underdeveloped distinction between artistic technique and technology blocked his view of the formal concerns of film production. Now, Adorno 'grants cinematic technique the status of aesthetic material – at least in the context of noncommercial film-making.'[27] By 1966, partly under the influence of Alexander Kluge, Adorno was prepared to consider the possibility that making films might be an alternative aesthetic practice within the context of modernist, self-conscious art.

Yet this is precisely the question: what happens to the modernist concept of art once the cinematic experiment of montage has been accepted as a viable project? Or, to put it differently, how is the concept of the culture industry affected by Adorno's reevaluation of cinematic production in his late writings? But even this question is not radical enough, since it suggests a simple linear development from a defensive to a more open and flexible attitude toward mass culture. As Miriam Hansen rightly suggests, 'Transparencies on Film' can also be seen as a reconfiguration of Adorno's earlier theory in which different strands come to the center – elements not quite compatible with the basic thesis of the culture industry chapter of *Dialectic of Enlightenment*. For instance, in his cooperative venture with Hanns Eisler, *Composing for the Films* (written originally in German), Adorno develops aspects of a theory of mass culture that do not fit into the later *Dialectic of Enlightenment*.[28] These moments cannot be explained by the influence or coauthorship of Eisler (who was much closer to Brecht); rather, the text, mostly written by Adorno, provides a different configuration – a configuration that to some extent resurfaces in 'Transparencies on Film.'

As can be expected, the problem of aesthetic autonomy becomes the touchstone for Adorno's reassessment of the film in 'Transparencies.' What is secured in the narrative process of a novel (Adorno uses the example of Robert Musil's early novel, *Die Verwirrungen des Zöglings Törless*, 1906) – namely, the distance of the representation from empirical reality – seems less persuasive in the case of a film. The viewer, Adorno assumes, conflates representation and reality, thereby losing the specific artistic element of cinematic production. Adorno notes: 'The late emergence of film makes it difficult to distinguish between technique and technology as clearly as is possible in music. . . . Film suggests the equation of technique and technology, since, as Benjamin observed, the cinema has no original which is then reproduced on a mass scale: the mass product is the thing itself.'[29] Adorno concludes that the lack of a firm distinction makes it impossible to develop film criticism analogous to music criticism, which is based on the analysis of technique. Hence, the most plausible approach seems to be one that focuses (following Kracauer) on the objects of representation. From there it is only one step, Adorno suggests, to a subjective approach: that is, a comprehensive analysis of the viewer's experience. By this, Adorno does not mean a study of film reception, however. What he is interested in is the correspondence between the experience of discontinuous images in the individual's mind and the technique of a representation of discontinuous images. Yet it is not, as one might expect, the element of montage that Adorno wants to underline; rather, it is the proximity to the beauty of nature (*das Naturschöne*). Hence, he focuses on the objects as signifiers of contradictory ideological constellations – messages to the viewers that are compatible only through their imaginary character.

Not surprisingly, Adorno argues that a theory of the film will of necessity contain a sociological component. Unlike music criticism, film analysis is concerned, Adorno suggests, with a social archaeology of images. This brings him back to his own concerns: the commodification of mass culture as an inevitable factor – which Benjamin did not sufficiently appreciate. It is against this commodification that progressive filmmaking must guard. Therefore, 'Tranparencies' suggests breaking radically with realistic conventions (including their technical means) by applying montage techniques. Such techniques have a very specific critical function. Through them, Adorno suggests, the necessary distance between cinematic representation (as an act of collective mimesis) and the individual viewer can be created. He expresses this function through a Freudian model: 'The liberated film would have to wrest its *a priori* collectivity from the mechanisms of unconscious and irrational influence and enlist this collectivity in the service of emancipatory intentions.'[30]

The valorization of film as a mode of critical intervention allows at least two alternative readings: either it represents an attempt on Adorno's part to incorporate the film into the avant-garde, or it reflects a different approach to the film medium in general. The essay's conclusion, which returns to Adorno's well-known critique of mass culture by underscoring the planned reproduction of untruth, speaks for the first reading; Adorno's willingness to explore the formal aspect of filmmaking and the possibility of a genuine film aesthetics speaks for the second. Many of his later writings, including parts of *Aesthetic Theory,* are compatible with the first interpretation. But if we privilege the intertextual link with *Composing for the Films,* a more radical interpretation gains plausibility, a reading that would undercut Adorno's binary opposition between mass culture and art.

From the very outset, *Composing for the Films* makes it clear that the culture industry is not identical with low or high art: 'The old opposition of serious and light art, low and high, autonomous art and entertainment, no longer describes the phenomenon' (GS 15:11). Autonomous art, Adorno suggests, is as much affected as show business; though its separate sphere may be maintained, under advanced capitalism it has become a reified *Kulturgut* (cultural commodity). The introduction, however, leaves no doubt that cinematic production is very much part of the culture industry. The film completes the late nineteenth-century drive toward the *Gesamtkunstwerk,* whose heterogeneous components are amalgamated in such a way that its total effect overwhelms the recipient. In this context, music conventionally functions as background or illustration without making radical use of its own technique. But *Composing for the Films* does not stop here; rather, it explores the possibilities of bringing together the cinematic medium and the advanced musical techniques developed by the avant-garde. Adorno's (and Eisler's) insistence on *Sachlichkeit* (functionally appropriate music) proposes a mode of cinematic production in which the music does not simply duplicate images and dialogue but creates additional meaning through its interaction with the images. 'What the new music can achieve through its specification is, of course, not the duplication of conceptually unmediated ideas as in, for instance, program music which has waterfalls thundering and sheep bleating. But it can strike the tone of a scene, its particular mood, its degree of seriousness or lightness, profundity or insouciance, authenticity or illusion – differences that are not provided for by the romantic store of props' (GS 15:41).

This passage articulates a task for the film in terms of seriousness and authenticity that cannot be subsumed under the category of culture industry. It is characteristic of Adorno that he sees the musical technique rather than the technology of the images as opening up space for a broader critical understanding of film production. Where a realist film aesthetic underscores the moment of mimesis, film's proximity to the real world, Adorno and Eisler suggest that the film should examine the reality of the routine in order to explore the tensions within reality that are covered up by the 'normal' perception of everyday life. These moments are captured through shots and sequences that defy the expectations of the viewers. Adorno believes that only the music of the avant-garde (for instance, Schönberg's) is capable of supporting the shock produced by such images (GS 15:43). In fact, he extends this argument by suggesting a remarkable correspondence between the tension (*Spannung*) of the film medium and the tension articulated by modern music. Whereas film technique is directed essentially at creating tension, the moment of tension plays only a subordinate role in traditional music, with its limited tolerance for dissonance – or this moment may be so outworn that in truth it no longer produces any tension at all. Tension is the essence of modern harmonics, however, which knows no chord that would not in itself bear and drive forward a 'tendency,' instead of reposing in itself like most conventional strains (GS 15:43).

Once Adorno becomes involved in a comparative analysis of music and film, the previous notion that film represents the culture industry clearly loses its power over the analysis. To put it differently, when Adorno begins to work with concrete texts, concentrating on their formal details, he ends by supporting a rather different theory of mass culture.[31]

One of this theory's most surprising features is its lack of interest in the model of industrial mass production, which is so prominent in *Dialectic of Enlightenment*. Instead, Adorno focuses on the language of the two media and their possible compatibility, a kind of analysis close to that of his *Philosophy of Modern Music* (*Philosophie der neuen Musik,* 1949), arguing for the historicity of the artistic material not only vis-à-vis music (where we would expect it) but also in regard to film. In this context, the inevitable apparatus of film production, its striking use of technology, can be acknowledged without the well-known gesture toward the concept of reification.

In thinking, together with Eisler, about film music and its appropriate form, Adorno can get closer to the problematic of film production without framing the issue within the concept of the culture industry. Through the analysis of dissonance in modern music, for instance, he works out for himself the legitimacy of filmic presentation: that is, the emphasis on tensions, breaks, and cuts that conventional film music, which emphasizes melody, must repress.[32] In fact, Adorno insists on radical solutions as the only way to counter the existing practice of the film industry. This position leads him to a critique of Sergei Eisenstein's film aesthetic, for the Soviet director grants film music only a supplementary role which, in Adorno's opinion, still duplicates the existing practice. More specifically, Adorno argues that Eisenstein's suggestion to render the Barcarolle from Jacques Offenbach's *Tales of Hoffmann* through the images of the 'approaching and receding movements of the water combined with the reflected scampering and retreating play of light over the surface of the canals' amounts ultimately to the same kind of 'absolute equivalence' that Eisenstein himself rejected (GS 15:67, 68).

What ultimately limits Adorno's vigorous film analysis in *Composing for the Films* – and keeps him from drawing the necessary conclusions – is his admitted unfamiliarity with the techniques of film production. He simply assumes that the composer of film music needs no more than a good understanding of the script and may leave the technical side – use of the camera, film editing, and so on – to the director and his or her team (GS 15:86). Yet this separation of tasks is largely responsible for the bad quality of existing film music; only a close cooperation of music and image production, based on a thorough comprehension of their respective techniques, will break up the conventional amalgamation. Later chapters (possibly written by Eisler) dealing with the practical aspects demonstrate to some extent this need for close cooperation, but they never question the priority of the cinematic production. The composer writes the music while looking at the completed film.

Adorno's lack of expertise in matters of film technique, for which he was severely criticized by the film critics of the 1970s and 1980s, led him back to a broad conceptual approach to the cinema in *Dialectic of Enlightenment* (written in the 1940s at more or less the same time as *Composing for the Films*). Here the institution of the film industry in Hollywood becomes the point of departure, and Hollywood's studio system serves as the paradigm for administered culture under advanced capitalism. By and large, the analysis of *Dialectic of Enlightenment* underscores the homology of mechanical industrial mass production and the highly predictable style of commercial films. Yet a critique of this interpretation remains unsatisfactory as long as it isolates the culture industry chapter and simply contrasts it with the complexity of the contemporary situation. Adorno and Horkheimer's conception of the culture industry owes its power to its contextualization within the book, specifically its relation to the radical critique of enlightenment developed in the first chapter. The analysis of the culture industry presupposes that the formation of mass culture is the logical result of the process of enlightenment, its pseudodemocratic expression. This link must be emphasized; otherwise, we are likely to misunderstand Adorno's critical charge, which has little to do with the preservation of traditional high culture. That the culture industry fully participates in the process of enlightenment underscores its modern (and postmodern) character, which is not compatible with traditional cultural stratification.

Although Adorno stressed this point several times, his critics have frequently misunderstood his approach, confusing his defense of autonomous (modern) art with a defense of high culture. In the context of *Dialectic of Enlightenment,* however, it becomes very clear that for him the principles of modern rationalism lead ultimately to the destruction of traditional culture, which is replaced with a new cultural formation based on commodity exchange. This new formation, while still competing with older forms during the eighteenth and nineteenth centuries, subsequently penetrates all aspects of the cultural sphere – by no means only low culture. The dialectic of enlightenment results in a peculiar transformation of the cultural sphere – namely, its standardization and commodification – a situation that also implicates the character of modernism. The resistance to this logic, however – the artwork's attempt to distance itself – remains part of this dialectic, which relies as much on the logic of enlightenment as does the entertainment industry.

Although it is true that the first chapter of *Dialectic of Enlight-*

enment and the chapter on the culture industry are systematically linked, there is a certain tension between the two. The latter makes use primarily of a Marxist model stressing commodification (emphasizing the economic system), whereas the former, together with the first excursus (on Homer), privileges the development of Western philosophy since Plato. In short, the focus of attention shifts. For Adorno and Horkheimer, the crisis of the human race begins with 'the separation of subject and object. When the tree is no longer approached as tree, but as evidence for an Other, as the location of *mana*, language expresses the contradiction that something is itself and at one and the same time something other than itself, identical and not identical' (DE 15; GS 3:31). The separation of subject and object, on one level, and the separation of concept and object, on another, mark the beginning of the process of reason that results in scientific classification and logical formalism. 'In its neo-positivist version science becomes aestheticism, a system of detached signs devoid of any intention that would transcend the system: It becomes the game which mathematicians have for long proudly asserted is their concern' (DE 18; GS 3:34). In this process the work of art plays an ambiguous role, either as integrated element or as the Other – the relic of a prerational world: 'The work of art still has something in common with enchantment: it posits its own self-enclosed area, which is withdrawn from the context of profane existence, and in which special laws apply' (DE 19; GS 3:35). This thesis, which is clearly indebted to Benjamin's concept of the aura, clashes with the theory of total commodification. But Adorno is in need of such a balance, because only through the notion of preserved enchantment can he uphold the critical moment in art: that is, the moment of its resistance to the process of enlightenment. Hence, the tension is worked out as the opposition between authentic art and its mechanical reproduction.

Yet this solution does not properly identify the problem at hand, which actually results from Adorno's use of two different ways to situate the artwork vis-à-vis the process of enlightenment. Insofar as *Dialectic of Enlightenment* privileges the moment of opposition in the artwork, the moment of participation is then relegated to inauthentic art: that is to say, to the culture industry. Two decades later, in *Aesthetic Theory,* Adorno reconsiders this problem and gives it a more persuasive solution. There he undercuts the dichotomy by arguing that the process of enlightenment leaves its imprint as much on the autonomous artwork of modernism and the avant-garde as on the products of the culture industry (GS 7:262–95, 334–57; AT 252–84, 320–36). This would mean that the question of opposition or affirmation does not coincide with the distinction between autonomous art and mass culture, but Adorno does not draw this conclusion; rather, in his late work he more forcefully develops the dialectic of the advanced artwork: its negation of modern social conditions through its formal characteristics, which are informed by the very rationality that they call into question.

From the perspective of New Criticism, Adorno and Horkheimer's approach to mass culture in *Dialectic of Enlightenment* might be labeled extrinsic. The authors construct a double frame in order to position and define modern mass culture: while its one side invokes the development of Western rationalism, its other aspect refers to the evolution of capitalism during the nineteenth and twentieth centuries. It is assumed that the two accounts are compatible: that is, that they represent different aspects of the same historical process. In this view, mass culture appears to be completely determined; its products seem to reflect the system – in economic as well as in ideological terms. Consequently, there is no need for individual analysis, since the result would be clear from the very beginning. Yet one must ask whether an intrinsic approach might not yield different results. With respect to autonomous art there is no doubt that Adorno favored intrinsic analysis, as clearly articulated, for instance, in his essay on poetry and society (NL 1:37–54). The early essay on the fetish character in music consumption (1938) could be considered an attempt to unravel the character of the culture industry from the inside by scrutinizing the structure of light music. The polemical nature of that essay, partly directed against Benjamin's theory of the distracted reception of artworks, uses much of the same rhetoric as the later culture industry chapter: 'All contemporary musical life is dominated by the commodity form,' Adorno asserts.[33]

Although the essay argues from the point of view of musical performance (more than production) and reception (listening), Adorno makes no serious attempt to read the scores of individual pieces; his statements remain mostly at the level of a generalized assessment and evaluation of typical situations. The commodification thesis, together with a psychoanalytical theory of regression, tends to block access to the concrete phenomena. Whenever Adorno looks more closely at the material of popular music, his understanding of modern music (such as Schönberg's) acts as a filter, with the result that popular music is moved to the margins.[34] Consider, for instance, the definition of 'serious music' in 'On Popular Music' (1941): 'Every detail derives its musical sense from the concrete totality of the piece which, in turn, consists of the life relationship of the details and never of a mere enforcement of a musical schema.'[35] This passage contrasts with Adorno's definition of popular music as different: 'Nothing corresponding . . . can happen in popular music. It would not affect the musical sense if any details were taken out of the context.'[36] Not surprisingly, then, Adorno emphasizes standardization as the crucial feature of popular music. In this scheme, popular music is designated as the Other against which the avant-garde can be measured. The dichotomy between serious and popular music is reinforced, because the difference is taken to define clearly demarcated spheres, each following separate laws and norms.

Adorno's music criticism, not unlike his film criticism, comes closest to a differentiated understanding of popular music and mass culture when his analyses deal with 'serious' music. As Andreas Huyssen has suggested, Adorno best succeeds in overcoming the binary opposition when he reads Richard Wagner. Taking the position that Adorno sees modernism and mass culture as related phenomena, Huyssen has pointed to the Wagner criticism as the missing link between Adorno's critique of the culture industry and his celebration of modern art.[37] But it is not a paradox that in evaluating Adorno's writing on mass culture we have to examine his critique of late nineteenth-century high culture: for Adorno, who insists on the conceptual totality of the historical process, the characteristics of modern civilization are to be found in various aspects of culture. Yet Huyssen is certainly correct when he argues that Adorno locates the emergence of modern mass culture within high culture – as a decline in technical rigor, a compromise with public taste.[38]

What makes Adorno's analysis of Wagner – the original essay (FW) was written in 1938 and published in 1939 – so important for the assessment of the culture industry is its emphasis on the composer's style and technique. In his encounter with Wagner, whose central importance for the development of modern music Adorno never belittles, he provides the intrinsic analysis of the textual material that is missing in the essay on popular music or the culture industry chapter of *Dialectic of Enlightenment*. The 1939 essay concentrates primarily on the libretti – *Tannhäuser, Die Meistersinger von Nürnberg, Der Ring des Nibelungen* (FW 1–24); the 1952 study (ISW; *Versuch über Wagner,* GS 5:7–149) focuses more rigorously on the musical aspects, especially on Wagner's use of the leitmotif, his preference for an orchestration that brings about special sound effects at the expense of the structural coherence of the music, and his propensity for the *Gesamtkunstwerk* as a means of completely overwhelming the listener. Noteworthy is a formulation in the early Wagner essay: 'The Wagnerian text bears witness to the early period of bourgeois decline. Its yearning for destruction anticipates that of society in parable form' (FW 45). Yet this decadence, as Nietzsche described it in *Der Fall Wagner* (The case of Wagner), remains for Adorno a dialectical process that contains a utopian dimension. Hence, the weakness of the subject (monad) that Adorno traces in Wagner's libretti is not only a symptom of decadence but also a move toward overcoming alienation: 'Their [the monads'] abandonment, however, not only helps the bad society to victory over their protests but also subverts the basis of the bad isolation itself' (FW 46). To put it differently, reification and commodification in Wagner's operas contain an element of negation – but this is precisely the aspect that is missing in Adorno's more explicit treatment of mass culture. Both the essays on popular music and the culture industry chapter reduce this dialectic to a notion of complete conformity when, for instance, the weakness of the individual subject (caused by modern industrial society) results in regression.

This shift, as I have suggested, does not necessarily reflect a development of Adorno's position; rather, it is the varying perspective of the essays that brings about the remarkable difference in attitude. The macrological approach, using the development of Western philosophy and evolution of modern capitalism as its foil, leads to an assessment of mass culture in which determining factors are emphasized, leaving little space for an internal dialectic, whereas the micrological approach, with its stress on technique and concrete motifs, permits greater flexibility.[39] Since Adorno privileges the second alternative when he focuses on autonomous art – for instance, on the canon of European modernism – the most interesting insights into mass culture in his writings occur at the borderline, when serious music or literature, as in the case of Richard Wagner or Richard Strauss, compromises in order to capture a broader audience. This approach reads the origin of modern mass culture as an inconsistency in the serious artwork. And this is precisely the locus where macrological and micrological approaches coincide, for Adorno does not view mass culture as a separate tradition but as a propensity of culture toward entertainment under the social conditions of advanced capitalism. Fordist capitalism, with its unmistakable emphasis on centralization and hierarchy, emerges as the ideal locus for the complete development of tendencies in the cultural sphere that had already become visible during the later nineteenth century.

Adorno's confrontation with Fordism in Germany and later in the United States clearly encouraged a reading of mass culture that underscores its systematic character and its functional nature for the manipulation of the masses. This specific historical environment – namely, the social as well as the political conditions of the 1930s and 1940s: the rise of fascism, the Great Depression and the New Deal in the United States, and the emergence of a totalitarian regime in the Soviet Union – stimulates but also limits Adorno's analysis. It is not accidental that recent mass culture theory has frequently rejected Adorno's position, in some instances without a clear insight into the changed historical premises. The polemical voices have used the social and political realities of the 1970s and 1980s to criticize Adorno's ambivalent attitude toward mass culture, commonly charging him, as we have seen, with elitism and aesthetic purism.

A *dogmatic* defense of Adorno's position(s) would be, I believe, the least fruitful response, since it would require two rather narrow strategies. First, such a defense would have to reduce Adorno's writings to a clearly defined position, thereby repressing crosscurrents and undercurrents in his writings; second, it would have to rely on Adorno's (sometimes implicit) understanding of advanced capitalism. A more differentiated reading of Adorno's theory is clearly possible.[40] Yet its limit seems to emerge as soon as we focus on the mediation between the economic and cultural spheres. As long as we perceive the economic system in terms of Fordist capitalism, the macrological assumptions of the Frankfurt School about mass culture appear to be plausible – but not from the perspective of the 1980s (under the sign of postmodernism). Contemporary mass culture does not confront us as a unified system speaking with one voice; its obvious variety in organization, recipients, styles, and formal structures calls for a different explanation. Further, it suggests that possibly even the period of Fordism (1920–70) allowed for more difference than Horkheimer and Adorno conceded in the culture industry chapter of *Dialectic of Enlightenment.*

Allowing for more complexity within the mass culture of the early twentieth century would certainly make it easier to account for the multifaceted structure of the late twentieth century. But it leaves us with a theoretical problem: how does Fordism generate variety that is not immediately serialized and replicated, as Horkheimer and Adorno suggest? One possible answer to this question would consist of canceling the basic (Marxist) model, thereby eliminating the need for mediation. Yet this strategy would either leave the phenomena undertheorized or call for a new theoretical paradigm. A more cautious response would foreground the internal contradictions within mass culture as the result of competing needs and interests among its recipients. This model would call for a critical reevaluation of Adorno's concept of the mass, which serves as a highly schematic instrument, leaving not much room for historical specificity. The tendency of the Frankfurt School to downplay traditional class concepts results in a poverty of socio-logical differentiation that discourages concrete descriptions of groups, their needs, and their unique way of participating in the cultural sphere. The emphasis on the concept of commodity as the universal key to the structure of modern mass culture blocks genuine interest in its products, since they are exclusively perceived as instrumentalized for manipulation through mass consumption.

For this reason Fredric Jameson has called for a reconsideration of the high-culture/mass-culture opposition, arguing for a more historical assessment in which the concept of high culture is speci-fied as nineteenth- and twentieth-century modernism.[41] Only with the emergence of modernism do we reach the binary oppo-sition of high and low. What both sides have in common, as Jameson points out, is the element of reification. But it must be noted that Adorno was quite aware of this shared feature. For him, the relationship between modern art and mass culture is dialecti-cal through and through. More relevant is Jameson's critique of Adorno's theory of consumption as manipulation, which tends to be undialectical insofar it conceives of consumers more or less exclusively as objects. Jameson suggests relating production and consumption in modern mass culture to the structure of older popular culture: 'The generic forms and signals of mass culture are very specifically to be understood as the historical reappro-priation and displacement of older structures in the service of the qualitatively very different situation of repetition.'[42] Yet it does not necessarily follow that the public of mass culture is atomized or serial. In stressing this feature of the audience, Jameson remains very much attached to Adorno's concept of the masses. But the serialized cultural production even of the early nineteenth century is thoroughly compatible with more traditional class structures. It is precisely the usage of the products of mass culture that has to be explored within specific historical configurations. Thus the gener-alized theory of reception that Jameson proposes, using the work of Norman Holland, would continue the notion of a unified mass audience whose needs and desires can be figured out. More fruit-ful, it seems to me, would be an approach that deconstructs the concept of the masses and the underlying theory of advanced capitalism (which Jameson leaves in place).

The shortcomings of Adorno's theory of the culture industry have less to do with his valorization of modernism (not to mention high culture in general) than with his theory of late capitalism, based on the circumstances of the 1930s and 1940s. This theory conceptualizes the development of culture as a dialectic between infra- and superstructure, using the category of reification as the mediating term. In Adorno's administered society the cultural sphere is perceived as unified and controlled. By extension, cultural production is conceived of as analogous to material production. The increasing opposition to this model (which of course allows considerable refinement) draws on significant structural changes in the base. With the emergence of post-Fordist capitalism during the 1970s, Adorno's definition of mass culture, especially its focus on industrial production, lost its general plausibility. As various critics have noted, during the 1970s the relationship between high and low culture began to take on a different form. With Scott Lash and John Urry, we can describe this transition as 'disorganized capitalism' characterized by cultural fragmentation and pluralism.[43] Instead of the concentration of capital, we see a dispersal of capitalist relations, which is connected with a decline in traditional industrial production. Instead of large plants and large industrial cities, we see a decline in plant size and increased subcontracting at peripheral places. E. Swyngedouw has specifically emphasized the changes in the production process and their results in the cultural system.[44] He brings together flexible small-batch production, a more horizontal labor organization, and individualized consumption in what he calls a 'spectacle' society.

Thus, from the point of view of postmodernist culture, the concept of the culture industry appears too rigid and inflexible. Postmodernist theory has offered a new matrix for the cultural sphere, according to which the enhanced flexibility of postmodernism is characterized by the radical use of fantasy and fiction. The material is replaced by the immaterial (money) and by fictitious images of capital. Instead of strict organization of production techniques and labor markets, we find chance and rapid adaptability. Postmodernist ideologies, with their explicit celebration of decentralization, multiple patterns of consumption, and lack of origins, necessarily challenge the cultural model of Fordist capitalism, in both its affirmative and its oppositional (Adornian) modes. From the postmodernist point of view, a modernist model of aesthetic opposition remains firmly linked to an outmoded concept of social reality.

Postmodernist polemic against the Frankfurt School is typical of this attitude.[45] For postmodernist critics, Horkheimer and Adorno remain attached to an untenable idea of culture as a distanced realm not accessible to the general population. In this context, the division of high and low culture implies a political opposition as well: namely, between a conservative and a progressive outlook. This conflation of cultural and political outlook relies on the notion of authenticity and its opposites: falsification, compromise, and regression. Jim Collins, for example, rightly assumes that the concept of authentic and autonomous art is at the core of Adorno's theory, but he overlooks the theoretical differentiation between older popular and modern mass culture in the Frankfurt School. As a result, he flattens out the specifically modernist character of Adorno's theory, confuses it with traditional dogmas of high culture, and thus makes the structural connection between monopoly capitalism and the mass production of culture invisible – leaving the reader with the impression that Adorno was simply prejudiced.

Without a more precise understanding of the transformation of capitalism since 1970, postmodernist charges remain abstract and arbitrary. What is missing in this critique is historical specificity: that is, an analysis of the concrete configuration of the 1940s to which Horkheimer and Adorno responded. As a local theory for Western industrial societies between 1920 and 1970, the theory of the culture industry can be defended as a perceptive, useful model. Trying to extend it beyond its original scope weakens its explanatory power.

This assessment, however, does not exhaust Adorno's criticism of mass culture. Especially at the level of micrological analysis (in the form of close reading), he succeeds in breaking away from binary oppositions such as high/low, authentic/inauthentic, true/false. And though the interrelationship of high and low culture is present in Adorno's criticism, it sometimes conflicts with the macrological approach also present in his work. This is why, from a postmodern perspective, Adorno's interpretations of modernist art tend to yield more insights into mass culture than do his essays specifically concerned with popular music. In the former, Adorno handles the aspect of reification more dialectically by showing the necessary demise of the cultural tradition through the rationality of the artwork, a rationality that is determined by social development in general and by the transition from liberal to organized capitalism in particular.

For Adorno, advanced capitalism remained identical with organized capitalism, since he died before the transformation from Fordism to post-Fordism became visible. On the whole, his outlook on the culture industry was defined by the parameters of Fordist capitalism – among them the close link between the economy and the state. For Adorno, who relied on the work of Pollock and Horkheimer, [46] industrial development and state intervention were inseparable; hence, he tended to simplify their relationship. His concept of the administered society reflected a notion of total penetration by bureaucracies.

Obviously, the concept of the culture industry fits this construct. Its danger lies in the generalized assumption that state control and capitalist production are more or less identical (as in the case of fascism). This view, however, misunderstands the interest of the state in regulating the cultural sphere not only through censorship but also through positive cultural planning. This kind of *Kulturpolitik* cannot be defined simply as an extension of capitalist mass production.[47] Its goals are not necessarily identical with those of the entertainment industry. To put it differently, the logic of capitalism (commodification of culture) competes with the logic of state planning, which operates at various levels and in various forms. Adorno and the Frankfurt School conflated these various institutions and organizations in one overarching apparatus.

In his *Late Marxism* (1990), Fredric Jameson underscores the historical limitations of Adorno's theory of mass culture. The new media society of the 1960s and 1970s, he says, goes far beyond the possibilities Adorno had in mind when he coauthored the culture industry chapter. Although this argument is plausible enough, it does not follow, as Jameson suggests, that *Dialectic of Enlightenment* offered not a theory of *culture* but a theory of *industry*.[48] To be sure, the conception of culture to which Adorno refers is primarily linked to the aesthetic sphere rather than to a total social fabric,[49] yet this older, specifically German definition by no means excludes the articulation of a theory of mass culture. It is precisely the imbrication of culture and capital (industry) that creates the sparks in a *dialectical* reading of culture in advanced capitalist societies. By deemphasizing the links between high culture (modernism) and mass culture, Jameson undercuts the central point of Adorno's theory: the dialectic of the artwork in advanced capitalism. As a result, he displaces the culture industry from the aesthetic sphere. But it is Adorno's central contention that aesthetic compromise – that is, the less than radical use of artistic techniques – leads to mass culture. In this respect, for Adorno, Hollywood's proximity to Hitler's Germany was not accidental. It followed from the logic of aesthetic instrumentalization.

7. The Social Dimension: Art and the Problem of Mediation

✳

THE initial debate over whether Theodor W. Adorno remained in the orbit of Marxist theory after he returned to Germany is ongoing. Those who argue that Adorno, despite his increasing hostility toward the Communist orthodoxy of the Eastern bloc, continued to accept basic tenets of Marxian theory will necessarily stress the importance of this aspect for his criticism of art and literature. Those, on the other hand, who claim that Adorno had already distanced himself in *Dialectic of Enlightenment* (1944) and discarded Marxist theory in his later years will find it somewhat more difficult to understand why Adorno continued to theorize about the relationship between art and society. There is no doubt that Adorno stressed the importance of this relationship in his writings on music and literature. His posthumously published *Aesthetic Theory* devotes an extensive chapter to the explicit and implicit correlation between art and society.

This may well be the least fashionable part of his oeuvre today, because it deals with questions that have been relegated to the margins of literary theory under the impact of poststructuralist thought. The reasons are not difficult to grasp: the suspicion of totalizing theories easily extends toward a sociological approach, since it appears to invoke the concept of totality in order to construct a link between aesthetic and social phenomena. The sociologist of art seems by definition to be a contextualist, someone who comes from the outside to superimpose totalizing concepts on the work of art. The obvious examples are Georg Lukács, Lucien Goldmann,[1] and (from a more subjective point of view) Jean-Paul Sartre. Especially the heavy-handed approach of the later Lukács, his insensitive determinism, has discredited this approach.

Although Adorno, as we will see, shared the skeptical attitude toward sociological criticism – he attacked both Lukács and the positivists who wanted to limit the sociology of art to empirical problems – he never denied the significance of the problems that Lukács and Goldmann tried to address. He argued against a contextual approach, asserting at the same time that a thorough textual analysis would also speak to the position of the artwork within the social system. He claimed to read the social meaning of the text from the inside, without cumbersome references to the historical 'background.' This claim does raise questions: if we think that the artwork contains a social meaning, we have to assume some sort of correlation between the social system and the system of the texts, some form of imprinting: for instance, a structural homology in Goldmann's sense, or a form of dialogue among author, text, and readers in which the text is a conscious response to a specific historical situation, as Hans Robert Jauss assumes.[2] Either case requires some implicit understanding of a larger context, a totality from which the artwork can be derived or deduced (Lukács, Goldmann) or to which it can at least be referred (Jauss).[3]

Can a sociological approach avoid these pitfalls? Adorno was clearly aware of the dangers. He spoke out against research that tries to situate the artwork by concentrating on its reception; similarly, he criticized readings that would simply impose social categories on the text. He did not, however, give up the concepts of society and history as necessary codeterminants for the aesthetic realm. His criticism is filled with a strong sense of social history as the condition under which artworks are produced and consumed. This is not a matter of the artwork *reflecting* social conditions but rather a matter of human labor. Although it would be hard to find a critic who insisted more on the autonomy of the authentic artwork, Adorno consistently argued in favor of human labor as the source of literature and music. In this respect he stood in clear opposition to Heidegger's assumptions about the origins of poetry (*Dichtung*). Adorno was prepared to argue that the artwork is not only expressive but has a truth content as well, but he resisted any claims for a transcendental grounding. This brings me back to the initial question of Adorno's allegiance to Marxist theory, in which the concept of human labor is, of course, an indispensable element. How does Adorno's theory relate to Marx's understanding of this concept? Is his concept of society identical to or compatible with the Marxist concept?

Before we pursue this question, however, a look at Adorno's conception of methodology may provide a better understanding of his procedure. The essay 'On Lyric Poetry and Society,' originally conceived as a radio lecture, can serve as a prime example, since it very self-consciously introduced Adorno's method to an audience of poetry readers who were convinced that there can be no link between poetic language and the material elements of the social system. The implied reader of the essay was the New Critic, who insisted on the strict separation of literature and history, and who believed that the value of poetry lies precisely in the fact that poetry is removed from the language of communication.

This gesture toward New Criticism serves as the foil for Adorno's argument. The essay attempts to demonstrate that this negative attitude contains an important moment of truth: that indeed poetry cannot be reduced to the level of ordinary statements about social phenomena; its intrinsically unique linguistic character has to be approached before the question of the social content (*Gehalt*) can be raised at all. At the same time, Adorno means to show that the blind spot of New Criticism (*Werkimmanenz*) is its dogmatic unwillingness to consider the social meaning within the text. New Criticism might be willing to consider the link between the author and the text, but it refuses to grasp the text's connection with so abstract a concept as society.

Against this conventional attitude, Adorno begins with two radical claims, which he then has to unfold. First, he maintains that the individual poem is always more than the expression of the author's individual experience; it participates in a social totality.

> For the substance of a poem is not merely an expression of individual impulses and experiences. Those become a matter of art only when they come to participate in something universal by virtue of the specificity they acquire in being given aesthetic form. . . . It thereby anticipates, spiritually, a situation in which no false universality, that is nothing profoundly particular, continues to fetter what is other than itself, the human. (NL 1:38; GS 11:50)

The participation in the universal is not, at least for Adorno, accidental; the aesthetic value of the poem depends on the link between individual expression and social participation. His second claim is that the peculiar truth content of poetry is reached through participation in the universal. Unlike philosophical discourse, however, the poetic discourse does not articulate the universal directly; rather, it is only through the unique language of the individual poem that the universal can be attained. Poetry explores, Adorno argues, those aspects of experience that have not yet been conceptualized, that have resisted the language of communication. From these broad assumptions the essay then proceeds to argue for the importance of the *social*: 'The universality of the lyric's substance . . . is social in nature' (NL 1:38; GS 11:50). For Adorno, totality is essentially social and grounded in history.

What makes the essay still interesting today is the fact that Adorno is fully aware of the problematical nature of his claims. Not only does he persuasively defend his method of reading, but he also addresses, although not systematically, the fundamental problem of universality and its impact on the individual poem. The method he favors is, by conventional standards, intrinsic: that is, a form of close reading. It could be called a social hermeneutics, a procedure clearly distinct from the research method of the empirical sociologist as well as from Lukácsian historicism or Karl Mannheim's sociology of knowledge. These approaches, Adorno argues, fail to think through and work out the problem of mediation. Art and society cannot be linked without mediation.

The concept of mediation (*Vermittlung*) has to be treated with great care in Adorno's criticism because it works on a number of levels. Occasionally he uses it in its traditional sense to mean that a third term (or several) is needed to make a connection between two ideas; in other instances, however, he makes a different use of the concept, stressing the element of negation. In Goethe's poem 'Wanderers Nachtlied,' an example that Adorno introduces, the social sphere is absent but makes itself felt through its very absence: 'The note of peacefulness attests to the fact that peace cannot be achieved with the dream disintegrating' (NL 1:41; GS 11:54). Through its negation, the social unrest takes on significance. The process of aesthetic imprinting works in such a way that the social forces are not reflected but translated, so to speak, into a linguistic form of entirely individual character. 'In every lyric poem the historical relationship of the subject to objectivity, of the individual to society, must have found its precipitate in the medium of a subjective spirit thrown back upon itself' (NL 1:42; GS 11:55). The relationship is a dialectical one: in the mediation of poetic language the subjective expression (of suffering) turns into objective meaning. In other words, language is the third term that makes a social hermeneutics possible. Language is twofold: an expression of the individual and the medium of concepts. Thus poetry, although distant from the social sphere, is connected with social problems through language itself. Hence, the reading must first and foremost concentrate on the linguistic form, as Adorno suggests when he interprets poems by Mörike and Stefan George in the second half of the essay.

The first step of this reading is fairly close to such traditional interpretations of Mörike as those of Emil Staiger;[4] it is an attempt to capture the mood and style of 'Auf einer Wanderung.' The decisive turn occurs when Adorno begins to focus on the actual moment of historical experience. The German classicists (Goethe and Schiller), Adorno argues, valued humanity in general and tended to disregard the particular and the individual because they were already responding to a capitalist society defined by exchange value. The romantics, by contrast, favored the private and the intimate in their response to the identical social configuration. What distinguishes Mörike's poem from classicism *and* romanticism is its precise but unconscious acknowledgment of the historical situation. In Adorno's words, the poem is a 'historicophilosophical sundial,' indicating the historical moment not in factual but in spiritual terms. Although Hegel's philosophy of history is not explicitly invoked, it is not hard to detect its presence – not surprisingly, of course, since Adorno was not only teaching Hegel but also working on his Hegel essays, which prepared the way for *Negative Dialectics* (1966).

In 'On Lyric Poetry and Society' Adorno insists that social hermeneutics has to proceed from within the text. Yet the essay does not fully explain how the reader can recognize the social meaning without reference to the context: that is, without knowledge of the social system and its history. Moreover, the suggestion that the poem functions as a historical sundial is not backed up by thorough analysis. It was only in *Aesthetic Theory* that Adorno came to a rigorously argued solution of this problem, after trial runs in the essay 'Theses on the Sociology of Art'[5] and in the chapter 'Mediation' in his 1962 work *Introduction to the Sociology of Music* (ISM 194–228; GS 14:394–421). The reason for the earlier lack of clarity may have been his uncertainty in the field of social theory, especially his ambivalence toward Marxist theory. While his theory of art, I believe, did not undergo major changes after his return to Germany, his social theory seemed to have changed in more significant ways. Helmut Dubiel and others have shown that the members of the Frankfurt School turned away from a more politically orthodox Marxist position during the 1940s[6] – a shift primarily motivated by the political configuration in Europe and North America: the rise of fascism in Germany, the rise of Stalin in the Soviet Union, and the fate of mass democracy in the United States. They lost faith in the revolutionary force of the proletariat and found it increasingly difficult to discover a social agent for historical change. Hence the concept of progress, as Benjamin's theses argued emphatically, had lost its meaning. Still, this skepticism, which Adorno certainly shared (and expressed most clearly in *Minima Moralia*), did not automatically cancel the Marxian concepts on which the Frankfurt School had relied in its analysis during the 1930s and early 1940s.

One can see that during the early 1940s not only much of the Marxist terminology was still intact for Adorno but also fundamental aspects of Marxist theory. The opening statement of his essay 'Reflexionen zur Klassentheorie' (Reflections on the theory of class) makes this clear: 'According to theory, history is the history of class conflicts' (GS 8:373). He is hardly interested in the conventional view, however, according to which class struggle will ultimately secure the victory of the proletariat over the bourgeoisie and thereby open the future for social progress. Rather, following Benjamin's 'Theses on the Philosophy of History,' he emphasizes the continued suffering – ultimately self-inflicted, of course – of the human species. History has become a repetition of the same; it is no more than *Vorgeschichte* (prehistory) (GS 8:374). The essay tries to rescue the notion of the dialectic in history from a concept of history that relies on 'evolution' rather than a Hegelian syllogism. 'The system of history – that is, the fixation of the temporal as a totality of meaning – through its systematic nature sublates time and reduces it to an abstract negation' (GS 8:375). Adorno extends his argument to the Marxian dialectic as well – with the important difference that Marx turns Hegel upside down 'by demarcating prehistory as the identical' (GS 8:375). Unlike Hegel, so Adorno argues, a truly Marxian theory of history stresses the negative element, the force of expropriation and violence. In this context, the appropriate metaphor for the historical situation of the 1940s is the maze – a place seemingly without an exit.

This position anticipates the theory of history developed in *Dialectic of Enlightenment,* yet it is quite obvious that Adorno's essay relies on the basic concepts of Marxian theory. Although Adorno explicitly drops, as hopelessly outdated, the notion of the revolutionary proletariat and suggests that the traditional concept of class antagonism has to be modified (GS 8:376), he still uses the Marxist analysis of capitalism based on such categories as forces of production, relations of production, use and exchange value. Similarly, he holds on to a traditional notion of the development of the economy from the phase of liberal capitalism to a monopoly capitalism in which competition has been largely eliminated. Finally, he links the stage of advanced capitalism with European fascism.

It is through a Marxist analysis that Adorno in 1942 subverts a position that would valorize the possibility of social and political progress. He tries, precisely with the help of Marxian theory, to fend off new versions of social theory that discredit the concept of class and class conflict. Adorno argues that advanced Marxist theory has to go beyond its own tradition in order to oppose the apologetic versions of bourgeois sociology. This is a strategy that Adorno certainly continued during the 1950s and 1960s when he faced the West German sociologists in the positivism dispute.

In 1942, Adorno suggests that certain parts of Marxist theory – especially *Verelendungstheorie* (theory of immiserization) – must be revised but insists at the same time on the validity of Marxian social theory. Advanced capitalist society, monopoly capitalism, follows the logic of Marx's analysis beyond the horizon of its author. The dividing line is not so much between wealth and poverty as between power and impotence: 'The site of the secret, you might say censured, poverty is political and social powerlessness' (GS 8:386). It is noteworthy that in 1942 Adorno emphatically calls for the removal (*Sturz*) of the power elite. As much as it may surprise anyone who is familiar with Adorno's later work, the essay 'Reflexionen zur Klassentheorie' offers a revolutionary perspective: the author anticipates the moment of the break when social suffering has become total. 'Only when the victims completely adopt the features of the dominant civilization do they become capable of stripping that civilization of domination' (GS 8:391). This sentence reflects Adorno's adamant refusal to accept the affirmation of the status quo in mainstream American sociology.

His resistance was equally strong in later essays written under very different circumstances in West Germany. Their aim was, by and large, to situate the position of the Frankfurt School within West German social theory and politics. Two essays from the 1960s may serve to illustrate the position of the late Adorno. In discussing them I will disregard, for the most part, their immediate historical context: for example, the student revolution of the late 1960s, which caught Adorno by surprise and changed his life in more than one way. These essays continue Adorno's vehement opposition to empirical social theory as it became more influential in Germany after World War II, through the impact of American and British sociology. Adorno realized that the majority of the younger generation of social scientists – among them figures such as Ralf Dahrendorf and Peter Ludz – felt more comfortable with empirical research methods. His essays leave no doubt as to why he was suspicious of this tendency: the new project moved toward affirmation. The elimination of 'traditional' sociological categories such as class and society in favor of more 'manageable' concepts such as group and *Schicht* (stratum) might assist close description but not critical distance. Hence, in his 1965 essay 'Gesellschaft' (Society), Adorno urges his readers to retain the concept of society as a necessary critical tool for the analysis of social processes. Clearly, he does not understand the term society (*Gesellschaft*) as merely empirical and descriptive; rather, he invokes the concept of society to signify the *totality* of all social relations. Thus, he sees it as a dynamic as well as functional category, one that allows the sociologist to theorize about the interdependence of the system and the individual.

A social theory as Adorno envisaged it in the 1960s would be closer to Max Weber than to Emile Durkheim; it would be a hermeneutically grounded theory, yet it would be – and this is crucial for Adorno – a theory of *nonidentity*. Social theory after World War II must understand the unimaginable, 'the advance of human beings into the inhuman'[7] – a test for which, Adorno rightly observes, traditional hermeneutics is not equipped.

What kind of theory, then, would be adequate for the task of critical interpretation? The second part of the short essay tries to define contemporary society. This sketch describes the world of the 1960s as a global system in which advanced capitalist and postcolonial Third World countries are interconnected through an economic system that is (still) constructed as a global market network. Adorno suggests that this society is as much motivated by profit as was nineteenth-century capitalism. Similarly, he defines it as a class society determined by class conflicts and structural antagonisms. In fact, he assumes that the differences between the classes (in objective terms) have increased rather than decreased during the ongoing process of economic concentration. As a result, society as a global social order moves toward a system with increasingly totalitarian tendencies, in both the First and Second Worlds.

Clearly, Adorno's analysis of contemporary society still owes its concepts largely to Marxist theory, without, however, affirming the socialist regimes of the Second World or the socialist movements of the Third. Thus Adorno finds it more difficult, if not impossible, to discover actual trends that would lead to a free society. 'A rational and genuinely free society could do without administration as little as it could do without division of labor itself. But all over the globe, administrations have tended under constraint towards a greater self-sufficiency and independence from their administered subjects, reducing the latter to objects of abstractly normed behavior.'[8] As a result, the situation of the individual has become objectively worse, although the masses may find the social conditions rather pleasant because they have become more dependent on the system and respond to its demands by a higher degree of submission (*Anpassung*).

A comparison between the 1942 and 1965 essays reveals a significant shift in Adorno's position but, at the same time, a surprising amount of continuity. Although Adorno's social theory rarely explicitly invokes the authority of Marx, it continues to use central categories from Marxist theory. This does not mean that Adorno is inclined to subscribe to the letter of Marx's analyses and prognoses; he concedes that much of that is no longer relevant for contemporary society. What he underlines, however – for instance, in the essay 'Spätkapitalismus oder Industriegesellschaft' (Late capitalism or industrial society) – is the relevance of the central Marxian concepts for a critical assessment. In his last address to the German *Soziologentag* (annual convention of sociologists) in 1968, Adorno stated this principle with great force: 'A dialectical theory of society focuses on structural laws, which determine the facts, as they manifest these facts and are modified by them. By structural laws such a theory understands tendencies that follow more or less stringently from the historical constituents of the total system' (GS 8:356).

Yet this touch of orthodoxy must not be confused with an affirmation of Soviet dialectical materialism. What makes Adorno's use of Marxian theory unique is his emphasis on the subjective element, which encourages a dialectical critique. 'To the fetishism of facts corresponds a fetishism of objective laws. A dialectic that has soaked in the painful experience [of the fact] that these objective laws prevail does not praise them; instead, it criticizes them as much as the illusion that the concrete and individual moment immediately determines the existing world' (GS 8:356). In other words, Adorno's social theory is neither descriptive nor classifying: hence his refusal to be satisfied with a concept of industrial society that is silent about the dominant mode of production. He holds on to the concept of forces of production as the primary and decisive category for the understanding of social systems, placing his emphasis on the limitations that result from the crystallization of these forces in specific relations of production. As we will see, his interest in these categories is by no means limited to the social system. They are equally important for his criticism of music and literature.

For mainstream sociology of art, one of the foremost tasks has been to define the field of investigation by demarcating its proper borders. During the 1950s a resurgent interest in sociology of art in West Germany, after the ban of any sociological criticism under Hitler, was accompanied by a concern with that demarcation. Among the musicologists it was Alfons Silbermann who strongly argued in favor of a clear line of division between music criticism and sociological studies.[9] Sociological research, he wrote, should be exclusively concerned with the reception of music – more specifically, with empirical investigations of listening and listeners. By the same token, the sociology of art is not involved in hermeneutical processes; the text is seen as a black box with input and output. Similar tendencies can be observed in West German literary criticism. In 1966 Hans Norbert Fügen, in his much-quoted book *Hauptrichtungen der Literatursoziologie,* proposed a distinction between sociological and hermeneutic criticism. Sociology of literature, Fügen argued, should focus on the contextual aspect of literature, either on production (author, publication) or on consumption (market, audience).[10] Both Silbermann and Fügen reaffirmed the traditional division of intrinsic and extrinsic studies.

In his 'Theses on the Sociology of Art' ('Thesen zur Kunstsoziologie,' first read as a paper in 1965), Adorno challenged this division with its conservative resistance to social change. For tactical reasons, he did not argue against empirical research; rather, he postulated from the very beginning that the sociology of art contains *all* aspects of the relationship between art and society. Empirical research must not claim a monopoly, because it is too limited in its approach to account for the more basic questions of meaning and function. To concentrate simply on the experience of art (*Kunsterlebnis*) would mean to overlook the social condition under which the production as well as the reception of music, for example, takes place.

Adorno's reservations about Silbermann's project are grounded in his broader understanding of the social. Bringing his concept of society to bear on matters of art criticism, he points to two areas of sociological investigation: first, the determination of the artwork by the production and consumption of art as it is socially organized; second, the social meaning of the artwork (*sozialer Gehalt*) as it can be derived from the work itself. To use a term that was later foregrounded by Peter Bürger, on one level sociological research deals with the question of the *institution*. Adorno advances the argument that popular music (as opposed to serious music) can be researched only in the larger context of the culture industry. The effect or impact of a piece of popular music depends on the framework of the institutional configuration. On another level, the sociologist would be concerned with the work of art itself. The social meaning of a text can be deciphered only through formal analysis and interpretation (close reading). In making this point, Adorno challenges the notion of quantitative empirical research as well as the New Critics' celebration of the autonomy of the artwork and anxious rejection of sociological analysis as extrinsic. This emphasis on the specific character of the individual work of art implies its aesthetic quality. The sociology of art and critical evaluation, Adorno claims, cannot be separated. Clearly, he rejects the Weberian notion of *Wertfreiheit* (indifference to value claims, neutrality) which underlay much of West German sociology at that time. A critical sociology of art must include the aspect of value by questioning the dogmatic value claims of art criticism and by criticizing the scientific claims of empirical sociological research.

In his 'Thesen zur Kunstsoziologie' Adorno outlines a theory and methodology of sociological criticism without, however, working out the details of the argument. The essay neither specifies the procedure of social interpretation nor confronts the question of exactly how the institution of art is grounded in the social system. Crucial questions remain unanswered. First, how is the correlation of art and society to be conceptualized? Conventional terms such as background, grounding, and so on, are ultimately unsatisfactory unless they can be unfolded in a coherent argument. Second, what specifically accounts for the assumption that there is a close connection between social history and the history of music or literature? If we take Adorno's sundial metaphor seriously, we have to investigate his theory of history. To be sure, he always warned against constructing unmediated links, but then, of course, the concept of mediation itself would also deserve closer scrutiny.

It is in the final chapter of his *Introduction to the Sociology of Music* that Adorno addresses these questions. In its stated methodology, his sociology of music stays fairly close to that of his 1965 'Theses.' In fact, the lectures on which the book is based preceded that essay by three years, and the subtitle 'twelve theoretical lectures' makes their claim apparent: the advancement of a sociological theory. The body of the study is concerned with specific social aspects of music; it is the last chapter that focuses on the most crucial methodological problem: 'the social deciphering of musical phenomena as such, an insight into their essential relation to the real society, into their inner social content and into their function' (ISM 194; GS 14:394). Using the example of Hector Berlioz, Adorno immediately points to the difficulty of an adequate solution: although it is persuasive to suggest that Berlioz's music – for instance, his way of using the orchestra (*Orchesterbehandlung*) – correlates with the beginnings of the industrial phase of capitalism in France, it is next to impossible to prove this claim through traditional sociological or historical methods. This argument works both ways: if the formal features of Berlioz's music cannot be correlated with specific elements of industrial capitalism, neither can the characteristics of advanced capitalism be easily traced in the works of composers as different as Claude Debussy, Gustav Mahler, and Giacomo Puccini. How can the critic transcend the level of suggestive, even persuasive analysis using terms such as *Zuordnung* (attribution) (ISM 196; GS 14:397)?

Adorno's answer relies on the distinction we observed in his 'Theses': the difference between the institutional and the textual level. The social content of the artwork is mediated through the institutional configuration that determines the production as well as the reception of music. As long as this configuration is not acknowledged, the seeming objectivity of empirical research is no more than an illusion. These institutional forces depend on the structure of the society in which they operate. Nineteenth-century musical institutions (for example, the social organization of music appreciation) – or literary institutions, for that matter – are determined by the central feature of the capitalist society: namely, the exchange value of a market economy.

Thus Adorno argues against a purely empirical concept of sociological institutions that restrict themselves to the level of facts. 'For the object itself is derivative, secondary, superficial. Because today the subjects are objects of society, not its substance' (ISM 198; GS 14:398–99). It is not surprising that Adorno, viewing the institution of music as grounded in the apparatus of the capitalist economy, places the emphasis on production and tends to see reception (listening) as a socially mediated epiphenomenon. As we will see, he by no means denies the significance of this aspect, but he refuses to conflate the social function of music with its consumption. From the very beginning, he is critical of the kind of administrative research that broadcasting companies organize to increase their control over their listeners and viewers. Corporate interests, as he observed, would hardly support critical studies.

Adorno's theory of the apparatus can easily account for the culture industry: that is, the social mediation of mass culture. More demanding is a sociological theory of advanced artworks (compositions), because it would be less than persuasive to derive the function of modern music from the structure of the social classes or the economy. Adorno assumes that all music, including 'serious' music, is grounded in social conditions; his problem is to develop a theory that specifies this general and admittedly vague assumption. He has to account for a relationship that a mechanical theory would describe as impact and a phenomenological theory would define as a correlation. In the last chapter of his

Introduction to the Sociology of Music he approaches this question primarily as a problem of *mediation*: he conceives of the composition of music – serious or popular – as a form of production and thereby as rooted in human, socially mediated labor. The artwork is something produced by an individual artist as part of the larger process of social production: 'However much the groups may be estranged by the division of labor, all individuals working in each phase are socially joined, no matter what they are working on. Their work, even the artist's most individual one in his own consciousness, is always "work in society"' (ISM 202; GS 14:403).

For Adorno, aesthetic production is specific but, at the same time, part of economic and social production. If the composition of music is subsumed under the category of production, it logically and historically follows the same laws. This understanding comes out most clearly in the following statement: 'Yet as in real society the productive forces take precedence over the circumstances of production which chain as well as enhance them, so will society's musical consciousness be finally determined by the production of music, by the work congealed in compositions, although the infinity of intermediaries is not altogether transparent' (ISM 202; GS 14:403). Compositions appear as *geronnene Arbeit* (congealed labor), a dynamic process that crystallizes in the context of specific relations of production.

It is noteworthy that Adorno stresses the difficulty of working out the details of the process of mediation. It is not quite clear whether he wants to apply the concept of production literally or as an analogy, since he distinguishes between superstructure (art) and material production. On the whole, he tends to downgrade the base/superstructure dichotomy, emphasizing instead the common ground of material and aesthetic production. This argument allows him to claim that there are similarities between social phenomena and artworks which do not depend on causal connections or the assumption of some form of *Zeitgeist*. Adorno is, of course, quite conscious of the dangers involved in this approach, as his critique of orthodox dialectical materialism demonstrates. Nowhere does he support a causal base/superstructure model or the reflection theory that goes with it; rather, he consistently insists on complex processes of mediation. For example, he recognizes the social contradiction between forces of production and relations of production as they emerge in the early stages of industrial capitalism, as well as the autonomous artwork as a subversion of conventional, socially accepted form. Thus, he argues that the central categories of the artistic construct are translatable into social categories. The German word he employs, *übersetzbar*, signifies not a form of reflection but a mode of working through the aesthetic material in such a way that the formal structure itself contains the moment of truth.

His attempt to find a materialist solution for the problem of correlation is not entirely consistent. At certain moments Adorno's argument makes use of a Hegelian concept of spirit (*Geist*) as the central category of mediation, yet the occasional allusions to *Geist* as the all-encompassing totality do not carry the same theoretical weight as the basic Marxist concepts. In any case, the approach of the *Introduction to the Sociology of Music*, favoring a Marxist concept of labor and production, remains fairly abstract when it comes to a sociological interpretation of the text. On the whole, his lectures are more concerned with the contextual and intertextual aspects of music than with the structure of compositions. In his *Aesthetic Theory*, as we will see, the emphasis is reversed: there the critical question refers to the social content (*Gehalt*) of the artwork itself.

The opera chapter of the *Introduction* can serve as an example of a combined intertextual and contextual approach. One might expect a sociological treatment of the opera to stress the dependence of the form on an extensive apparatus, originally growing out of the court theater of the seventeenth and eighteenth centuries. But Adorno takes most of this for granted and examines first and foremost two related aspects of the opera: the crisis of the form in the twentieth century, and its inadequate reception by an audience that is no longer competent to experience its aesthetic quality. Thus, the opera appears as a genre that functions successfully in a social and cultural environment in which it has lost its purpose – or, to be more precise, in which its original functions have been replaced by secondary considerations that were quite alien to the time of its production and first consumption. If the opera, as Adorno points out, is the most illusionary theatrical form, then today's reception of it involves the additional illusion of a stable and reliable cultural tradition in which its conservative admirers can take refuge.

It is noteworthy that Adorno begins the chapter with a historical consideration: 'Neither from the musical nor from the aesthetic point of view can we avoid the impression that the operatic form is obsolete' (ISM 71; GS 14:254). He goes on not only to recount the history of the opera in terms of a decline after 1910 (with Strauss's *Der Rosenkavalier* as the last instance of a harmonious unity between composition, performance, and audience) but also to hint at the social changes that caused the growing rift between the needs and desires of the audience and the aesthetic appeal of the operatic form. The modern opera, Adorno argues, lacks the public support on which composers of the nineteenth century could necessarily count. Even though the operas of Schönberg, Alban Berg, and others responded to the challenge of modernism, audiences did not. They remained loyal to the repertoire of the nineteenth century and its implicit definition of high culture, thereby handing the form over to the culture industry and losing the very culture they wanted to protect. For Adorno, the genre can be continued only through the negation of its tradition, but this act of subversion also destabilizes the social and cultural environment of the genre. As much as the form expressed the ideology of the bourgeois audience during the nineteenth century, its modernist version, undercutting this ideology, was bound to lose this audience. Adorno notes: 'In the opera, at any rate, a self-assured bourgeoisie could celebrate and enjoy itself for a long time. On the musical stage the symbols of its power and material ascent combined with the rituals of the fading, but arch-bourgeois, idea of liberated nature' (ISM 80; GS 14:264).

This argument explains the crisis of the opera after 1920 but hardly the revival of opera as an institution after 1945. The repertoire of European opera houses, Adorno observes, seems as stable as ever, now including rather than excluding modern operas. In response to this development, Adorno draws on the theory of the culture industry. Traditional high culture functions in a new way: it offers the recipient the illusion of participating in a culture that does not exist any more. The consumption focuses as much on the ambience of *Kultur* as on the work itself, so that the operas have their audience but at the expense of their own substance. Such a paradoxical situation goes beyond alienation; it marks an affirmative consumption of the moment of alienation. The audience desires the illusion of a culture that was already an illusion at the time of its production.

Adorno regards it as futile to research the interests and the taste of this postwar opera audience without simultaneously reflecting on the history of the genre – its formal as well as its institutional aspects – and it is this intertwinement of contextual and intertextual considerations that distinguishes his approach from empirical sociology. Obviously, his method refuses quantification and its appearance of objectivity, even in those areas where he is exclusively concerned with social situations. Neither the chapter on the conductor nor the following essay on the organization of music life makes use of statistical procedures. Adorno's observations on the role of the conductor are anything but descriptive; they concentrate on the representation of power in the relationship between leader and orchestra. The division of labor in the performance of music thus becomes an allegory for social power relations. Serious music, which by its own definition is above or immune to social conflicts, is at the same time an extension of those conflicts. The performance requires a hierarchy among the performing artists that the text might possibly challenge. In other words, the institution itself cannot be conceived without an element of conflict and repression that aesthetic freedom tries to overcome. Even chamber music, Adorno points out, is by no means excluded from this dialectic. Music performance is always involved in the very social problems to which the composition responds on its own terms.

What distinguishes Adorno's use of contextual material from empirical sociology is his insistence on integrating the 'outside facts' into the discussion of the text and its intertextual configuration. In fact, just as he disregarded the conventional borderlines between sociology and psychology, his essays rarely uphold rigid methodological distinctions. Through the dialectical structure of their argument they prefer to explore invisible, even seemingly improbable connections, frequently using a minor detail as the point of departure. The insignificant detail speaks to the larger issue; it leads Adorno to the nodal points of the social system. The unsystematic procedure of his essays, their seeming lack of a straightforward argument that would lend itself to a neat summary, are part of his theoretical position; a theory whose logic follows the social system reproduces the reification of the system itself. The theorist is part of the social situation that he or she describes. The suspicion of scientific systematization, which certainly runs through Adorno's oeuvre, must not be confused, with a belief in arbitrary situations, dead ends, or discontinuities, however. Adorno remained convinced that history could be conceptualized, that its various moments and strands, although they will not easily fit together and produce a harmonious whole, are related to one another. His resistance to sociological positivism is ultimately rooted in this conviction – a conviction for which his own theory is the objective correlative.

The crucial question, then, is this: does Adorno presuppose a center from which the various elements can be derived? His work does not seem to give us an unambiguous answer. There is no attempt to argue for a center, a point from which a society can be fully reconstructed and understood, but there are numerous suggestions that social organization follows a logic that unfolds in history.[11] The moment comes out most clearly in his understanding of European capitalism: he consistently argues that modern (post-eighteenth-century) art must be understood in the context of a society determined by exchange and, as a consequence, by reification. Yet even here Adorno's answer is not unambiguous, because he typically does not argue from the perspective of economic history but searches for a point where the economy and art connect. There is, I think, a tension in Adorno's criticism that can be formulated in the following way: on the one hand, he assumes that social as well as cultural phenomena are part of a larger whole; on the other hand, he refuses to reproduce the logic of that larger whole in his theory. His theory and methodology are expected to expose the totality and undermine it at the same time. Adorno developed this intricate and certainly unstable relationship most radically in his late work, especially *Aesthetic Theory*.

We have to remind ourselves that because the author died before *Aesthetic Theory* was completed, its present organization and chapter division were determined by the editors.[12] According to the schema, which hardly agrees with Adorno's intentions, the last chapter concerns the sociological aspects of aesthetic theory. But such a focus is deceptive because it represses the presence of many sociological problems in the preceding chapters. For Adorno, the separation of the social and the aesthetic is already the result of a false consciousness and has to be questioned. Therefore, any analysis of Adorno's work that singles out a particular aspect is in danger of presenting a reified structure, whereas his thought insists on an open and continuous process of dialectic. More rigorously than in the *Introduction to the Sociology of Music*, Adorno is here concerned with two aspects: on the one hand, the historicity of art, its participation in the process of human history; and on the other, art's own intrinsic history, the development of the aesthetic material and technique. One result of this dual focus is a renewed assessment of the problem of engagement that was at the center of his polemical essay 'Commitment,'[13] but from today's point of view, Adorno's response to a dogmatic Marxist position (that of Brecht) comes across as equally dogmatic. Another result is a renewed interest in the status of mass culture, especially its relationship to high culture and the avant-garde; however, this discussion does not go significantly beyond his earlier work.

At the center of his concern is the fundamental insight of Hegel: the historical nature of the aesthetic. Therefore, what mainstream criticism takes for granted comes under scrutiny: for Adorno the autonomy of art and the sanctity of aesthetic considerations are no longer the unquestioned ground for criticism; rather, they constitute the point of departure for an analysis of historical roots. Adorno argues that there were two significant changes in the history of art and literature between the Renaissance and the later twentieth century: the first occurred during the eighteenth century and was closely connected with the rise of capitalism; the second took place during the late nineteenth century when liberal capitalism changed into monopoly capitalism. In neither case does Adorno press for dates or try to pinpoint specific works of art. What is important to him is the insight into the changing parameters of the production and reception of art and literature.

It was only through capitalism, a market economy determined by exchange, that autonomy became the institutional parameter (to use a later terminology) explicitly formulated in the theories of Gotthold Lessing, Johann Gottfried Herder, and Kant. This shift also changed the relationship between art and society. Under feudalism or even absolutism, art was more immediately a social phenomenon than in the modern period. Art had an immediate social function that was recognized by producers and recipients alike. Accepted control mechanisms were part of this function, as well as exemplary ways of using art as social criticism (for instance, in the work of Aristophanes). Hence, this relationship can be described in positive and affirmative terms. Adorno maintains that modern art, on the other hand (after the eighteenth century), cannot be so defined. What is called the 'emancipation of the arts and literature' implies that the immediate social function has been canceled; thus art becomes 'asocial.' 'By crystallizing in its own right, instead of accommodating itself to existing social norms and thereby proving itself to be "socially useful," [art] critiques society through its mere being' (GS 7:335; AT 321). Hence the art-society correlation of capitalist societies, according to Adorno, can be defined only in terms of 'concrete negation.' With the emergence of aesthetic autonomy as a principle, the older definition becomes ideological. At the same time, however, as Adorno rightly points out, the distancing of the autonomous artwork from the social structure contains its own element of ideology: the distance precludes social praxis.

We have to note that for Adorno any discussion of the art-society relationship has to be historically specific, since he sees this relationship as part of the historical process. Adorno resists theories that attempt to generalize in terms of time and place. Hence, it is important to read his arguments in their context. His claim, for instance, that in art, social elements do not appear unmediated has to be understood as a statement on *modern* art, as does his distinction between truth and ideology in art, and his denial of social praxis in the work of art. Adorno's opposition to the postulate of engaged art is grounded in his assumption that the aesthetic cannot be translated into the social. When the mediation can be defined exclusively in terms of negativity, the notion of an immediate social application misses the crucial point: that is, the elevated status of advanced art in a modern society.

With respect to modern art, then, *Aesthetic Theory* makes two seemingly contradictory assumptions: on the one hand, Adorno holds that art becomes autonomous and therefore separate from social history; on the other hand, he insists on the involvement of art and the individual artwork in history. The contradiction disappears, however, when we realize that these assumptions operate on different levels: the latter one refers to a broad temporal spectrum, the former specifically to modern European history. Nevertheless, with regard to the last two centuries, the contradiction still has to be accounted for.

Post-Adornian critical theory – for instance, that of Habermas or of Peter Bürger – has dealt with this problem by referring to Max Weber's theory of modern rationalization: in a differentiated modern society, art becomes a separate sphere with its own institutions. In Weber's theory it is the process of rationalization itself that produces the autonomy of art. Occasionally, Adorno may describe this process in similar terms; by and large, however, his theoretical explanation uses a different set of concepts. Modern art, he argues, has to be understood in terms of exchange value. The autonomy of art is the equivalent of a split between exchange value and use value in a capitalist economy. Such a split creates a world of fetishized objects (commodities) – among them, works of art. Artworks owe their autonomy to the very fact that also endangers their autonomy: they have become commodities. As commodities they have an exchange value vis-à-vis the social system. Both producer and recipient relate to the social fact of the artwork as a commodity with a specific exchange value; this external side is determined by the relations of production. The internal side, by contrast, is supposed to be free from this constraint, to rely on pure use value. But use value disappears under the conditions of advanced capitalism; instead, the purity of the artwork is fetishized. It claims to be pure art with no outside function, thus relegating the commodity aspect to the margins.

If used undialectically, this argument tends to favor a causal determinism in which capitalist art is easily reduced to the status of a commodity. But Adorno's dialectical approach understands the fetishism of the commodified artwork as the means of resistance and subversion: 'That art works, in their fetishism, are culpable, does not mean that they can be dismissed, as little as one can dismiss anything that is culpable; for in a world totally mediated by society, nothing exists outside of the context of culpability. The fetish character of works of art is actually a condition of their truth content, which is also their social truth' (GS 7:337; AT 323). As fetishes they are *also* objects outside the market economy, not reducible to profit. In this respect they operate like cult objects from a premodern world, taken out of the context of ordinary life.

Adorno's model emphasizes the intertwinement of art and society. More specifically, it claims that society is not outside but inside the artwork: 'The essential social relationship in art is in the immanence of society in the work itself rather than the immanence of art in society' (GS 7:345; AT 330). Clearly, Adorno favors the textual level, in this instance, over the institutional level. As we have seen in the *Introduction to the Sociology of Music*, however, he is quite willing to discuss and take seriously the institutional aspect as well. His preference for the textual level forces him to work out a conceptual frame for a rigorous argument. When he claims that social struggle and class conflict leave their imprint in the structure of artworks, we are left with a number of difficult questions. First of all, what does 'imprint' (*abdrücken*) mean in this context? Since Adorno consistently rejects reflection theory, the meaning of the term needs to be specified. Second, what allows us to assume this kind of intrinsic connection? Is there a prestabilized harmony between social history and the history of music or literature? Hegel's philosophy of *Geist* could make this assumption, but does Adorno fall back on Hegelian idealism in order to defend his model?

I begin with the second question, since it will lead us back to the first one. Adorno is quite conscious of the problem addressed in the second question. The presupposition of a harmony smacks of mystification, yet he maintains that there is an adequate theoretical solution. It makes use of Gottfried Leibniz's category of the *monad*: 'The process [of mediation] which takes place within artworks and which is then arrested in them should be conceived of as analogous with the social process to which they are upheld' (GS 7:350; AT 335). Adorno argues that there is an affinity between the formal configuration of the artwork and the structure of the social system. This claim clarifies his intention but still leaves us with the question of why such a correlation should occur. At this point, Adorno reverts to the materialist Marxist model and argues that the stated intertwinement is grounded in the dialectical relations between forces of production and relations of production. The site of aesthetic production is the intersection between productive forces and social conditions articulated as norms and conventions (style). When the aesthetic productive forces transcend conventions, the result will be an authentic artwork. But in two respects the work remains tied to the existing relations of production: first, in a market economy it will always be a potential commodity; second, its own authenticity includes the struggle with conventional heterogeneous norms. Hence, Adorno insists that no work of art can be pure truth; it will always also be, in part, ideology.

The secret of the artwork is not that it discloses truth but that it is produced under specific historical conditions and – we might add – has to exist in history through complex processes of appropriation. When art claims the status of absolute purity and self-containment, as in the modernist *l'art pour l'art* theory, the claim is ideological and true only indirectly, insofar as it articulates the opposition of advanced art against the pressure of social alienation. 'The ideological moment of the *l'art pour l'art* principle is not grounded in its vigorous antithesis of art to the empirical world, but rather in the abstract and facile character of this antith-

esis' (GS 7:351–52; AT 336). The example of turn-of-the-century
authors (Rilke, George, Oscar Wilde, and so on) is useful here:
Adorno not only stresses the moment of production in art but
also emphasizes the need for historical specificity; thus, he argues
that fin-de-siècle literature responds to and contains the elements
of advanced capitalism. Postliberal capitalism, with its emphasis
on the concentration of capital (monopoly), turns away from
competition in the marketplace. This trend affects the status of
commodities: they become more fetishized. The increased reification (as Max Weber and the early Lukács argued) of the total
society finds its negative equivalent in the conscious attempt of
Jugendstil artists to remove the work from the marketplace. The
result is the opposite of what the writers and artists intended,
however: subjective differentiation and the refinement of aesthetic sensations become the material of the emerging culture
industry.

The answer to the second question provides the key to the first
as well. Since Adorno's notion of the 'imprint' does not depend on
a concept of reflection, there are two possible answers to the question of the term's meaning. One relies on the category of *productive forces*; it presupposes an affinity, however mediated, between
material and aesthetic production. Given this meaning, Adorno's
model would be fairly close to Lucien Goldmann's homology
model, which assumes that the form of literature (not the context)
is the equivalent of a specific social structure.[14] Some of Adorno's
formulations suggest a similar view, but he did not limit himself to
this position. Of equal if not greater importance is the concept of
negation as a critical tool. In this case, the absence of a specific
social moment in the text can be as telling as its presence. The
process of mediation becomes almost invisible, insofar as even
terms such as 'traces' and 'imprints' are actually too undifferentiated to articulate the proper relationship. The monad is perhaps
the best image that Adorno could use for his model; at least its lack
of windows makes any notion of communication or reflection
and imitation impossible. The communication of the work of art
with its environment, with the outside world, Adorno stresses,
occurs only in the form of noncommunication. Thus the first

chapter of *Aesthetic Theory* defines the mimetic structure of the artwork as the dialectic of nature and control over nature, which, of course, also determines the social world. More specifically, in the sphere of aesthetic production it becomes the dialectic of technique and material – a tradition of negativity in which, according to Adorno, the works are each other's mortal enemies. The traces of the authentic work of art that we find in its material point to *modernity as a necessary trajectory*. The production of the work, Adorno suggests, is concerned primarily with internal problems of technique; solving these problems simultaneously offers a critical view of the social environment.

As strange as it may sound, Adorno's understanding of social criticism is much closer to Marxist theory than is generally assumed. Although the majority of recent historians of the Frankfurt School have come to the conclusion that Critical Theory backed away from orthodox Marxism during the 1940s and completely lost contact with it during the 1950s and 1960s, a closer look at Adorno's texts reveals that this assessment – which is valid with respect to politics – does not do justice to his aesthetic theory. As much as Adorno consistently criticized mechanical versions of Marxist theory and their undialectical notions of the base/superstructure model or reflection theory (he accuses Lukács of both), he relied on core Marxian concepts – forces of production, relation of production, commodity fetishism, reification – in his sociological as well as his aesthetic writings. Paul Piccone's assertion that there was still a great deal of Marxism in the Frankfurt School in the 1960s is not far from the truth,[15] at least as far as Adorno is concerned. One could argue that it was only members of the second generation of the Frankfurt School – in particular, Jürgen Habermas – who consciously revised and ultimately turned away from Marxist theory.

Outside observers have frequently regarded Adorno as a 'revisionist' because of the emphasis of his theory, especially its lack of a political project. The late Adorno was unable to detect any oppositional class or group that had the potential for revolutionary struggle; in fact, he could not envision a revolution at all. Similarly, he argued against engaged art: that is, art as a tool in the political struggle. For him, the oppositional force of the artwork is independent of its author as well as its recipients. It offers, so to speak, a critical commentary without being able to interfere in the social world. *Aesthetic Theory* makes the point again and again that works of art cannot change the world directly. In short, Adorno's increasing resistance to political activism gives his theory the appearance of being removed from the site that Marxism traditionally claimed as its own. The necessary question, then becomes, where exactly is Adorno's social theory situated?

With respect to the history of Marxist theory, Adorno's writings have been grouped with the members of the Frankfurt School as part of Western Marxism, the Hegelian revival of Marxian thought. More specifically, it is impossible to overlook the impact of the early Lukács. Adorno owes two elements of his model to Lukács: from *Theory of the Novel* he could take over the historicization of orthodox theory, and from *History and Class Consciousness* the specific emphasis on commodity fetishism and reification. Additional work on Hegel after World War II strengthened these elements in Adorno's writings. Rethinking Hegel's dialectic became one of his most important preoccupations. Still, it seems inadequate to situate Adorno's social theory and his critical approach to art squarely within the tradition of Hegelian Marxism, for other influences on his work complicate the assessment – most notably the impact of Benjamin, but also his connection with Siegfried Kracauer and Max Horkheimer.

These intersections should warn us against premature conclusions. More important, the crucial question is not so much Adorno's debt to his predecessors as his place in contemporary criticism. A generation after his premature death, this question has to be asked – not only in Germany, where there was a general feeling of hostility toward Adorno during the 1970s, but also in the United States, where his reception has been somewhat uneven.

My discussion in response to that question will limit itself to a comparison with two strands of Marxist theory: structuralist Marxism as it was developed by Althusser and his British disciples; and Western Marxism, especially its American version in the writings of Fredric Jameson. Clearly, Jameson's project is much closer to Adorno's theory than is the literary theory of Althusserians such as Terry Eagleton and Perry Anderson. Jameson is not only aware of Adorno but sees his own work in the same tradition: the position he takes in *The Political Unconscious* is partly a response to Adorno and the Frankfurt School.[16] Eagleton, on the other hand, comes to the Frankfurt School rather late and through Benjamin, rather than through Adorno and Horkheimer.[17] What Jameson and Eagleton face, as critics writing in the 1970s and later, is an environment of theoretical suspicion that Adorno did not encounter. Among other things, this suspicion questions the concept of totality – a central category for the Marxist tradition. The arguments against totalizing theory would touch both models of Marxism. But can Marxist theory do without the concept of totality?

In both his 1981 and 1990 books, Jameson argues that Marxian theory cannot dispense with this category and defends its undogmatic use against deconstructionist attacks. He does, however, acknowledge the importance of hermeneutics as a theoretical touchstone, thus displaying a sensitivity to the problem of close reading that was alien to large parts of the Marxist tradition. It is precisely in this area that his project intersects with the writings of Adorno – and, inversely, with the theory of Althusser, who is seen as the opponent of hermeneutics.

The Althusserian distinction between mechanical causality, expressive causality (Hegel), and structural causality allows Jameson to redefine the problem of reading in terms compatible with Adorno's strategy of immanent reading. Jameson's willingness to accept Althusser's critique of expressive causality and the idea of a seamless totality, especially in regard to the concept of historical periods, is in fact fairly close to Adorno's suspicion of idealist concepts of history relying on the concept of spirit (*Geist*) as the central category. This suspicion would, incidentally, call certain uses of the concept of mediation into question as well. In view of Althusser's critique of historicism and the causality of expression,[18] Jameson proposes a revision of the conventional base/superstructure model that would overcome the allegorical functions of Marxist criticism (Lukács). Instead of distinguishing levels (base and superstructure), Jameson, following Althusser, unfolds the model of production in such a way that the economy is no longer privileged over culture and ideology; culture and ideology have their own access to the base (structure) as the absent cause. The structure in this revised Marxist model, as Jameson points out, is a totality (but not a ground or origin) with the various fields (legal, cultural, economic) as semi-autonomous systems. Assuming a semi-autonomous status for culture (literature and art) implies a special relationship of simultaneous dependence and autonomy – traditionally called mediation. Mediation, as Jameson defines it, is 'the classical dialectical term for the establishment of relationships between, say, the formal analysis of a work of art and its social ground.'[19] Traditional mediation is seen as a way of connecting by establishing identity (homology). Jameson wants to replace this understanding of mediation with the concept of transcoding as a way of reconnecting a fragmented world of special codes. Proper mediation, then, means the interrelatedness of all elements of the structure – a strategy that makes Hegel less an opponent than an ally of Althusser.

Clearly, Jameson focuses on theoretical problems that are also fundamental to Adorno's theory. His solutions, however, differ in significant respects. Adorno favors the category of the forces of production over the mode of production and would probably not agree to a concept of mediation as transcoding. As a result, he is not faced, as Althusser and Jameson are, with the thorny problem of semi-autonomy. A schema of Adorno's position would look like this: instead of beginning with the mode of production, he starts with the concept of labor as a way of relating to nature. Human control over nature is at the same time a necessary condition for human communities and a potential threat to these communities. This dialectic of progress is played out in history through the tension between the forces of production and the relations of productions. For Adorno, the forces of production are not limited to the economic sphere; they are equally operative in the cultural sphere. This broader concept eliminates the traditional base/superstructure problem. It also extends the dialectic between the forces of production and the relations of production to the cultural sphere – for instance, to music and literature. Here the dialectic is reformulated as the tension between material and technique or, on a different level, between style (conventions) and subjective innovative impulses. In any given historical situation, the production of music or literature partakes of the larger dialectic of productive forces and the dominant relations of production. As a human activity, writing poems or plays cannot escape this dialectic. It always occurs under specific conditions and is part of a prevailing mode of production – not because this activity is causally or expressively determined by the base or a center but rather because it is a form of human labor.

To this interpretation I want to add a cautionary reminder in order to avoid misunderstandings. The emphasis on human labor does not imply the possibility of pure human creativity, or a notion of unimpeded communality. For Adorno there is no access to a prehistorical and presocial state that can serve as a foil for the conception of alienation in history (as there is in Lukács's *Theory of the Novel*). Aesthetic production is specialized production and thereby alienated.[20] Moreover, as specialized production it increasingly follows its own 'laws': that is, its own dialectic between the relations of production (conventions) and forces of production (innovative techniques). Adorno seems to assume that this particular dialectic corresponds to the dialectic in the economic and social realm. To give an example that he uses a number of times: Beethoven's music, working on the material of classicism, develops new techniques that correspond to the social forces expressed in the French Revolution (ISM 209–15; GS 14:401–18). Yet it would be insufficient to claim that Beethoven's music is revolutionary in aesthetic and political terms; the point of Adorno's argument is that it also contains the elements of bourgeois domination and control.

When Adorno constructs a correlation between the dialectic operating in a work of art and that of the social system, as he does in the example of Beethoven, he is left with the problem of accounting for the correspondence without referring to the dominant mode of production as the determining factor. He would have to take into consideration the possibility that the historical dialectic of Europe's music or literature is separate from, or not in tune with, that of the social system. Kracauer made that point some years ago when he distinguished special histories from general history and insisted that these special histories do not neatly add up to a single general history in a Hegelian fashion. What would happen to the Adornian model if one were to drop the idea of a general history determined by a dominant mode of production? The result would be that any guarantee of correspondence would disappear. Its occurrence would be strictly an empirical fact, and we would never be certain that the reading of a poem or a musical composition would also (necessarily) articulate the conditions of its time. To put it differently, the reading could not proceed strictly immanently, as Adorno originally claimed.

Canceling the idea of a general history, however, would not eliminate the possibility of a negative dialectic, as suggested by Adorno in his reading of Goethe'e poem 'Wanderers Nachtlied' (NL 1:41–42; GS 11:53–55). Instead of a homology or affinity, we would emphasize nonidentity: the incompatibility of Goethe's poetic language and the moment of social history that is absent from the poem. The link is the human suffering that the poem does not articulate. The Adornian model could function even without the premise of a total structure as an absent cause. There is no need for folding one level into another on positive terms, directly or indirectly. Adorno's model of negation would not share Jameson's understanding of the dialectic as difference viewed against a background of identity.[21] For Jameson, this definition of mediation as transcoding is crucial, because it allows him to break out of formalism. For Adorno, by contrast, it is not a necessary strategy, because he locates the dialectic of the forces of production and the relations of production within the work of art. The critic who restricts himself or herself to a definition of mediation that relies firmly and exclusively on a negative dialectic does not need to refer to a general mode of production. There are only concrete, particular instances involved.

Comparing Adorno's theory with that of a 'poststructuralist' Marxism brings certain aspects of his model into the foreground; a comparison with post-Althusserian British Marxism will stress different aspects. In terms of theoretical traditions, Jameson's writings are much closer to Adorno's than is recent British Marxism with its strong emphasis on a general theory of production and consumption that systematically includes literary production. What is illuminating, however, is Terry Eagleton's systematic distinction between the general mode of production (as the totality) and the literary mode of production, since this distinction assumes that literature has its own productive forces as well as relations of production (apparatus). This assumption is possibly closer to Adorno's model than to Jameson's version of Althusser.

Unlike Adorno, however, Terry Eagleton systematically unfolds the general-mode-of-production / literary-mode-of-production (GMP / LMP) differentiation and thereby arrives at some conclusions that throw interesting light on Adorno's theory. Eagleton specifies the activity of producing literature (orally or in writing) as a subordinate but semi-autonomous sphere of production. Most significant is his insistence that this mode of production is not necessarily cosynchronous with the general mode of production or, for that matter, with other coexistent literary modes of production: 'Structurally conflictual LMPs may thus coexist within particular social formations.'[22] Following orthodox Marxist theory, Eagleton argues that 'the forces of production of the LMP are naturally provided by the GMP itself, of which the LMP is a particular substructure.'[23] Still, he sees this relationship as a dialectical one that allows for a considerable amount of flexibility between the spheres of production. In particular, it argues for an asymmetry between GMPs and LMPs. In Eagleton's model it is conceivable that a precapitalist literary mode of production might survive in a capitalist society. Inversely, it would be possible to argue that an LMP is more advanced than the GMP, since the literary mode is not simply a dependent factor of the general production but relies on its own dialectic, constituted 'by the modes of literary distribution, exchange and consumption.'[24] Thus Eagleton approximates Adorno by claiming that the forces of literary production are historical through and through, as they are determined by the mode of literary distribution, exchange, and consumption – and determine these moments as well.

What clearly distinguishes British Marxism from Adorno's position is the theoretical focus. Adorno argues first and foremost for the internal dialectic of the text; Eagleton subsumes the text under the concept of the literary mode of production and is therefore less specific when it comes to the level of the text, although he explicitly makes room for the internal side: 'Every literary text in some sense internalizes its social relations of production.'[25] The moment of internalization is then articulated through the conventions and codes that provide the framework for the reception of the text.

Eagleton's theoretical model contains two components that are of particular interest with respect to Adorno. First, his distinction between the general mode of production and the literary mode of production enables him to back away from the constraints of homology in a more radical way than Adorno does (or Jameson, for that matter). To be sure, Adorno would never accept a mechanical solution that subordinates the artwork to the social formation, but his model does not systematically unfold this relationship; there is, for instance, no provision for the legitimate coexistence of different literary modes of production under the roof of the same general mode of production. Because of his conception of history (negative telos), Adorno tends to think of the 'more advanced' literary mode of production as the only legitimate mode. For him the significance of Bach's music, for example, can be explained in terms of its affinity to a modern capitalist division of labor rather than its historical location within the baroque tradition.

Second, Eagleton insists on the involvement of the text in the literary mode of production. This, of course, touches on the core of Adorno's position: when Adorno calls the text a 'historico-philosophical sundial,' he affirms its meaning for the social formation, mediated through the literary mode of production. For post-Althusserian Marxism this is a matter of *ideology* formation in which both general and aesthetic ideology come into play, whereas for Adorno the subsumption of the text under the concept of ideology without attention to its potential truth value is unacceptable. In their aesthetic theory, then, Eagleton and Adorno have little in common. A significant affinity, however, can be found on the level of the forces of production in literature (or music). Unlike proponents of traditional Marxist theory (and unlike Jameson), they both locate the productive forces within literature itself rather than within the economy, thus emphasizing production rather than reflection.

In comparing Adorno's model of sociological criticism with poststructuralist Marxism, I have tried to foreground not only affinities and differences but, most of all, those aspects of more recent theories that confront similar problems and sometimes develop solutions where Adorno's work remains merely suggestive. Although Critical Theory and Althusserian Marxism are generally perceived as opposite poles within Marxism (with respect to the role of the subject and to ideology), a comparison that focuses on problems rather than preconceived positions yields more interesting results. Through the moment of contrast, it highlights – and this is my intention – the specificity of Adorno's approach, especially his use of the Marxist tradition and the relevance of his theoretical model in the context of a poststructuralist Marxist paradigm. In the transformed intellectual climate of the 1980s and 1990s, I contend, Adorno's dialectial version of sociology of art has remained a viable option. Although Adorno's thought, taken as a paradigm, could not work out a solution for all the questions posed by structuralist and poststructuralist Marxism, he did focus on the internal dialectic of the artwork and, by extension, on its institutional setting. In doing so, he both historically grounded and specified the nature of the work of art to such an extent that the idea of a sociological method was also called into question. Adorno's resistance to a scientific and ready-made method, frequently criticized by empiricists and orthodox Marxists alike, proved to be an asset, since it helped him avoid the methodological reification to which much of the sociology of art developed during the 1960s and early 1970s fell prey.

PART THREE: MODES OF THEORY

8. The Philosophy of Art and Its Discontents

THE initial reception of Adorno's posthumously published *Aesthetic Theory* (1970) was both ambiguous and controversial. Although it emerged as his most important contribution to the 1980s debate in aesthetic theory and literary criticism, its first German readers were frequently puzzled by the presentation and the structure of the text. Of course, Adorno's German audience was used to his complex and convoluted style and the opacity of his terminology, yet this late work appeared to go even beyond *Negative Dialectics*. Critics felt that the text ultimately failed to present a coherent, systematic argument; it looked more like a collection of heterogeneous fragments put together in an idiosyncratic manner. For the uninitiated reader it was not easy to define Adorno's position, since there seemed to be many contradictory claims which were not worked out within a consistent and logical system.

By the standards of the early 1970s, Adorno's *Aesthetic Theory* was an untimely work. Beyond not satisfying traditional expectations of a positive treatment of the aesthetic that would affirm the role of the arts in the modern world, the study disappointed even Adorno's disciples, especially those from the radical left, because it refused to support the politicization of aesthetic theory that they demanded. On the whole, the book was more positively reviewed by conservative critics than by members of the Marxist camp. In fact, it raised once more the fundamental question as to whether Adorno could be considered a Marxist at all. During the early 1970s, by and large, the answer to this question was negative, and thus Adorno's late work was excluded from the corpus of master texts that informed the critical left discourse of the early 1970s in West Germany.

The neglect of Adorno's posthumous work in the United States had rather different causes. Apart from the severe problem of linguistic inaccessibility (the first translation did not appear until

1984), *Aesthetic Theory* at the time of its publication did not fit easily into the American intellectual constellation, where post-structuralist theories with a largely anti-Marxist bias were beginning to influence critical discourse. In this context, Critical Theory and Adorno seemed to stand in opposition to the various strands of French theory. If there was a major German figure whose work directly and indirectly shaped the American intellectual scene, it was Martin Heidegger rather than Adorno. In the American transition from modernism to postmodernism, Adorno's aesthetic theory did not offer the appropriate key terms for participating in the ensuing debate about the fate of literature and the arts in the late twentieth century. Although Adorno's theory was very much concerned with the historical configuration after the breakdown of the European avant-garde of the early twentieth century, his way of articulating it differed so markedly from the postmodernist debate of the 1970s and 1980s that the similarities were not immediately recognizable. Nor was it the collapse of modernism during the 1960s that provided the back-drop for his theory; rather, he reflected on the rise of modernism during the later nineteenth and early twentieth centuries in France and Germany (with music as his central example) and its downfall during the 1940s and 1950s. In other words, both Adorno's material and his way of thinking about it overlapped only partly with the postmodernist discourse in America.

Moreover, many of Adorno's concerns were specifically rooted in the West German configuration of the 1950s, in which both traditional academic theory and phenomenological approaches by and large repressed the radically historical nature of art. In this intellectual climate, Adorno still felt obliged to confront the residues of an older German tradition that did not adequately respond to problems of formal structure. These concerns were hardly significant for the American discussion of the 1970s, which presupposed the demise of the formalist agenda of the New Criticism. Hence, a superficial reading of *Aesthetic Theory* might have rejected it out of hand as a belated defense of a New Critical position – and not entirely without reason, since Adorno's emphatic affirmation of the autonomy of the artwork partially coincided with the interest of New Criticism in setting the work of art apart from historical reality.[1] Even the fact that Adorno did not share this interest at all did not bring him closer to the American discourse of the 1970s, because his own theoretical articulation of the mediation between art and society relied on Marxist concepts that were not favored by deconstructive criticism.

In short, immediately after its publication *Aesthetic Theory* – even had there been a reliable translation – could hardly have found wide acceptance in this country. In the postmodernist debate Adorno seems to take sides with the modernist camp, not only in his defense of aesthetic autonomy but also in his continued use of the concept of the work of art and its particular emphasis on the truth content (as the core of the artwork). His insistence on the redemptive power of the artwork clearly does not confirm postmodern notions of playful stylistic eclecticism as a solution to the barren closure of the modernist work of art. Jameson is certainly correct in asserting that Adorno's posthumous text could not speak to the 1970s or 1980s.[2] Whether it provides the answers for the 1990s, as Jameson maintains, depends on the specific focus of the reading. One possible solution would be an appropriation through poststructuralist theory, especially through the work of Derrida and Lacan, whereby Adorno would become a forerunner or German version of poststructuralist theory. Another version, favored by Jameson, for instance, would foreground the essentially Marxist conceptual framework not as a dogmatic statement but rather as a radical working-through of a dialectical theory in which the theoretical articulation is as much a part of the question as the object of study. In either case, the status of Adorno's analysis would take on a new significance and a different meaning. Readers of the 1970s frequently emphasized the belatedness of Adorno's theory, but both a poststructuralist reading and a dialectical interpretation would stress the advanced character of Adorno's text – not only in its philosophical position but also in its textual presentation. What has come into the foreground only more recently is the transitional character of Adorno's late work – its emphasis on the problematic boundaries of philosophical discourse as well as those of aesthetic production.

For this reason, a renewed interest in *Aesthetic Theory* must start with the original introduction, which Adorno later discarded as inadequate for the formal articulation of the problem at hand. This introduction, probably written during the late 1950s or early 1960s, moves toward the fundamental problem of a philosophy of art after the demise of traditional aesthetic theory – without, however, transcending the traditional philosophical discourse. In this respect it remains within the realm of philosophical concepts and arguments.

The old introduction focuses on the contemporary situation of aesthetic theory, more precisely on the apparent lack of any recent viable systematic treatment of aesthetic problems. Aesthetics as a philosophical discipline has, Adorno suggests, lost not only its rigor but, more important, its raison d'être. It has decayed into an academic subdiscipline that has little to offer to contemporary art criticism. Aesthetic theory that relies on the traditional role of the observer, Adorno argues, cannot do justice to the modern artwork. The contemplative attitude of the older academic tradition has become incompatible with the nature of modern art, which through its own formal structure frowns on distanced contemplation and rejects an approach that highlights the moment of pleasure (*Genuß*). Modernism, especially its radical phase in the early twentieth century, subverted the systematic foundations of traditional aesthetic theory through its aesthetic dynamics (processes of radical innovation). For Adorno, the philosophy of art reaches its nominalist state in the work of Benedetto Croce, where the substantial transhistorical categories of the aesthetic tradition are radically questioned, essentially leaving the critic with the individual artwork as the object as well as the norm of criticism.

In the old introduction, Croce's writings figure as the appropriate transition from a philosophical to a modernist aesthetics quite apart from their author's personal taste. The subversion in Croce's criticism is ultimately a matter not so much of his approach or method as of a close connection with the historical situation of art around the turn of the century. In other words, the radical articulation of the modernist work of art is not compatible with a normative and systematic development of aesthetic theory, because during the later nineteenth century, with the emergence of modernism, philosophy and art – as different versions of the spirit (*Geist*) – separated to the point of mutual hostility (GS 7:496; AT 458). For this reason, eighteenth- and nineteenth-century philosophies of art, in particular Kant's and Hegel's, remain the unsurpassed models of aesthetic theory, for in their writings (to a much lesser extent still in Friedrich Vischer's) Adorno finds the most adequate articulation of the truth content of contemporary artworks.

Yet even this formulation, he points out, is problematic. From the vantage point of the late twentieth century, both Kant and Hegel failed in their attempt to define the aesthetic through general concepts; more specifically, they failed in an inevitable attempt to synthesize the moment of nonidentity of art with a philosophical discourse based on universal concepts. Although Adorno stresses a principal incompatibility that philosophy was unable to recognize, he equally underlines the need for conceptual reconstructions to provide a rigorous elaboration of the aesthetic features of the artwork without relying on pure *Einfühlung* (empathy). Thus Adorno points to two incompatible approaches that nevertheless have to be combined. Aesthetic criticism as a form of knowledge, he notes, is either grounded in a rigorous conceptual apparatus, which refuses even to acknowledge the complexity of the material, or based on what he calls a form of 'consciousless consciousness [*bewußtloses Bewußtsein*]' (GS 7:497; AT 459) operating within the phenomena. Emphatic distance and emphatic closeness are the only viable attitudes toward the work of art.

It is characteristic of the old introduction that Adorno follows the development of modern aesthetic theory to the point where the historical constellation breaks down; that introduction does not, however, transcend the gap between conceptual constructs and close readings, between a rigorously immanent approach and the use of transcendental categories that constitute art as the foundation for the artwork. Therefore, the original introduction remains largely concerned with the negative aspect of aesthetic theory: namely, the failure of previous attempts to grasp what Adorno sees as the ultimate goal of speculative art theory – the truth content (*Wahrheitsgehalt*) of the artwork. By emphasizing the centrality of the truth content, Adorno distances himself from empirical and positivist or even structuralist theories in which the work of art is reduced to the status of material and robbed of what ultimately is most important for him – its moment of subjectivity.

Adorno's concern about the adequacy of aesthetic theorizing takes on the form of a historical analysis of the changes in the artwork during the nineteenth century on the one hand, and a review of contemporary philosophy of art on the other. What motivates this parallel treatment is Hegel's dictum that art had reached its end as the articulation of the objective spirit. Adorno's emphatic disagreement with this verdict (anticipated by Heinrich Heine, whose modernity Adorno was unable to recognize)[3] takes issue with central categories of traditional aesthetics: namely, *Anschaulichkeit* (concreteness) and naiveté. As Adorno notes, the history of art after Hegel has brought home to us the error in Hegel's premature aesthetic eschatology. Adorno faults Hegel for carrying along the conventional baggage of aesthetic naiveté (GS 7:501; AT 462). Against this notion of art as merely *abbildend* (imitating), Adorno stresses the moment of reflection and abstraction in modern art (beginning with the Renaissance) and thereby the entwinement of aesthetic and philosophical discourses which, from the perspective of the discipline of philosophy, he questioned at the beginning of the old introduction. There is no doubt that the entwinement of philosophy and art remains a crucial issue for his own endeavor; in fact, it remains the very foundation of his criticism of music and literature.

The elucidation of the truth content, however, has to come to terms with a historical process of aesthetic production in which the articulation of meaning in the modern artwork tends toward a point zero. The most radical moment of the first introduction consists of defining, although in abstract terms, the impending death of art as the historically undeniable truth; any attempt to suppress this moment would lead either to an embrace of the existing conditions or to a merely impotent stress on the uplifting character of the artwork. This means that the truth content of the advanced artwork can be demonstrated only through its negativity, in the way it subverts its own ground.

The old introduction reaches its own limits where it both claims and subverts the importance of philosophy for aesthetic criticism. The truth content of the artwork, Adorno notes, is in need of philosophy, since art and philosophy converge in that truth content (GS 7:507; AT 468). At the same time, he stresses the incompatibility of abstract categories and concrete, individual works of art, since in principle the latter resist a strategy of subsuming their structure under concepts and do not respond to the logic of identity. Yet the articulation of this crucial insight relies on the very philosophical discourse that the artwork calls into question. Hence, the old introduction emphasizes an aporetic situation: aesthetic theory can neither rely on a transcendental logic of deduction nor legitimize itself through pure and intuitive experience (GS 7:510; AT 471). This reformulation of the problem displaces it to the level of methodology, however, whereas the earlier definition had rightly focused on the problematic nature of the philosophical discourse itself. The difference between art and philosophy cannot be expressed by philosophy without recourse to the very discourse whose inadequacy was assumed in the first place.

This line of questioning would suggest a break with traditional philosophical discourse, but the first introduction appears to avoid that conclusion by invoking the difference between Kant's formalist and Hegel's content-oriented approach to art. In other words, the old introduction once more, although critically, invokes the philosophical tradition and reinstates its categories and arguments, such as Hegel's concept of *Geist*. Adorno notes: 'The supreme task of aesthetic theory is to explore the spiritual essence of works of art; this task is the more important since aesthetic theory cannot borrow the category of spirit from philosophy' (GS 7:513; AT 473). Thus, Hegel's philosophy serves as a frame for the discussion without, however, being used dogmatically. The invocation of the philosophical tradition, especially of German aesthetic theory of the early nineteenth century, has a problematic status. By suggesting answers and solutions without dogmatically claiming them, aesthetic theory can articulate itself philosophically – that is to say, through philosophical concepts and arguments – in order to reach insights that do not exclusively apply to a particular work of art; simultaneously, it can resist the closure of the philosophical system.

This position leads necessarily to a hermeneutic of the artwork. The disclosure of the truth content as the ultimate goal of aesthetic theory can be achieved, Adorno concludes from his discussion of the relationship of art and philosophy, only through an approach in which experience and reflection are completely entwined. Only immanent criticism would be able to achieve this goal. A complete understanding of the artwork is reached only when its experience can be defined in terms of truth or untruth. For this reason, as Adorno stresses, the element of critique is not imposed from the outside; rather, it is part and parcel of the aesthetic experience. Again, the old introduction deflects Adorno's central problem, the incompatibility of philosophy and art, to the level of adequate *Verstehen* (understanding) of the artwork. This reformulation of the problem reinstates the legitimacy of the theoretical discourse that was questioned by the original definition of the problem. The insistence on *Werkimmanenz* (immanent analysis) (GS 7:517; AT 477) is not, as Adorno suggests in the old introduction, a reliable solution to the problem at hand. In fact, he will assert in the later version of *Aesthetic Theory*, the very opposite is true: the power of immanent criticism, its rigorous attention to the concrete artwork – that is, to its formal construct as well as its thematic character – subverts the philosophical discourse it is supposed to protect and affirm. The result is the paradoxical character of aesthetic theory: it claims what it cannot claim. By making a philosophical claim through concepts and arguments, aesthetic theory would violate the nature of the aesthetic.

In light of the fundamental paradox in the methodology of the old introduction, which relies on the legitimacy of the philosophical discourse, the question of style or articulation becomes crucial. This question points to one of the most fundamental problems of Adorno's late work: the presentation of philosophical thought after the demise of philosophy. In the second version of the text he comes to a more adequate understanding of this question precisely by avoiding a conventional introduction and by giving up the traditional architecture of systematic theory. Adorno accepts and embraces the fragmentary character of the work, in which all parts point to the same center but do not form a harmonious whole – a tour de force that must necessarily be both enlightening and frustrating. In this respect his *Aesthetic Theory* converges with the artwork: it refuses purity and harmony; it calls attention to its contradictory nature. Moreover, it sustains itself by pointing to its own impossibility. In its last version *Aesthetic Theory* self-consciously addresses its own status; it subverts what it sets out to do. This radical self-questioning has encouraged some critics to view it as an exposition of postmodern theory which has broken away from the modernist tradition. In this reading Adorno's stress on the negativity of the artwork has been received as a critique of the grand designs of modernism and the politicization of the artwork in the European avant-garde. Yet Adorno's concern with the autonomy of art, equally strongly articulated in *Aesthetic Theory,* should warn us against selective readings that focus exclusively on postmodernist themes and motifs.

In fact, it is the transition from nineteenth-century art to early twentieth-century modern art that Adorno marks as the decisive turningpoint in the history of art and aesthetic theory. In German literature he invokes the work of the early Hofmannsthal, in particular the letter of Lord Chandos ('Ein Brief,' 1902), to demonstrate the decay of traditional aesthetic materials, the coming apart of language and meaning. This argument captures the belated modernism of German and Austrian culture, as well as its potential for rapid radicalization in the expressionist movement, which remained for Adorno, in more than one way, the touchstone for the complete separation between advanced art and mass culture (the culture industry). It is not accidental that a preliminary discussion of the culture industry coincides with the discussion of the break between the nineteenth century and the modernist tendencies of the early twentieth century. Adorno's aesthetic theory is primarily concerned with those movements and tendencies within autonomous art that celebrate the new, the unexpected, in the organization of the material: 'The moment of violence in the new work of art, for which the term experiment has been introduced, must not be ascribed to the subjective opinion or the psychological make-up of the artist; in a situation where this tendency (*Drang*) does not find a secure basis in form and content, the objective constellation compels productive artists to experiment' (GS 7:42; AT 35). Typically, this passage highlights the objective character of a historical process that cannot be reduced to the personal convictions of the productive artist. The inherent dialectic unfolds as a process of working through the aesthetic material that the artist encounters. In this perspective the modernist project – beginning with Baudelaire – extends to expressionism, dadaism, and surrealism, while in the field of music Adorno remains focused chiefly on the new music of the Vienna school (Schönberg, Berg, and so on), although he occasionally includes postwar composers such as Karlheinz Stockhausen.

We have to note that any attempt to differentiate carefully between modernism and the avant-garde does not find a clear correspondence in the work of Adorno. Whereas for Peter Bürger the distinction is important, since it allows him to define the task of the avant-garde as a turn against art and the category of aesthetic autonomy,[4] for Adorno the difference remains relative. He sees the radical movements from expressionism to surrealism, for which he uses the term avant-garde, as part of the modernist project – its most radical articulation, so to speak: the most advanced artistic position of groups and schools. Hence, Adorno carefully resists the fundamental distinction between modernism and the avant-garde, which Bürger foregrounds. Although he notes that French surrealism challenges the concept of art, Adorno emphasizes the aesthetic nature of this provocation and argues that at its core the provocation consists of a predominance of art (as an institution) over the work of art. This argument differentiates art and the artwork in order to affirm the aesthetic rather than to deconstruct the aesthetic project of modernism, as Bürger claims in his interpretation of French surrealism.[5] For Adorno, the institutional side remains secondary. He sees the abolition of art as a futile gesture of the avant-garde to mark its polemical distancing from the social – futile because it cannot truly overcome the social and cultural conditions that have caused the gap in the first place. The raison d'être of the aesthetic in the modernist project is, Adorno suggests, the continuation of human suffering. The aesthetic therefore functions as a marker for the human condition.

The extended concept of modernism, as we have seen, is the core of Adorno's project. Its historical boundaries are the demise of the romantic concept of art as pure expression of the absolute on the one hand, and the aging of modern art after World War II on the other. Still, these boundaries must not be understood as chronological markers. For Adorno, the historical dialectic operates as a logic of negativity both inside and outside the artwork. What the old introduction claimed for the situation of aesthetic theory – namely, its end as a systematic discipline – converges in *Aesthetic Theory* with the notion of the possible end of art: that is, the end of the aesthetic project. Adorno's attention, as much as he contemplates the entire modernist project, concentrates on its precarious decline, the potential abolition of art, and the disappearance of aesthetic autonomy.

> The idea that art should be abolished shows respect insofar as it honors art's truth claim. Still, the survival of disintegrated art signifies more than a cultural lag, that is, the overly slow transformation of the superstructure. Art has its power of resistance in that the realization of materialism would include its own abolition, that is, the abolition of the domination of material interests. (GS 7:50; AT 43).

In Beckett's prose, for instance, Adorno recognizes a form of resistance to a social process that resulted in a totally administered society. He characterizes Beckett's prose as a prose of the zero point, closer to the reality of atomic physics than to traditional forms of perception, yet precise in its concentrated expression of collective historical experience. For Adorno, the coarseness and shabbiness of Beckett's allegories have the force of negative realism, the negative imprint of a totally administered world (GS 7:53; AT 46). Not the oppositional but the marginal position of art in a late capitalist society serves as the paradigm for the second boundary: that of a final exit. Adorno's polemical stance toward Brecht is, at least in part, related to this concern. What he sees in Brecht's later plays is an attempt to preserve the radical gesture of the earlier avant-garde, its anti-psychologism, even though objective social conditions have already subverted these forms of opposition.

Consequently, Adorno resists theoretical constructs of the modernist aesthetic project which celebrate the origin of art. In fact, he explicitly rejects an ontology of art. Art must be conceptualized on the basis of historically changing configurations of elements, its conception defies any formal definition. For Adorno, this means that art cannot be deduced from a predetermined origin. Because there is no primal level (*Grundschicht*) on which subsequent elements can be erected, he rejects as late romantic the claim that archaic artworks are the purest and most perfect (GS 7:11; AT 3). The insistence on specific historical configurations as the only ground of aesthetic production underlines both the transitory nature of art and the artwork and the unstable situation of an aesthetic theory that cannot retreat from the historical character of its object. This, indeed, is one reason the question of Adorno's proximity to postmodern theory is a legitimate one that has to be explored – not only with respect to his concept of the work of art but, more important, in regard to the structure of his writings.

It would be premature, however, to assert that Adorno's theory is postmodern because it emphasizes the impact of late capitalism on aesthetic practice. This more general historical argument could just as well be used to defend the modernist character of Adorno's aesthetic theory. The concept of the totally administered society would clearly point to a conception of capitalism characterized first and foremost by entrepreneurial concentration on all levels. This Fordist model of capitalist production, as it dominated the early twentieth century, was by and large concurrent with modernist aesthetics rather than with postmodernist notions of art.[6] Not surprisingly then, Adorno's theory of mass culture in *Dialectic of Enlightenment* constructs a close and causal connection between the structure of capitalist enterprises and the structure of the culture produced for the masses. In that construct the concept of the advanced autonomous artwork serves as the opposite pole: that is, the negation of reified cultural production. During the 1940s Adorno's polarization of mass culture and autonomous art is predicated on a modernist model in which autonomy of art designates the oppositional force of the artwork, although not necessarily the oppositional stance of the institution of art.

The question must be asked, then, to what extent the concept of the artwork and, in particular, the idea of autonomy change in Adorno's late work. Are there any indications that the modernist model has been modified or replaced? With great force, *Aesthetic Theory* underlines once more the separation of art and reality. Only on the basis of its distance from the empirical world – a separation that enables art to organize the relation of parts and whole according to its own needs – can the work of art reach a higher form of being (GS 7:14; AT 5). Only through their distance to empirical reality do works of art refer to and communicate with this reality. For Adorno, this communication (as distinct from that of mass culture) consists of the refusal to communicate. To conceptualize this double bind, he develops the category of the monad, in which the inside and outside are correlated without causal links.

Adorno's theory of the artwork openly and explicitly harks back to German idealism, especially to the theories of Kant and Hegel. By bringing together their positions, without trying to eliminate the contradiction between formalist aesthetics and content aesthetics, Adorno prepares the dialectical articulation of his own theory, whereby the deficiencies of the earlier approaches are utilized to confront the enigmatic character of the advanced work of art. The voices of Kant and Hegel – to which we have to add, of course, those of Marx, Nietzsche, and Freud – are not harmonized; rather, they are used contrapuntally – each adds to the quality of the composition. In this way, Adorno carefully avoids the temptation to synthesize their positions in order to reach his own point of view as a final step of theoretical articulation. Instead, *Aesthetic Theory* works out a pattern of oppositions and tensions, contradictions and similarities, which suggest a totality without ever defining it. Hence, the concept of truth in theory is no longer stable but shifts according to the chosen perspective, while these individual perspectives are never allowed to dominate the whole. Consequently, in a reversal of Hegel's dictum, the whole is untruth.

In this respect, Adorno's aesthetic theory corresponds to the constitution of the artwork. If the work of art is conceived of as a dynamic rather than a fixed constellation, its theoretical articulation calls for a perspectivist approach that can do justice to the dynamic mode of the category:

> That artworks are not 'being' [*Sein*] but 'becoming' [*Werden*] can be grasped technologically. Their continuity is teleologically required by their individual moments. For this reason, art mocks formal definition. The mode through which art constitutes itself as being, is itself, as a mode of behavior, dynamic – a mode of behavior which points toward objectivity, as it both retreats from it, takes up a relation to it, and, modified by it, holds on to it. (GS 7:263; AT 253–54).

The artwork strives for its identity by bringing together (*synthetisieren*) heterogeneous, nonidentical moments. As Adorno remarks, this unity is processual and momentary, not a magic formula for the whole. Hence, the artwork represents not only the identity of the nonidentical but also, on a higher level, the identity of the nonidentical and the identical.

The definition of the artwork as a dialectical process also throws light on a very important component of Adorno's theory: namely, its temporal core (*Zeitkern*). The momentary and ephemeral character of the artwork, which links it with phenomena such as fashion, underscores the antitraditional and anticlassical nature of the advanced, modern artwork. Any notion of a positive tradition and of timelessness is for Adorno incompatible with the process of extreme aesthetic articulation within the work of art. What Russian formalism described as the necessary quality of difference in the history of literature takes on a more radical meaning in Adorno's aesthetic theory, for in Adorno the truth content of the artifact depends on its engagement with empirical reality – not through a reflection of reality, as Lukács prescribed, but through the configuration of its own formal and thematic moments. The polemical confrontation remains strictly immanent.

This interpretation highlights the unstable character of the artwork but fails to grasp another, equally important aspect of what Adorno means by *Zeitkern*. He argues that the work of art, since it is not anything fixed or definite but something dynamic, shares its immanent temporality with both the whole and its parts by unfolding their relations through time. Just as artworks, given their processual nature, exist in history, they also vanish within the process of history (GS 7:266; AT 255). What Adorno suggests is more than the conventional notion that the reception of artworks changes with time, that the reception has its own history. Instead, he makes the much stronger claim that the essence or spirit of the artwork, for which he uses the term *Geist*, is exposed to historical time. There is no timeless idea of the masterpiece; hence, it can expire like any other human product.

Adorno's insistence on the *Verzeitlichung* of the artwork and of modern art in general radically undermines two aspects of nineteenth-century aesthetics: first, it calls into question the notion that stable traditions can serve as a background for the concept of autonomous art; second, it subverts the use of the concept of genius (or, more generally, creativity) as a way of distinguishing authentic artworks from conventional ones. The activity of the genius artist, modeled on the concept of a transcendent god, is not, as such, more important or valuable than other human activities. Rather, it is precisely the separation of the result of the creative process from the creative process itself – the innovative configuration of the received materials – that defines the authenticity of the artwork. What makes this configuration new and valuable is contained within the objective process. By the same token, the concept of tradition breaks down as a meaningful category for thinking about continuity and permanence in art – a category that was crucial for nineteenth-century aesthetic theory, despite the fact that the historicization of art and literature had already severely undermined the idea of the classical.

In *Aesthetic Theory* the dialectic between the institution of art and the individual work is decided in favor of the latter. The institution – for instance, the rules of genres and forms – has lost most of its normative force (except its role as the opposite of the authentic). It functions instead as the bearer of tradition and convention: that which is determined by the force of past constellations. In a remarkable passage Adorno therefore polemicizes against Nietzsche's celebration of conventions and the conventional. Nietzsche, he says, misread conventions by taking them literally as a form of consensus. They appear as contingent and therefore, from a different point of view, as arbitrary. For this reason, as Adorno points out, Nietzsche overlooked the historical power of conventions and treated them like playful arrangements. He underestimated the aspect of violence in their existence (GS 7:303; AT 291). Clearly, Adorno's intention in this passage is not to restore or affirm the power of conventions for aesthetic production; rather, he wants to call attention to the weight of diminished traditions in modern history which, in spite of their contingent character, codetermine the act of aesthetic production.

For the modern author, conventions, quite apart from their legitimacy, mark the border. Thus the breakdown of institutional traditions (for example, of genres) increases the freedom of the artist vis-à-vis the received material. But, as Adorno notes, this tendency also weakens the difference between the expectations set by the genre and the articulation of the individual artwork. At the same time, however, *Aesthetic Theory* argues against a Nietzschean celebration of style as a legitimate common denominator for aesthetic production: 'What has been irrevocably exposed is that the authoritative validity of styles was a reflex of the repressive quality of society from which mankind has sought to emancipate itself, so far without permanent success; without the objective structure of a closed and therefore repressive society, an obligatory style is unthinkable' (GS 7:307; AT 295). A normative style is a reflex of the repressive nature of society, a configuration that humankind has tried to overcome, although it remains always threatened by relapses. Thus, obligatory stylistic norms are inconceivable without the objective force of a closed and thereby repressive social structure. What is left in the modernist project is the radical articulation of the individual work, something that ultimately liquidates style.

For this reason, Adorno clings to the idea of aesthetic progress, the idea of development – sometimes even linear development. The concept of progress is grounded in notions of material and control over the material, not in the idea of timeless quality (GS 7:313; AT 300). Hence, for Adorno the concept of progress is closely linked to the concept of *technē* and free choice of the artistic means. Conscious and free choice, in contrast to the traditionalism under the cover of which this moment of freedom was prepared, marks the process of progress that constitutes the history of modern art. It is the dialectic of technique and received materials (in which the artist functions as a mediator) that defines the process called the history of art and literature. Yet it would be hasty and inadequate to understand the historical process exclusively in technical terms. As Adorno makes clear in his discussion of the transition from Bach's compositions to those of Beethoven, it is the truth content that ultimately legitimates the process.

As we have seen, the categories of both genius and tradition are significantly affected by Adorno's understanding of the specific temporality of the artwork. Its lack of permanence, far from being a mark of deficiency, defines its force and historical impact (at the risk of expiring). By the same token, the category of the truth content, which stands at the core of *Aesthetic Theory,* is equally affected. Obviously, this concept does not denote, in any crude sense, an abstract value based on the content of the artwork: for example, a message that could be communicated to the recipient, or an idea that could be expressed in another way. Adorno criticizes this possible misunderstanding as it appeared in vulgarized forms of Hegel's aesthetic. At the end of the section on the enigmatic character of the artwork, Adorno suggests a comparison between the artwork and *Schrift* (writing). In neither case is the meaning (*Sinn*) immediately given. The most radical way to conceive the enigmatic character is to pose the question of whether there is meaning or not. For no work of art exists without its context, however varied, and this context, because of the objective nature of the artifact, also posits the objectivity of meaning.[7] Hence, the quest for meaning is a quest for the solution of the artwork's enigma. It is precisely the concern for the enigmatic meaning that Adorno defines as the truth content. The objective solution to the enigma of the artwork is its truth content. By insisting on a solution of its own enigma, the artwork points to the truth content.

Adorno's attempt to unfold the concept of truth content proceeds negatively by excluding a variety of traditional approaches: for example, its existence or its structure (*Logizität*), its idea or its participation in a broader mode of expression (such as the tragic). What these approaches have in common is an abstract notion of truth that would remove the truth content from the temporal realm and assign it a permanent conceptual identity. Yet for Adorno, it is the nonidentity that marks the structure of the truth content. The truth content cannot be identified without mediation. Just as it can be recognized only indirectly, it is in itself mediated (GS 7:195; AT 187).

What has to be clarified is the nature of the mediation, since it would be misleading to apply a strictly Hegelian understanding to this passage. From the point of view of a philosophical – that is, conceptual – discourse, the difficulty of finding a solution that does justice to the specificity of the artwork is grounded in the very limitation of this discourse, which operates through the mediation of concepts. It cannot grasp the otherness of aesthetic appearance without imposing its own procedures. At the same time, the moment of truth in the work of art remains unacknowledged unless it is extracted and affirmed through a process of interpretation that cannot proceed without language and concepts: that is, universal elements.

For Adorno, the possibility of a convergence of art and philosophy is decisive because only in this convergence can the truth content of the artwork be constituted. Adorno argues that convergence between art and philosophy rests entirely on the moment of universality, which art offers through its own language (GS 7:197; AT 189). Yet even this definition of the truth content's condition of possibility remains too abstract, since it misses the distinction between meaning and truth, the concrete constellation of the elements and the moment of emphatic truth through which the artwork – at least momentarily – transcends itself. The truth content of the artwork must be articulated through the language of criticism, but it is not identical with its concept; rather, the truth content relies on aesthetic appearance (*Schein*). The search for the truth of an artifact is none other than the search for the moment of truth in aesthetic illusion: that is, its redemption as the appearance of truth. Thus, the truth content is not to be confused with the artifact.

This definition comes considerably closer to an adequate solution of the problem, but again it does not completely articulate the dialectical process, since it posits aesthetic appearance without defining its specific status and function. The following formulation makes this clear: 'Art has truth to the extent that it is an illusion of the non-illusory [*Schein des Scheinlosen*]. In the best analysis, to experience art is to recognize that its truth content is not null and void; each artwork, and especially the uncompromisingly negative one, says silently "*non confundar*" ' (GS 7:199; AT 191–92). The definition of art as illusion is incomplete. Aesthetic truth must be defined as the illusion of something that is not an illusion. Hence, aesthetic appearance may be the only legitimate medium for the truth content but is not its goal, which is *scheinlos*, non-illusory. As Adorno remarks, there is a strong tension between the work of art and its truth content. The rigorous, critical unfolding of the truth content ultimately destroys the artwork; every artwork as an artifact cancels itself in its truth content.

It is important to note that the radical nominalist stance Adorno adopts with regard to art does not imply a relativist position. Quite the contrary: Adorno argues consistently for a historical approach that would dissolve all notions of timeless values, and he simultaneously stresses the possibility of a truth content contained within the structure of the historically determined, concrete artwork. This he can do because the truth content of the artwork does not depend on the validity of universal aesthetic values or norms. As I have suggested, *Aesthetic Theory* carefully avoids the claim that the truth is located in philosophical concepts that have been extracted from the artwork. It is for this reason that a historical and an antirelativist position are compatible. Especially in the chapter 'Allgemeines und Besonderes' (Universal and particular), Adorno develops a specific character of the history of art which is not simply to be subsumed under the category of the social or political. Hence, for him, the 'progress' of art is not automatically synonymous with progress in history. The concept of general history (in a striking parallel to the late Siegfried Kracauer) breaks down. The history of music or literature, the history of specific forms and genres, allows only for partial reconstructions – developments that break off or expire, links between works that seem far apart. The difficulty in assessing the progress of art in general has to do with the structure of its history: it is not homogeneous. The various strands do not easily find a common denominator. For this reason, totality is not immediately accessible in historical reconstruction, either at the level of the individual artwork or at the level of larger constructs (genre, period). Instead, the concept of totality can serve only as a negative category that enables the historian to articulate the problem of reconstruction.

Although his discussion of aesthetic 'progress' through artistic control over the material subverts conventional notions of linear history, Adorno remains committed to the nexus between the aesthetic and the social. Here the concept of the monad serves as the model for articulating this relationship without recourse to reflection theory. In the monad the internal and the external – that is, the aesthetic and the social – come together in a process of imprinting in which the organization of the artwork, in its very negation of the social, hints at the social deficit. Still, when Adorno argues in favor of the nonhomogeneity of history, the alienation characteristic of modern society is only one aspect of the problem. Equally important is the tension between archaic elements in the artwork and the rationality of modern society. Philosophically speaking, the artwork does not synchronize with rational explanations of reality. From the point of view of modern science (as seen through the lens of positivism), art is an embarrassment because its truth claims cannot be proved. Positivism can deal with art only by relegating it to the realm of the emotions. But for Adorno, the archaic nature of art, its proximity to magic, contains the moment of critique that modern rationalism (in the form of instrumental reason) is unable to generate. In Adorno's theory, for this reason, the aspect of the artwork's untimeliness deserves closer scrutiny.

Adorno's reflections about the origins of art ('Theorien über den Ursprung der Kunst') in *Aesthetic Theory* may be an appropriate point of departure. In reviewing the critical literature on this subject, Adorno emphasizes the historical moment when art begins to separate from magic. Hence, he speculates about prepaleolithic paintings in which the aspect of mimesis completely dominates the expression. Archaic painting was preceded by a mimetic attitude toward reality, the wish to become similar to the Other (though this does not necessarily coincide with the superstition of an immediate impact). If a sense of the difference between image and reality had not already been evolving for a long time, the astounding elements of autonomous form would be inexplicable.[8] From this observation or, better, from this interpretation of cave paintings, Adorno does not draw the obvious conclusion that in such paintings, where the aesthetic moment is already clearly recognizable, the mimetic phase has been overcome. On the contrary, he suggests that the element of mimesis will remain a significant moment of later art as well and therefore result in a nonhomogeneous configuration. A moment of regression cannot be denied in the artwork, yet the moment of regression, he emphasizes, is the locus of resistance against the rationality of civilization and its repression of human suffering. This interpretation of early art suggests a dichotomy between rational civilization and irrational art. In a surprising turn, however, Adorno undercuts his own argument by pointing to the moment of rationality within the artwork itself. For him, art is from the very beginning codetermined by a principle of rationality, a form of the rational that excludes instrumental reason and retrieves mimesis. What characterizes the aesthetic response is its ability to see more in things than they are; it is this insight into the invisible that is transformed into an image (GS 7:488; AT 453).

Being out of step with the process of civilization is characteristic of the artwork; it both resists the logic of the civilizational process and, as Adorno tries to illuminate through the concept of the monad, responds to it. This tension between two incompatible tendencies comes across as either an archaic or an advanced element, containing either residues of a precivilized stage or an articulation of the very modernity that conventional discursive language fails to capture. In his discussion of the ugly (*das Häßliche*) as an aesthetic category, Adorno touches on the relationship between modern art and the archaic artwork, which can be seen as offensive and distasteful from a later historical juncture when its specific cultural function is no longer needed. Again, the point of this discussion is not, as one might expect, the celebration of the beautiful in the autonomous work of art; rather, Adorno wants to underscore the inseparable link between the archaic and the modern. 'Archaic ugliness, the cannibalistically threatening cult masks, were an element of a content – that is, the mimesis of fear – which they surrounded themselves with for the purpose of atonement.' Even at a later stage, long after the demise of mythical fear and retribution, the archaic artwork haunts the viewer, for 'the old images of fear live on in a history which has not redeemed the promise of freedom, and in which the subject, as the agent of unfreedom, has perpetuated the mythical spell, against which it rebels, and to which it submits' (GS 7:76; AT 70). Obviously, this passage retrieves an argument from *Dialectic of Enlightenment*. In *Aesthetic Theory*, however, the argument has a somewhat different function: it points to the multifaceted nature of the artwork, its simultaneous presence at different historical levels – a configuration that makes it frequently unacceptable to modern rationality. Accordingly, nineteenth-century aesthetic theory eliminated the historical dynamic of primitive art, especially the threat of the archaic and barbaric, in order to focus our attention on the beautiful.

This emphasis was grounded, as Adorno underlines approvingly, in the concept of autonomy, but this concept tends to repress its origin. Therefore, Adorno is interested in retrieving the darker aspect contained in the concept of the beautiful: 'The image of the beautiful as the one and undivided emerges with man's emancipation from his fear of the overwhelming totality and undifferentiated character of nature. This tremor of fear is preserved in the beautiful on the basis of its separation from immediate presence and the constitution of a realm of the untouchable' (GS 7:82; AT 76). Only where this *Schauer* (shudder) is still felt, where the emancipation of the artwork from magical practice is still noticed, can the force of the beautiful be adequately received.[9] The terrible and the offensive are always contained within the beautiful as its repressed and forgotten elements. For Adorno, this is, of course, one reason a discussion of modern art cannot be carried out successfully on the basis of a traditional concept of the beautiful. In the modernist project the advanced artwork deliberately transcends the boundaries of the beautiful as the proper realm for autonomous art and follows the logic of its material precisely to the point where the repressed and forgotten moments of the aesthetic experience again appear.

For this reason, the link between the advanced artwork and the archaic one is crucial. It marks the irreducible untimeliness of the work, as well as its resistance to the laws of technological progress. The radical industrialization of art, its complete adjustment to the highest attainable standards, collides with those elements that resist incorporation. If technology moves toward industrialization, it does so at the expense of immanent formal articulation and thereby at the expense of technique itself. This tendency gives art an element of the archaic, which compromises art (GS 7:322; AT 309). Modern artworks in particular, such as the early piano pieces of Schönberg, deliberately expose their barbaric side and thus refuse the rich texture and tonality of the late romantics. Hence, the moment of *Vergeistigung* (spirituality) – for Adorno undoubtedly the center of his theory – cannot be construed as linear progress. Instead, he connects the spiritual essence of the work with its archaic side – which, again, is closely related to the moment of mimesis. Thus, Adorno's theory of mimesis is the key to his understanding of the untimely character of art.

It goes without saying that in *Aesthetic Theory* the concept of mimesis is not grounded in reflection theory; there is no attempt on Adorno's part to define art as imitation. Mimesis is defined as 'a nonconceptual affinity between that produced by the subject and its unposited (objective) other' (GS 7:86–87; AT 80); in the specific case of the artwork, it refers to the magic act of creating an identity between the image and the thing through an articulation that precedes the subject-object division. Regression to the magic stage is the artwork's path to knowledge, a form of rationality which at the same time blocks itself through its own procedure. In this manner art compliments the process of objective knowledge, yet it also subverts the objective character of knowledge through its prerational, magic form. As a result, dogmatic rationalism is bound to reject the moment of knowledge in art, excluding it, as the irrational, from the realm of precise and grounded knowledge. Hence, the aporia of modern art can be described in Weberian terms as the inevitable enchantment of a disenchanted world, since the artwork cannot be completely separated from its mimetic impulse.

This is one reason Adorno remained skeptical with regard to the tendencies of the European avant-garde during the 1920s and 1930s to conflate industrial technology and technique in the artwork. The model of technological progress, as it was used by Russian constructivism to legitimate the project of modernity, is in Adorno's aesthetic theory always characterized as problematic and one-sided; at best it can serve as a moment within a dialectical process. By the same token, he is equally skeptical of any uncritical celebration of the mimetic impulse in art. For Adorno, who relentlessly insists on the historical perspective, the process of secularization as the core of the project of modernity cannot be eliminated through primitivist or nostalgic theories. This means that art will also be measured in terms of philosophical knowledge; more specifically, aesthetic expression ought to be interpreted with regard to its truth content. Here Adorno defines the moment of artistic expression as a compromise: expression 'aims at the trans-subjective; it is a form of knowledge that preceded the dichotomy of subject and object and therefore does not recognize this polarity as definitive' (GS 7:170; AT 163). Aesthetic expression tendentiously strives for the moment of knowledge, but not through discursive language; rather, expression objectifies what is abstract and, in doing so, makes it *ungegenständlich* (not available as object). As Adorno puts it, 'the true language of art is nonverbal, its nonverbal moment has priority over the element of signification in literature, a moment that is also not completely absent from music' (GS 7:171; AT 164).

The archaic element in the artwork, as it is located in the mimetic impulse, is both indispensable for a theory of the artwork and a stumbling block, for it undercuts the integration of aesthetic modernism into the project of modernity. Their histories intersect and overlap, but they cannot be construed as parallel developments. Consequently, Adorno's theory does not easily support a trajectory that moves from traditional art via modernism and the avant-garde to postmodernism. In each of these phases (if we assume for a moment that Adorno would recognize their legitimacy) the tension between the modern and the archaic resurfaces, but in rather different ways. Although Adorno clearly differentiates phases within the modernist project, his theory does not immediately respond to contemporary questions. Hence, the fashionable question as to whether Adorno's theory anticipates the postmodernist condition cannot be answered by simply pointing to those elements that seem to fit the description or by stressing those aspects that seem to oppose it. Methodologically, both procedures are ultimately inadequate because they impose a conceptual framework from without, presupposing a metatheoretical narrative for the present condition.

Fredric Jameson has argued that Adorno's theory, including his philosophy of art, is at least compatible with the postmodernist condition.[10] To be sure, Jameson does not deny the Marxist grounding of Adorno's work; in fact, he strongly emphasizes it against possible readings that would move Adorno closer to such authors as Heidegger and Derrida. But he perceives the Marxism of Adorno as a way out of the confines of the modernist project, rather than its mere confirmation. For Jameson, Adorno's music criticism – his support of the activities of the Cologne radio station, as well as his books on Mahler and Berg – speaks in favor of a postmodern sensibility. By the same token, he argues against the more traditional assumption that Adorno's position was bound up with the modernism of Schönberg and the Vienna School.[11]

One might expect Jameson to appropriate Adorno's late philosophy, in the same manner, as the expression of a cultural transition toward the postmodern. Jameson resists this move, however, arguing instead that in an odd way Adorno's philosophical style and old-fashioned understanding of the economy simultaneously undercut and fit into the contemporary intellectual situation. He extends Adorno's grim and relentless fight against positivism into the present by suggesting that the positivism of the 1950s and 1960s turned into the postmodernism of the 1970s and 1980s. For Jameson, in short, Adorno turns out to be the most appropriate critic of the 1990s, since he combines a postmodern sensibility – or at least an openness to the postmodern condition – with a stern resistance to its false theoretical and political promises.

This synthetic sweep tends to downgrade the tensions and contradictions that encouraged divergent readings of Adorno during the 1980s. There are persuasive arguments for instance, that *Aesthetic Theory* on the whole represents a modernist aesthetics, the most obvious point being Adorno's consistent use of the concept of the artwork. Although he problematizes it by differentiating traditional and modern works of art (specifically, romanticism and modernism), he nevertheless clings to this concept. For him the individual artwork, more than movements or periods, represents the essential achievement of art. In keeping with his aesthetic nominalism, Adorno clearly gives priority to the concrete artifact as the basis for aesthetic theorizing. His emphasis on the objective status of the artwork, on its structural and material features, in contradistinction to a reception- or producer-oriented approach, could be perceived as specifically modernist. This argument can be supported by Adorno's emphatic stress on the autonomy of art, which occasionally borders on a celebratory attitude. The autonomous status of the artwork is not only significant for Adorno's theory but systematically indispensable. If the unfolding of the truth content is the ultimate goal of aesthetic reflection, the categorical difference between aesthetic and empirical reality remains crucial. For Adorno, art without autonomy would lose its negative, critical force and become a mere instrument for either political activism or affirmative decoration of the status quo.

Since the centrality of the autonomous artwork for the modernist project is undeniable, from this perspective *Aesthetic Theory* reads like a defense of modernism and therefore an implicit critique of the more radical avant-garde.[12] This argument could easily be supplemented by pointing out that Adorno's historical analyses of modern music and modern literature focus, by and large, on the early stages of modern art and show a noticeable reluctance to give theoretical support to specifically avant-gardist movements such as dadaism and surrealism. His ongoing debate with Walter Benjamin about the role of technology and montage in the avant-garde and especially his defense of the aura, against Benjamin's critique, might serve as additional proof of Adorno's more conservative modernist stance.[13] Looking back from the vantage point of contemporary discourse, one might therefore stress the historical limitations of Adorno's position.[14]

In keeping with this argument are two features of Adorno's theory that are at odds with the contemporary debate: its occasionally blatant though unacknowledged economism (its emphasis on the impact of the forces of production), and its strong insistence on the need for a philosophical discourse. In *Aesthetic Theory* Adorno defends a philosophy of art as distinct from structuralist criticism, or close readings that stay on the level of descriptive analysis, in very obvious terms. Although in the old introduction he questions the viability of a traditional philosophy of art, in the later version he explicitly defends a philosophical project of aesthetic criticism by arguing for a 'synthesis' of art and philosophy: philosophical reflection is still necessary to redeem the artwork.

In the same way, Adorno's understanding of modern society seems incompatible with the contemporary debate. This aspect is of course less noticeable in *Aesthetic Theory*, where social theory tends to stay in the background, than in *Dialectic of Enlightenment*. In the earlier work the concept of the culture industry is predicated on a Marxist understanding of monopoly capitalism, which is perceived as the determining factor for the structure of modern mass culture. But even in the late work, including *Aesthetic Theory*, the concept of the totally administered society from which social forces of resistance have been expurgated shapes Adorno's discussion of the role of art in modern society. His consistent critique of the explicit politicization of the artwork is obviously linked to the notion of a closed social system. If we follow the argument of David Harvey in *The Condition of Postmodernity* (1989) that modernism (as distinct from postmodernism) is rooted in a form of capitalism exemplified by the Fordist enterprise,[15] then Adorno's position must strike us as clearly modernist.

The line of argument presented so far has a certain plausibility in that it brings together elements of Adorno's theory that are clearly not isolated features but structurally important components. Adorno's economism is linked to a specific notion of the social, which again is connected with his understanding of social resistance – especially through the artwork – and, finally, with his concept of aesthetic autonomy as indispensable for the critical force of the artwork. Still, it is doubtful whether such a summary contains the essence of Adorno's aesthetic theory. This interpretation seriously underrates the moment of self-reflexivity in his late work, especially his rigorous questioning of the traditional logic of theory. For this reason, more recent readings have brought into the foreground precisely those elements that he seems to share with contemporary poststructuralist theory. Here we find a very different approach to Adorno. The obvious point of departure for this endeavor is the category of negative dialectics: Adorno's attempt to rescue Hegelian dialectics through a thorough critique from within. The refusal to synthesize and thereby harmonize totality in *Negative Dialectics* shows considerable affinity with poststructuralist attacks on Western logocentrism. As Rainer Nägele has pointed out, Adorno shares with the poststructuralist project its antihumanism, antitotality thinking, and thorough critique of the Enlightenment.[16] There is an even more fundamental similarity in their stance vis-à-vis Heidegger: one could argue that Adorno's critique of Heidegger in *Negative Dialectics* anticipates Derrida's. What Adorno has in common with poststructuralism, according to this argument, is a relentless critique of all forms of ontology – not in the name of yet another ontology but in the name of pure difference.

In the light of this criticism, certain features of Adorno's writings that have not attracted the special attention of Habermas and other members of the second generation of the Frankfurt School in Germany come into the foreground: a more skeptical, if not negative stance toward the subject and the expectations of ego-psychology; an understanding of language that cannot be confined to communication (and the Enlightenment tradition); an emphasis on the nonconceptual and particular; and a similar stress on nondeductive logic (parataxis and metonymy). Once these appear, the distance between *Negative Dialectics* and Derrida's *Of Grammatology* seems smaller than that between Adorno's late work and Habermas's *Theory of Communicative Action*. Invoking the proximity of Adorno to the philosophical criticism of early German romantics such as Friedrich Schlegel and Novalis, Jochen Hörisch has attempted to demonstrate the common ground of romantic theory, Critical Theory (Adorno), and French poststructuralism; he points to the critique of subject philosophy (Fichte, Hegel, Edmund Husserl) as a common theme that allows the aesthetic sphere to preserve the right of the particular and nonconceptual.[17]

This attempt to see Adorno's *Aesthetic Theory* as a postmodernist text, one that responds to changes occurring during the 1960s in the spheres of the arts and literature, must seize on certain elements and use the text as a kind of storehouse for topics and themes that confirm a postmodernist attitude. At the same time, this approach must neglect or underrate Adorno's connections with the modernist project. Hence, more persuasive than a simple postmodernist reading, I believe, is the argument that Adorno's late work, although constructed with modernism in mind (if we may presume Adorno's intentions), transcends the boundaries of the classical modernist project. It radicalizes certain modernist characteristics to the point of clearly subverting the architecture of a modernist aesthetics. The late work does this not necessarily by forcing the avant-gardist aspect (technology, montage, cancellation of the artwork) but rather by foregrounding the latent contradictions of the modernist project itself. For this reason, a programmatic distinction between modernism and the avant-garde tends to obscure the tendency of Adorno's late work, since it superimposes an evolutionary scheme (the move from modernism to the avant-garde) that is not compatible with the internal problematic of Adorno's text. Precisely because Adorno is fixated on the concept of the autonomous artwork, he must examine the history of modern art in the light of the radical subversion of this concept. Not only is the autonomy of the artwork always questionable and doubtful, but the objective meaning of the artwork – its function as a crystallized artifact produced for a specific historical moment – cannot be captured with certainty because, as Adorno underlines, this meaning shifts within the process of history. In addition, we have to note that this process cannot be construed as a linear evolution. Yet Adorno's critique of universal history and its concomitant category of totality must not be confused with sheer abandonment or cancellation. Rather, totality remains the absent term that influences the trajectory of negative dialectics, giving significance to the breaks and gaps of the various processes for which the term 'history' is problematic shorthand.

The integration of Adorno into the postmodernist condition, then, as proposed by poststructuralists but also in a curious way by Jameson (Adorno as the theorist of the 1990s!), has to remove important elements of Adorno's theory in order to succeed. One of them is Adorno's understanding of the subject-object relation – to put it historically, the question of his appropriation and critique of Hegel. Although it is certainly correct that Adorno is critical of Hegel's use of dialectics and unwilling to subscribe to Hegel's aesthetic theory, it would be misleading to argue that Adorno abandons or cancels dialectical thought. In fact, he claims that Hegel's philosophy of art was not dialectical enough, that in spite of its program it tended to freeze the classical tradition into a static system.

By the same token, the desubjectification that poststructuralist commentators have celebrated in Adorno must be read as part of a dialectical relationship in which the objectivication of the subject results in alienation, not simply as a strategy of decentering and fragmentation. For this reason, Hegel (and by implication Marx) remains an important dialogical partner in Adorno's late writings. Accordingly, *Aesthetic Theory* as a whole maintains a critical stance toward the reality of advanced capitalism and tends to view the advanced work of art as a significant oppositional force. But this moment cannot, as Adorno's more dogmatic readers have suggested, be completely subsumed under the category of modernism (or, for that matter, of the avant-garde). It defies the logic of simple periodization.

9. The Discourse of Philosophy and the Problem of Language

MORE than one commentator has remarked that Adorno approaches truth as something mediated through language. For this reason, it is not uncommon to link his thought to the linguistic turn of cultural theory and propose a special proximity between Adornian theory and poststructuralist attempts to rethink the role of language in contemporary philosophy. As tempting as it may be to interpret Adorno's position as close to and compatible with poststructuralist thought by using the category of negative dialectics as the mediating term, this path would ultimately lead us away from Adorno's conception, since it neglects the specific constellation out of which his concept of truth emerged. Although it is certainly correct that Adorno would not separate truth from linguistic considerations, his approach does not easily fit the more recent description of a general linguistic turn in matters of epistemology and criticism. An indication of the difference is Adorno's continued insistence on the need for conceptual language in the discourse of criticism. As we have seen, the original introduction to *Aesthetic Theory* underscores the impossibility of a traditional systematic philosophy of art, but Adorno holds on to the requirement of conceptual rigor and epistemological reflection. For him, the question of language (which he certainly took more seriously than did most other members of the Frankfurt School) is embedded in the larger question of the status of philosophy, and, specifically, of logic. His concern with the logical aspect goes back to the 1930s and 1940s, when he discussed problems of logical theory with Horkheimer. In any event, we can locate Adorno's (mostly implicit) theory of language most easily, I believe, by looking first at his critique of traditional philosophy.

We have to keep in mind that the beginnings of Adorno's philosophical writings coincided with a more general change in the perception of language. In a number of crucial areas the conventional understanding of language as a means of communication and a tool for attaining knowledge came under scrutiny. Specifically, the problematization of language imposed itself on literary, philosophical, and religious discourse. In the critical discourse on literature, for instance, Hofmannsthal's letter of Lord Chandos (1902) called into question the signifying power of language. Fifteen years later, from a different viewpoint, the literary experiments of the dadaists radically undermined traditional assumptions about poetic meaning. At the same time, within the discourse of philosophy, Lukács's *History and Class Consciousness* developed a rigorous critique of linguistic reification, and from a different perspective, Ludwig Wittgenstein's early work implied a complete rejection of the neo-Kantian model of epistemology. Furthermore, and particularly important for Adorno (who was trained in the neo-Kantian tradition), Walter Benjamin reconceived the epistemological parameters of philosophy in his early essays, especially in 'On Language as Such and the Language of Man' (1916) and 'On the Program of the Coming Philosophy' (1918). Adorno came to follow the path of his older friend and mentor, who set out to reformulate the task of philosophy in the light of the limitation of Kant's theory of knowledge and the recurrence of these limits in neo-Kantian attempts to salvage the transcendental epistemology. Against the Kantian insistence on the subject, Benjamin underscored the objective and divine character of truth and therefore characterized Kant's theory of knowledge as modern mythology. For this reason, Benjamin accentuated the linguistic aspect of philosophy and argued that philosophy must be grounded in a theological theory of language.[1]

Particularly instructive are two essays in which Adorno explicitly raises questions about philosophical discourse: the early (1931) essay 'Die Aktualität der Philosophie' ('The Actuality of Philosophy') and the lecture 'Wozu noch Philosophie?' ('Why Philosophy?') published in 1962. These can serve as a frame for Adorno's philosophical oeuvre. Though they differ considerably in tone and mood – the later one being obviously more pessimistic than the earlier one – they share a radical critique of systematic philosophy, a critique that draws on the immanent evolution of philosophy after Hegel as well as on the historical context of the philosophical project within advanced Western societies.

In the 1962 essay, Adorno underscores objective aspects by offering a critical analysis of existing philosophical schools; only then does he point to the remaining path of philosophical reflection: namely, a dialectical procedure that resists the lure of closure. Clearly, however, he rejects the reduction of philosophy to a methodology of science that is exclusively concerned with formal problems. In this respect, Adorno is prepared to defend the metaphysical tradition against its scientific critique. At the same time, he takes issue with two versions of philosophy that dominated the West German discourse after 1945: the renewal of ontology in Heidegger's philosophy, and the existentialist project of Sartre and his German disciples. What these approaches have in common with positivism, Adorno argues, is their polemical stance against metaphysics.

> In both positivist theory and that of Heidegger – in his later work, at all events – the current is set against speculation. The idea which arises independently from, and indicatively of, the facts, and cannot be separated from them without leaving a residue behind – a remainder, as it were – is stigmatized as vain and idle cerebration: according to Heidegger, however, ways of thinking that follow the typical pattern prescribed by the historical evolution of thought in the West at bottom fall short of the real truth. The latter comes to light of itself, and stands revealed: correct thinking is no more than the ability to perceive it.[2]

Adorno's critique is twofold. First, it stresses the problematic implications of the antimetaphysical attitude: the naive acceptance of that which is given, and the passivity of the subject toward truth – both the result of unmediated thought. Second, it underscores immanent problems, especially in Heidegger's philosophy. For Adorno, Heidegger's understanding of truth misses the mediation of the concept[3] or, more precisely, the moment of mediation in conceptual work. 'Thought itself, of which all ideas are a function, cannot be represented in the absence of thinking activity, which the word thought designates.'[4]

This is not the place to pursue Adorno's critique of Heidegger in more detail; it may suffice to note the importance of its linguistic aspect. For Adorno, Heidegger's ontology misrepresents the nature and function of human language. At no point can Adorno overlook the involvement of philosophical thought in language, not only as an instrument of theoretical articulation but also – emphatically – as a self-conscious reflection of its own historical character. Thus, both positivism and ontology, historically situated, must be recognized as forms of reified thought. Adorno's project can be defined at least in part as a relentless self-conscious critique of ossification as it is reflected in the language of positivism or ontology, exposing the jargon of ontological murmuring that mystifies its actual function in the social realm. Clearly, this project extends to the Marxist tradition as well; its orthodox strands, as Adorno stresses, are no less reified than scientific positivism.

Yet Adorno's position in 1962 cannot be summarized as a mere critical continuation of the dialectical tradition. As much as the later Adorno holds on to the Hegelian tradition, he does not see himself as a neo-Hegelian; rather, his critique includes all forms of idealism, especially of absolute idealism. Under these conditions, philosophical thought, after losing its hegemony, is restricted to negativity, to a refusal of fulfilling a positive function. 'Because philosophy is good for nothing, it is not yet outmoded.'[5] Adorno hastens to add that even this program is not reliable and safe; it is as much open to criticism as any traditional theoretical position.

Adorno's 'Why Philosophy?' isolates certain moments in his thought without, however, fully articulating his reservations against the claims of systematic philosophy. It is in *Aesthetic Theory* that the radical moment of this critique comes into the foreground. In particular, the original introduction, written in the late 1950s, underscores the fundamental impossibility of systematic philosophy with regard to works of art. But as Adorno makes clear at the very beginning, the problems of aesthetic theory are closely related to fundamental epistemological problems, which almost immediately resurface in aesthetic theory, since the material of aesthetic theory depends in principle on the concepts of subject and object provided by epistemology. What Adorno calls the 'extreme nominalism' of modern art – that is, its resistance to pre-conceived genres and forms – seriously undermines the form of traditional aesthetic theory, which stressed systematic categories. Consequently, Adorno has to deal with the fundamental contradiction between the conceptual apparatus (which includes, of course, the concept of the artwork) and the concrete piece of music or literary text. Conceptual language is, Adorno maintains, at the same time inadequate and indispensable: inadequate for the task of rendering the individual artwork; necessary, however, for disclosing its truth content (*Wahrheitsgehalt*). 'The truth content of a work of art calls for philosophy. It is only in philosophy that philosophy converges with or expires in art. The way to this point is that of the most immanent reflection of works of art, not the external application of philosophical tenets' (GS 7:507; AT 468). Yet this typical Adornian strategy, stressing the need for immanence, does not solve the dilemma of aesthetic theory, since it does not automatically provide the mediating moment. One could certainly argue that the concrete artwork is not open to philosophical articulation at all, that any transition from one discourse to the other is impossible. This would leave Adorno with a fundamental gap between art and philosophy, the aesthetic and truth. For Adorno, however, it is language after all that makes the mediation possible, since language is not limited to a model of identity (*a* is *b*) but can, through negativity, articulate difference.

In his late writings Adorno stubbornly defends the task of philosophy without giving it a positive program, without even assuming an unquestionable legitimacy. At one level, this strategy proposes an ongoing critique of the philosophical tradition (Kant, Hegel, Marx, Husserl) which balances its claims by emphasizing its internal tensions and contradictions – which cannot simply be taken as proof of errors but must also be seen as aspects of truth. At another level, however, *Aesthetic Theory* introduces an even more radical critique of the philosophical project by calling into question the nature of conceptual language, suggesting not only its inadequacy for the articulation of the meaning of art but also its incompatibility with the expressive quality of art. For Adorno, the advanced work of art is the most radical challenge to the philosophical discourse and its claim to truth: 'The truth of discursive knowledge is undisguised, but for that reason it does not have the truth. The knowledge which is art has the truth, but as something with which it is incommensurable' (GS 7:19; AT 19). What distinguishes the truth content of the artwork from the concept of truth in philosophy is, according to Adorno, its nonconceptual logic: 'Although works of art are not conceptual and do not judge, they are logical' (GS 7:205; AT 197). Ultimately, as much as he questions the idea of the rounded artwork, Adorno gives greater importance to art than to philosophy as a bearer of (historical) truth. 'It can be said of philosophy, and of theoretical thought in general, that it suffers from an idealistic prejudgment insofar as it has only concepts at its disposal. Solely through them can it deal with what it reaches for, but never grasps' (GS 7:382; AT 365). Therefore, the Hegelian subsumption of art under philosophy has to be reworked: philosophy now may help to disclose aesthetic appearance, the 'enigmatic quality' (*Rätselcharakter*) of the work of art.

Aesthetic Theory does not explicitly develop a comprehensive theory of language, but it is shot through with reflections and notes on the problem of language and its relationship to knowledge on the one hand, and to expression on the other. In *Aesthetic Theory*, more than in *Negative Dialectics*, Adorno retrieves essential elements of his original philosophical project of the early 1930s. Both 'Die Aktualität der Philosophie' and 'Thesen über die Sprache des Philosophen' are early but important attempts to respond to Benjamin's language theory and, at the same time, to refute the claims of Heidegger as the legitimate heir and 'conqueror' (*Überwinder*) of Husserl.

At this juncture, we can disregard Adorno's map of contemporary philosophy and concentrate on his 'program,' which stresses the dialectical movement of philosophical discourse. Unlike the late Adorno, the young Adorno – at this point very much under the influence of Walter Benjamin's *Ursprung des deutschen Trauer-*

spiel (*The Origin of German Tragic Drama*) – was prepared to offer a programmatic statement in his inaugural lecture at Frankfurt University. Quite consciously, already setting himself off against positivism on the one hand and ontology on the other, he harks back to an earlier model of philosophy (for which the name of Leibniz has to stand in): 'The organon of this ars inveniendi [art of invention] is fantasy. An exact fantasy; fantasy which abides strictly within the material which the sciences present to it, and reaches beyond them only in the smallest aspect of their arrangement.'[6] But what Adorno has in mind has little to do with a return to older models; rather, it is his unmistakable distance from axiomatic grounding that propels him toward essayistic models such as those of Francis Bacon and Leibniz.

Although the inaugural lecture focuses on the methodological aspect, it does not spell out the linguistic consequences for the philosophical discourse. In his 'Thesen über die Sprache des Philosophen' (GS 1:366 f.), Adorno explores some of the implications of an 'essayistic' position. The short essay contains a radical break with the linguistic model that guided the Enlightenment and idealist philosophy – a model in which semiotic and semantic levels are clearly distinguished and in which, furthermore, the sign is defined as arbitrary. As a result, subject philosophy concentrates on consciousness as the unifying principle and leaves objective reality out as a sphere that can be reached only indirectly through linguistic constructs (concepts). 'For a way of thinking that conceives of things exclusively as functions of thought, names have become arbitrary: they are freely posited by consciousness' (GS 1:366). The modern linguistic model (as clearly articulated by Ferdinand de Saussure, for instance) is to be replaced with a paradigm in which signs and reality, language and history are thoroughly intertwined. Only through language, Adorno suggests, does history partake of truth. Words are never mere signifiers for what can be conceptualized; rather, words are penetrated by as well as filled with history, and truth is the result of this fusion. 'The share of history in the word absolutely determines the choice of the word because history and truth meet in the word' (GS 1:366–67).

Adorno's suggestion appears to be out of touch with modern linguistic theory, and his insistence on the semantic reality of language collides so obviously with contemporary practice that further explanation is needed. His argument takes the latter objection into account by suggesting that linguistic models are historically determined. His own model would pertain only to a premodern society, whereas modern societies are characterized by a reified model that splits signs and referents. For Adorno, under the sign of modernity the retreat to a prehistorical realm of linguistic purity is impossible – a point that he makes against Heidegger's attempts to escape traditional philosophical terminology.

Adorno's proposal remains ambivalent; it follows two strategies that are not easily compatible. On the one hand, he criticizes modern linguistic theory, postulating a semantically grounded understanding of language; on the other hand, he insists on the historicity of language and polemicizes against any attempt to return to an older paradigm. The task of the philosopher is to confront the decay of present-day philosophical language: '[The philosopher's] material is the ruins of the words to which history binds [him]' (GS 1:368). Adorno's later work follows up both sides of the argument but not necessarily by keeping them together. Well known, of course, is his critique of philosophical jargon as a form of reified language and his discussion of the limits of conceptual language. Less known is his attempt to unfold an alternative model.

In 'Theses on the Language of the Philosopher,' Adorno suggests a 'dialectical' solution that makes use of objective configurations. To use his own language: words are supposed to 'surround' truth; their configuration is expected to articulate the 'new' truth. 'The procedure is not to be identified with the intention to "explain" new truths with conventional words; on the contrary, configurative language will have to avoid entirely the explicit procedure that presupposes the unbroken dignity of words. As against conventional words and the speechless [*sprachlosen*] subjective intention, configuration is a third way' (GS 1:369). It is worth noting that Adorno speaks here of a dialectical procedure but not of mediation. A configuration, in other words, is not the result of a mediation between oppositional concepts. Adorno conceives of the disclosure of truth not as a formal and conceptual process but as an aesthetic event. Thus knowledge and art begin to converge: 'The growing significance of the philosophical critique of language can be formulated as the onset of a convergence between art and knowledge' (GS 1:370). Some four decades later, Adorno's *Aesthetic Theory* unfolds precisely this program.

As Susan Buck-Morss and others have shown,[7] the first attempts of the young Adorno to work out the problem of truth and language owed a great deal to Walter Benjamin's writings of the 1920s, especially to his study of the baroque tragic drama. In the introduction to that study Benjamin had introduced the concept of the configuration in order to redefine the truth content of works of art without falling back on a historicist approach. In the context of my argument, however, Benjamin's influence is less important than Adorno's response, which takes the form of a double-edged critique of language. Adorno takes issue not only with an ontological approach to language but also with a formalist-semiotic approach that underscores the arbitrary nature of signification. This means that he is equally opposed to Heidegger's and Saussure's models of language. For Adorno, the critique of the reified linguistic theory of semiotics is as crucial as the critique of ontology, since both approaches share an inability to take the historical moment seriously. The Marxist theory of reification enables him to pinpoint the element of ossification in modern language theory, just as Lukács had emphasized the moment of ossification in Kant's philosophical discourse. As a result, Adorno's own model of language and truth does not fit easily into conventional linguistic or philosophical discourses. Attempts to integrate his thought into existing models have a tendency, therefore, to pressure his approach one way or the other. This unique position creates certain problems when Adorno carries out his own epistemological project in *Against Epistemology* and *Negative Dialectics*, since his critiques of Husserl and Heidegger are not launched from the perspective of the expected opposition – that is, semiotics.

Already in *Against Epistemology*, partly written in 1937–38 and completed in the early 1950s, Adorno's earlier program has become less visible, replaced to a large extent by a more traditional critique of phenomenology from a Hegelian point of view (albeit a Hegel without idealism). Especially the introduction grounds its critique of 'foundational philosophy' (*Ursprungsphilosophie*), from Plato to Husserl, in a historical dialectic that basically follows Hegel's critique of Kant's rationalist formalism but radicalizes this critique to the extent that its own method is equally drawn into the problematic sphere of epistemology.[8] Internal criticism, following up on given premises and implications, remains locked into the system and can be overcome only through attention to the language of the argument itself, its figures and tropes. For instance, Husserl's preference for juridical and contractual language still links him to 'the myth of the first' (AE 26; GS 5:34). Adorno's critique of Husserl's 'categorical intuition' (*kategorische Anschauung*), as a crucial element of his epistemology, relies on Hegel's critique of immediacy and his insistence on mediation. For Adorno, Husserl's 'doctrine of ideation' (*Lehre von der Ideation*) has fallen behind Hegel: 'The equivocal usage steps in for the immanent movement of the concept. In Husserl's antecedent, "being" is used in the most universal, abstract, and mediated sense. The conclusion substitutes entities for being as the immediately intuitive moment of whatever sort which attains categorization' (AE 207–8; GS 5:210–11).

What Adorno, with the help of Hegelian dialectics, wants to isolate in Husserl's use of language is its static, almost passive understanding of description as a way to grasp 'things' (*Dinge*). Husserl's ideal of description undercuts arguments: 'Phenomenology gives notice, provisionally and inadequately, of the end of the discussion' (AE 210; GS 5:212). Adorno is not interested simply in maintaining 'the discussion,' in which language serves in its traditional role as a tool; rather, the point of his criticism is the static character of Husserl's model, in which statements are expected to approximate facts (*Sachverhalte*) and the subject-object relation remains fixed and undialectical. As a result, Husserl's phenomenology is doomed. Despite its desire to get closer to things (*Sachen*), it cannot overcome the gap between the conceptual apparatus and the facts: 'One concept is evolved out of another so that contradictions may be corrected in ordered succession, but none would come closer to the "thing" than the first one. Indeed each falls deeper into the thicket of invention' (AE 211; GS 5:214). In other words, for Adorno the failure of Husserl's project, the failure of renewed idealism, is closely related to the latter's understanding of language and the language-truth relation where the levels of sign and referent are set apart. Husserl's discourse aims at descriptions not unlike those of the scientist who organizes the world according to types and systems of types.

As much as Adorno criticizes the propensity toward a systematic approach, especially in Husserl's later writings, in *Against Epistemology* he more or less refrains from presenting an alternative position. The mode of criticism is mostly immanent, with an emphasis on the late bourgeois character of Husserl's thought, the search for ultimate security in an age in which security is no longer available. Only occasionally does Adorno's interest in the fragmentary, unresolvable nature and the dialectics of language come to the fore – in his preference for Husserl's isolated phenomenological analyses, for instance, which exhibit an antisystematic character. In this context, Adorno points at least in passing to Freud's resistance to the traditional opposition of logic and intuition (shared by Husserl) and underscores the logic of the intuitive as part of the rational (AE 46; GS 5:54). By and large, however, in his struggle with the phenomenological model and especially with its postulate of absolute grounding, Adorno does not unfold his own position.

This is where the later *Negative Dialectics* goes a decisive step beyond *Against Epistemology*; here the scope of the questioning has significantly widened and with it the problematization of traditional philosophical language. The later study, however, also extends the involvement with conceptual language, as Adorno states at the very beginning. In his definition of dialectics he stresses the moment of difference between objects (*Gegenstände*) and concepts and, therefore, the problematic attempt of all philosophy to establish identity through statements. Hence, Adorno's interest in dialectics emphasizes contradictions rather than synthesis as a way of reestablishing identity: 'Contradiction is non-identity from the viewpoint of identity; the primacy of the principle of contradiction in the dialectic measures the heterogenous against identity-thinking' (ND 5; GS 6:17). Thus, dialectics emerges as the radical consciousness of nonidentity. Yet this consciousness has to be expressed in a philosophical – that is, conceptual – language. The introduction insists emphatically on the necessity as well as feasibility of this task, turning against Henri Bergson and Ludwig Wittgenstein, who want to limit the scope of philosophical discourse.

> The plain contradiction of this yearning [for transparent language] is that of philosophy itself: it is qualified as dialectics before it becomes entangled in its particular contradictions. The labor of self-reflection consists in unravelling those paradoxes. Everything else is signification, second-hand construction, and today – as in Hegel's day – prephilosophical. (ND 9; GS 6:21)

The language of philosophy is predicated on the problematic but inevitable desire to get closer to a prelinguistic realm. This attempt, Adorno points out, does violence to the nonconceptual (*Begriffslose*) by repressing, marginalizing, and eliminating it through its stamp of identity.

Despite his critique of mystical or irrational approaches to epistemology, Adorno does not mean simply to restate the traditional domain of philosophy and its language. Rather, in *Negative Dialectics,* he describes philosophical reflection as consistently confronting its own limits and its own culpability. Far from defining dialectics as a mediated path to truth, Adorno calls it an 'ontology of the false state of affairs' (ND 11; GS 6:22), which can be overcome only through reflection on its own state. Knowledge of 'reality,' in other words, depends entirely on language but cannot place its trust in concepts. For this reason, Adorno rejects both the empirical and the rationalist model of language; that is, he opposes equally a model of reflection and a model of conceptual autonomy (where empirical reality does not really matter). Philosophical discourse, he suggests, strives toward the Other without being allowed to leave its own domain. 'Philosophy which realizes that, which annuls the autarchy of the concept, wipes the scales from its eyes' (ND 12; GS 6:23–24). To put it differently, philosophy can survive only by questioning its survival. But in this procedure of questioning it remains tied to its own tradition. For this reason, Adorno is especially critical of programs that seek a completely new beginning or a return to a past state, as does Heidegger's ontology. For Adorno, Heidegger's demand for a reorientation in philosophy misses the present condition of philosophical discourse; it postulates a new language and new categories without reflecting on the need for and the limits of conceptual language.

Ontology, to summarize Adorno's critique in part 2 of *Negative Dialectics,* is the refusal to accept the paradox of philosophical language: that its task is to do what it cannot do by reconstituting the realm of the absolute under the category of Being (*Sein*). In Heidegger, absolute knowledge is disclosed not through the dialectical process of conceptual work but through 'intellectual intuition [*intellektuelle Anschauung*]' (ND 62; GS 6:70), where mediation is no longer necessary. In this framework, ontology presents itself as a solution to modern problems without working through these problems. Adorno treats ontology as a form of ideology that has a specific political and social function in postwar Germany: 'In the categories to which fundamental ontology owes its resonance – and which it therefore either disavows or so sublimates that they no longer serve for an unwelcome confrontation – one can read how much they are the imprints of something lacking that is not to be produced, how much they are its complementary ideology' (ND 65; GS 6:73).

Yet for the purposes of my argument, this critique is less central than the immanent critique of Heidegger's categories presented in the second chapter. Here Adorno focuses on the conceptual apparatus of ontology and its (almost desperate) attempt to overcome the boundaries of conceptual language. He demonstrates the very abstractness of the category of Being as the supposed origin: 'If one tries to accomplish Heidegger's differentiation of Being from the concept that logically circumscribes it, one is left – after subtracting entity as well as the categories of abstraction – with an unknown which has only the pathos of its invocation over the Kantian concept of the transcendent thing-in-itself' (ND 98; GS 6:105). In fact, as Adorno points out, Being derives its significance and power from a strategy of hypostatization applied to the copula 'is.' 'Heidegger, in misplacing it beyond the sole source of its meaning, succumbs to that reified thought to which he took exception' (ND 101; GS 6:108). In this setup, Heidegger – very much against his intention, of course – remains caught in an obsolete model where 'subject, copula, and predicate would again – as in obsolete logic – be hermetic, completed details after the model of things [*Sachen*]' (ND 101; GS 6:108). Against this model Adorno sets his own, in which the copula has a very different function: namely, that of a 'promissory note on particularization' (ND 101; GS 6:108). In other words, the copula in a statement is designed not only to identify subject and predicate but also to bring about the characterization of the particular which it can only claim to accomplish.

As we can see, Adorno's critique of Heidegger is very much involved in a critique of Heidegger's language, not only at the level of its jargon but, more centrally, at the level of Heidegger's most basic category, which provides the ground for his ontology. Yet one must not overlook the fact that Adorno does share with Heidegger certain concerns and presuppositions that neither analytic philosophy nor contemporary semiotics would necessarily grant. He shares with Heidegger the belief that language is more than signification (ND 101; GS 6:109) and that facts (reality) and language (signs) are not independent of each other. Still, he refuses to follow Heidegger's elevation of the copula 'is' to a first principle of origin in the argument that the judgment '*A* is *X*' contains an irreducible element that can be abstracted as Being. The following passage presents the crucial point in Adorno's critique:

> Heidegger gets as far as the borderline of dialectical insight into the non-identity in identity. But he does not carry through the contradiction in the concept of Being. He suppresses it. What can somehow be conceived as Being mocks the notion of an identity between the concept and that which

it means, but Heidegger treats it as identity, as pure Being itself, devoid of its otherness. (ND 104; GS 6:110)

Whereas Heidegger tries to transcend the dualism of the judgment in his striving for Being, Adorno resolutely reminds his reader that the moment of nonidentity in the judgment must not be repressed; in fact, it must be foregrounded so that the subject-object dialectic becomes visible. In other words, he rigorously holds on to the process of conceptual procedures (work) that he himself had described as problematic.

For Adorno, the problematic side of the philosophical discourse is at the same time its strength, the relentless attempt 'to express what cannot be articulated [*das Unausdrückbare auszudrücken*]' (ND 106; GS 6:114). Of course, this task must not be confused with a search for the irrational; rather, Adorno's postulate must be understood as a way of distinguishing philosophy from the sciences (including the historical sciences). Philosophy shares with the sciences, of course, the methodological use of language, but it proceeds in a mode that Adorno refers to as a 'suspended state' (*Schwebende*), and 'the determinant of its suspended state is that even while keeping its distance from the verifying type of cognition it is not noncommittal – that the life it leads has a stringency of its own' (ND 109; GS 6:115). Where Heidegger went wrong, Adorno suggests, was in his attempt to articulate *das Schwebende*, to bring it into the form of a definitely worked-out terminology and thus to claim for it a 'quasi-superior rank' (ND 109; GS 6:116).

It is, of course, not accidental that Adorno compares *das Schwebende* of the philosophical discourse to music: that is, to a medium without concepts, one in which truth cannot be achieved through the method of judgment. Likewise, the language of philosophy cannot be satisfied with a positive doctrine or a deduction of such a doctrine (*Lehre*) from first principles. Even the category of reflection, which carries a great deal of weight in *Negative Dialectics*, does not quite suffice to express the inexpressible. For this reason, Adorno's relentless critique of Heidegger can never quite come to grips with the nature of philosophical discourse, since it is limited by its own object: that is, the ontological model of Being. The legitimacy of philosophy, which Adorno treats as questionable but not hopeless, depends on the possibility of re-functioning elements of the metaphysical tradition, without, however, buying into its dogmatic side. To put it differently, Adorno assumes that philosophical discourse can no longer be grounded in first principles, nor can it rely on universal concepts deduced from these principles (ND 136; GS 6:140). Consequently, a positive concept of totality is no longer available. This leaves philosophy with an arduous task for which it is not quite adequately equipped: to discover how concepts and 'the nonconceptual' (*das Nichtbegriffliche*) come together (ND 137; GS 6:141).

At this juncture we have to focus on Adorno's literary essays of the 1950s and 1960s, which approach the same problem from a different angle. Their center is, of course, precisely *das Nichtbegriffliche* in works of art, the moment that escapes conceptual construction. This opposition is crucial for Adorno's music criticism, but in his literary criticism it comes into the foreground as the problem of language. The problem articulates itself in two different ways. First of all, art criticism is concerned with the epistemological status of art and literature: can art and literature contain cognitive truth, or are they (exclusively) expressive? Second, given the difference between literary and philosophical discourse, how can criticism articulate the nonconceptuality of the artwork?

Adorno's famous essay on the essay, 'Der Essay als Form' ('The Essay as Form') addresses primarily the latter question by arguing for a nonsystematic treatment of aesthetic issues, but it also speaks to the larger problem of the truth content in works of art and the difference between conceptual claims and *das Nichtbegriffliche* as the Other, which does not seem to fit traditional philosophical discourse. Adorno directs his essay (typically enough for the 1950s) against the scientific and systematic claims of traditional academic criticism, which is concerned with both the factual aspects of the artwork and the aesthetic features of the individual text. Like the early Lukács, Adorno underscores the special character of the essay: its deliberate incompleteness, the fragmentary quality that resists the demands of systematic treatment and refuses to take its cues from philological research. Taking the factual side for granted, the essay concentrates instead on the moment of reflection; it is concerned with precisely those aspects that tend to get lost in scientific or philosophical approaches. Still, we have to note that Adorno does not give up on the conceptual element in criticism. His scorn for the journalistic feuilleton and the fashionable existentialist criticism of the 1950s (Heidegger) is unmistakable: 'With a peasant cunning that justifies itself as primordiality, it refuses to honor the obligations of conceptual thought, to which, however, it had subscribed when it used concepts in its propositions and judgments. At the same time, its aesthetic element consists of merely watered down, second-hand reminiscences of Hölderlin or Expressionism' (NL 1:6–7; GS 11:13).

More rigorously than the young Lukács, Adorno insists on the difference between the essay form and poetry (*Dichtung*), notably in their use of language. The pseudo-poetic, an attempt to lose itself in its object by imitating its language, is the temptation (*Versuchung*) of the essay. For Adorno, the essay must preserve a precarious balance between conceptual and poetic language. But this formulation does not quite do justice to his radical notion. It leaves out the moment of transcendence: 'In the emphatic essay thought divests itself of the traditional idea of truth' (NL 1:11; GS 11:18). The essay does not state truth, nor is it merely a matter of (poetic) expression; rather, it 'seeks the truth contents (*Wahrheitsgehalte*) as themselves historical. It does not seek any primordial given, thus spiting a societalized (*vergesellschaftete*) society that, because it does not tolerate anything that does not bear its stamp, tolerates least of all anything that reminds it of its own ubiquity' (NL 1:11; GS 11:19).

Adorno's rigorous defense of conceptual criticism, however, must not be confused with a return to a traditional philosophical discourse. For him, concepts fulfill a different function in the essay: they may remain undefined; they approach truth by forming a specific configuration through which the nonconceptual Other can be articulated. In this context he offers a crucial formulation for the character and use of concepts: 'In actuality, all concepts are already implicitly concretized through the language in which they stand. The essay starts with these meanings, and, being essentially language itself, takes them farther; it wants to help language in its relation to concepts, to take them in reflection as they have been named unreflectingly in language' (NL 1:12; GS 11:20). The essay form takes back and reverses the linguistic ossification implied in scientific discourse. Thus, the essay presents a paradox: a process of defining its particular object through nondefinitions, thereby creating a nonfetishized language. What Adorno celebrates is not only the essay's open form and conscious lack of a dogmatic position but ultimately its lack of intellectual security, its lack of an affirmative ideal of truth. The anti-Cartesian tendency is unmistakable.

It is not accidental, of course, that Adorno refers to Leibniz's concept of the monad in order to suggest how language and truth may be related. He defines this relationship as a configuration that does not follow the conventional distinction between the parts and the whole. The essay, as Adorno notes, does not allow a search for its elements or for origins. Its moments are not strictly derived from its totality, nor do its individual parts lead to the whole. As an anti-Cartesian form (and method), Adorno stresses, the essay does not instrumentalize its own language. Instead, it allows and encourages a full articulation of the object through a linguistic differentiation that radically appropriates contradictions and discontinuities. The essay form, Adorno notes, is characterized by breaks and gaps, following the breaks and gaps of reality itself; it reaches its unity by acknowledging these moments rather than by harmonizing them.

In its antisystematic mode, the essay form frees itself from the pressure to use language as a means of identification. In fact, the essayist's awareness that representation through language is not identical with the object (*Sache*) provides the essay with critical energy. For Adorno, essayistic language is critical language par excellence – not because it defines a position but because it refuses to define a position, because it undercuts all positions including its own. As a consequence, truth cannot be defined as the correspondence (*Übereinstimmung*) of language and reality. In the essay, Adorno suggests (and the suggestion could be extended to critical writing in general), truth can and must be articulated through untruth.

The essay's defiance of discursive logic, its keen interest in associations and equivocations (*Äquivokationen*), brings it close to aesthetic language. The essay, Adorno submits, partakes of the possibilities of the nonconceptual without becoming art. This means that concerns for 'rightness' (*Stimmigkeit*) are of greater importance than rules of discursive logic. Does this indicate that Adorno returns to a romantic position, which celebrates art at the expense of rational philosophical arguments? The proximity to the romantic fragment is obvious enough. But there is no attempt to restore the ideology of originality as embodied in the artistic genius. Hence, Adorno does not mean to reinforce an irrational idea of poetic language as pure expression; rather, he sees poetic language as objective structure following its own internal logic.

In 'On Lyric Poetry and Society' Adorno offered the first analysis of this structure by emphasizing the social aspect of poetry. By and large, that essay has been read as Adorno's contribution to a sociological method; less attention has been paid to the essay's equally important emphasis on language, especially since this topic receives a more thorough and more differentiated treatment later in *Aesthetic Theory*. Methodologically speaking, the essay on poetry owes its force to the dichotomy of the particular (poem) and the general (society), which is subsequently unfolded dialectically. Adorno wants to demonstrate the universal quality in the individual poem. More relevant in our context, however, are his remarks about the character of poetic language. Adorno underscores its noncommunicative nature: 'Not that what the lyric poem expresses must be immediately equivalent to what everyone experiences. Its universality is no *volonté de tous,* not the universality of simply communicating what others are unable to communicate' (NL 1:38; GS 11:50). Instead, he suggests, the poem is expected to preserve the individual moment, the moment that has not yet been subsumed under the concept. In doing so, in concentrating on the particular, the poem reaches the level of the universal (*Allgemeine*).

Adorno's polemic against theories of communicative poetic

language, however, does not cancel a model of poetic language as expression (*Ausdruck*). What he wants to eliminate is the traditional use that directly links the poem and the emotions of its author; he sees the language of the poem rather as the objective correlate of its specific social conditions. This means that for Adorno there is a referent outside the semiotic system but a referent that cannot be communicated directly. Only a mediated correspondence is possible: the speaking subject of the poem can suggest meaning through a specific configuration of words. 'The "I" whose voice is heard in the lyric is an "I" that defines and expresses itself as something opposed to the collective, to objectivity; it is not immediately at one with the nature to which its expression refers' (NL 1:41; GS 11:53). For Adorno, both poetry and society are mediated through language (NL 1:43; GS 11:56). By emphasizing the expressive aspect of poetry, which crystallizes in language, Adorno brings together a subjective and an objective model of language. He describes language as a twofold phenomenon (*Doppeltes*) that simultaneously molds the subjective reactions and feelings and articulates concepts along with their relationship.

The core of Adorno's concern is his interest in redemption (*Versöhnung*): that is, his interest in nonreified language. In the poetry essay this means first and foremost a critique of Heidegger's ontological conception of language, which celebrates poetry as the language of Being. Adorno's concept of poetic language, by contrast, reintegrates – at least in its moment of redemption – subject and linguistic system. In this respect, the poetry essay reiterates a concern that Adorno had already expressed in the early 1930s: the need for a language theory that does not simply reflect the actual reification of language in modern society. In *Aesthetic Theory* he more rigorously unfolds these questions, although even there he does not offer a systematic treatment.

Aesthetic Theory does differentiate two aspects of the concept of language that were not separated in the poetry essay: language as a means of communication, and language as artistic expression. The essay defined them dialectically; *Aesthetic Theory* emphasizes their fundamental distinction. It is characteristic for the work of art, Adorno suggests, to transcend the language of communication; in fact, it is no longer compatible with communication. 'The true language (*Sprache*) of art is speechless (*sprachlos*). Art's speechless moment has priority over the signifying one of poetry – a moment which is not entirely lacking even from music' (GS 7:171; AT 164). The expressive moment of art, aesthetic articulation, does not coincide with its conceptual aspect. Hence, the language of art moves to a metaphorical level – at least from the point of view of modern linguistics. Yet for Adorno this metaphorical use is the older and more fundamental mode: a prediscursive, mimetic use in which the work of art has a special affinity to the subject. For expression does not communicate the subject's concerns; rather, works of art 'reverberate with the prehistory of subjectivity – that of ensoulment [*Beseelung*]' (GS 7:172; AT 165). Hence, for the late Adorno the concept of poetic language cannot be exhausted by rational and logical considerations; its core is the element of mimesis 'as imagining objectivity' (GS 7:172; AT 165). *Aesthetic Theory* underscores the nondiscursive character of the artwork: 'Only by withholding its verdict does art judge; that is the defense for great naturalism' (GS 7:188; AT 181). The implication is that works of art cannot be pinned down to define their truth content. It is the peculiar nature of their linguistic code that they cannot be decoded; they are like hieroglyphs whose code is unknown or lost. 'Works of art speak only as handwriting [*Schrift*]' (GS 7:189; AT 182).

More than before, the late Adorno emphasizes the enigmatic character (*Rätselcharakter*) of the artwork, its incompatibility with discursive knowledge. But at the same time, he insists on the element of truth in the work of art, which cannot be dismissed simply as reflection (imitation) or illusion, as much as these elements do play a significant structural role. The mode of art is disclosure without the certainty of disclosure. 'As a mimetic struggle against taboo, art attempts to give the answer and gives it as an answer free of judgment – but then again not; thereby, the answer becomes enigmatic, like the dread of the primordial world which changes, but does not disappear' (GS 7:193; AT 85). It is precisely this enigmatic character of art that calls for philosophical reflection and thereby reintroduces discursive language. Only philosophical reflection, which must rely on concepts, can articulate the truth content of art. The artwork also needs to be deciphered, and that deciphering is the task of criticism.

This solution seems to bring us back to a hermeneutic model: the disclosure of truth in the artwork can be achieved through interpretation; in the process of close reading the truth content can be disclosed – though only indirectly. As Adorno notes: 'The truth content of works of art is not something to be immediately identified. Just as it is only discerned in a mediated manner, so is it in itself mediated' (GS 7:195; AT 187). This suggests that art and philosophy ultimately converge insofar as the truth of the artwork is no other than the truth of philosophical reflection; what Adorno initially separated in *Aesthetic Theory* finally comes together again.

This integration is not without problems, however, since Adorno's most radical formulations about the nature of the work of art, in particular its existence as *Schrift* (writing), make it difficult to superimpose philosophical reflection as a means of revealing the truth content. *Schrift* remains elusive and ambiguous vis-à-vis conceptual cognition. Adorno achieves the integration by conflating the two concepts of language that he uses in *Aesthetic Theory*. Insisting that language contains always a universal aspect, he postulates the convergence of art and philosophy in a collective subject that clearly transcends the individual aesthetic experience. This (metaphysical) grounding allows him to bridge the gap between the discourse of philosophy and the language of the artwork. But this solution does not take into account that, for Adorno, the language of the work of art is not compatible with identifying judgments. Hence, the truth content of the artwork must remain a paradox: 'Works of art are in the most extreme tension with their truth content. While the nonconceptual truth content does not appear otherwise than in the product, it negates the product' (GS 7:199; AT 191). The truth content is not, as one might expect, simply contained in the work of art; rather, artwork and truth content remain in a state of extreme tension. The truth content, Adorno suggests, although it must appear through the product, negates the artwork as a product. To put it differently, the truth content is conceived of rigorously as a negation of the product (*das Gemachte*). The integration of the artwork and philosophical language can be achieved, as Adorno underscores, only by admitting this hiatus. Consequently, the artwork's authenticity is always problematic – not so much because it only 'imitates' reality as because it postulates what is not there and what therefore must be illusion.

As I have argued, the ultimate testing ground for Adorno's theory of language is the work of art. It is here that he forces together conceptual discourse and aesthetic expression in the concept of the truth content (*Wahrheitsgehalt*). Ultimately, this construct is bound to fail because it must conflate two incompatible notions of language: whereas conceptual language cannot escape the moment of identification in the process of making judgments (*Urteile*), the logic of the artwork is exclusively based on the configuration of its material. The more Adorno underscores its 'lack of conceptuality' (*Begriffslosigkeit*), the more he widens the gap. Hence, he must postulate a rapprochement between art's immanent logic and discursive thought; he does so either via the idea of negation or through the analogy with mathematics (GS 7:205; AT 197–98), which integrates formal logic and pure configurations without referent. Yet Adorno does not want to cancel the referent, for without empirical reality, art would lose its counterweight and hence its authenticity. Therefore, *Aesthetic Theory* must attempt to resolve this dilemma and undermine its solution at the same time. Even as he celebrates the undecidability of art, Adorno insists on the possibility of its redemption in philosophical reflection.

More than other members of the Frankfurt School such as Horkheimer or Marcuse, Adorno was keenly aware of the embeddedness of philosophy in language, especially of the linguistic constraints of philosophical discourse. In this respect he was indebted, without explicitly saying so, to Nietzsche's critique of traditional metaphysics and its linguistic models. Insofar as Nietzsche's philosophy has provided a new linguistic paradigm, traditional models of signification have become problematic: the quest for truth is no longer firmly grounded in concepts. Clearly, however, Adorno did not follow Nietzsche's path of language critique, which foregrounds the arbitrary nature of signs. As much as he questioned the legitimacy of traditional philosophical discourse and stressed the problem of the copula in any judgment (*Urteil*), Adorno did not want to sever signifiers, meaning, and referents. In other words, he did not follow modern linguistics as it was developed by Saussure and then radicalized in poststructuralist thought. The structuralist model had no appeal for him because it separates semiotic and semantic aspects, whereas Adorno maintained the need for concepts and categories as modes of conveying thought. Although skeptical of conventional philosophical language, he did not share the fundamental doubt that philosophical categories are the mere result of language: that is, the result of an effect produced in a particular language such as Greek or German. With Kant and Hegel, he maintained the legitimacy of reason against radical nominalism and positivism.

Still, Adorno was neither a Kantian nor a Hegelian in any dogmatic sense. His affinity to German idealism, I suggest, was not based on dogmatic faith in Kant's and Hegel's positions; rather, it reflected his commitment to rational conceptual operations – despite their problematic nature. At the same time, he emphasized the deficiency of traditional logic in its desire to impose identity at the expense of both the subject and the object. This distancing from traditional logic is already clear during the early 1940s in his discussions with Horkheimer, and it is also strongly articulated in *Dialectic of Enlightenment* (1944). Adorno's resistance to the philosophical discourse takes the form of foregrounding an oppositional discourse, which he found almost exclusively in art and literature. As Susan Buck-Morss has suggested, his counterdiscourse or countermodel was deeply indebted to Benjamin's writing of the 1920s, notably the study of the German *Trauerspiel*.[9] The logic of mimesis (*unsinnliche Ähnlichkeit*) complements and corrects conceptual logic.

Benjamin's pre-Marxist texts rely on mystical inspiration rather than on modern linguistic theory. As he remarks in his essay 'On Language as Such and on the Language of Man,' for Benjamin 'every expression of human mental life can be understood as a kind of language.'[10] More important, Benjamin stresses the distinction between spiritual character (*geistiges Wesen*) and strictly linguistic character (*sprachliches Wesen*), which serves as a tool to express and communicate the spiritual character. But insofar as the spiritual essence can be communicated, it becomes identical with its linguistic character, which means that 'all language communicates itself.'[11] For Benjamin, persons and things articulate themselves *in* language rather than *through* language. The distinction is crucial because it separates the conventional theory of language, which defines the word as a tool, and a theological theory in which God's creation becomes complete when humans give names to things. Ultimately, for Benjamin, the nature of language can be understood only in the context of a theological model grounded in sacrifice.

It seems that Adorno was less interested in the theological aspects of Benjamin's work than in its implicit critique of conventional secular linguistic theories. Furthermore, for Adorno the music critic, Benjamin's notion of a variety of languages (painting, sculpture, poetry) was particularly important because it enabled him to relate music to the discourse of philosophy. More specifically, the symbolic nature of artistic languages (expression) – for Benjamin the supplement of communication (*Mitteilung*) – allowed the articulation of that which cannot be communicated (*das Nicht-Mitteilbare*). In this context the idea of mimesis played an important role in Adorno's late writings. Especially in *Aesthetic Theory* he relies on the notion of mimesis in order to differentiate between conceptual language and the language of art, which he sees as an older, even archaic mode of expression.[12]

Adorno underscores the mimetic element in modern art as well: works of the avant-garde are involved in the transformation of communicative language into mimetic language (GS 7:171; AT 164). Although he never offers a formal definition of mimesis, his frequent use of the term in *Aesthetic Theory* suggests a sharp distinction between the 'language' of the artwork – which remains without language (*sprachlos*) – and any form of discursive language. Mimetic language precedes – in archaic as well as modern artworks – the split between subject and object implied in the

241

signifying use of discursive language. For Adorno, mimesis invokes the primal history of the subject and its link to nature. Hence, he suggests the proximity of the aesthetic to mimesis in archaic art and underscores the link between magic and mimesis. In magical praxis the agent seeks not to imitate but to approximate nature, thereby creating a moment of close affinity. Through mimesis the work of art remains connected to nature beyond the principle of imitation. The act of mimesis is bound up with art's prespiritual aspect (*das Vorgeistige*), while the spiritual moment is linked to the aspect of construction in the artwork. Both are indispensable. In art, Adorno argues, mimesis enables expression, not as an arbitrary articulation of the subject but as an alternative form of knowledge (GS 7:87; AT 80–81). Where Benjamin emphasized the religious ground, Adorno stresses the dualistic nature of language: its conceptual nature on the one hand, and its mimetic moment on the other. For Adorno this dualism remains an unresolved dialectial opposition. Each mode of language validates the other without the possibility of synthesis.

10. Epilogue: Critical Theory after Adorno

✳

THE inner form of Adorno's writings makes it difficult if not impossible to offer a conclusion that summarizes his ideas. These remarks aim, instead, to explore the impact on his work of the present historical and theoretical constellation. Since the mid-1980s Adorno's status within the discourse of philosophy has changed; he has turned, it seems, into a classic. Although he has not necessarily become less controversial, the ongoing and at times heated debates about his work have taken on a different character. Admitting that one can no longer either accept or reject his claims on the basis of their dogmatic judgments, the discussion has increasingly been concerned with the process of appropriating Adorno, with discerning his legacy for the present.

This shift has clearly not led to a purely historicist attitude toward Adorno, but it has altered the parameters and the spirit of the discussion. Twenty-five years after his death, his work is distant enough to allow for competing approaches that strive to connect his negative dialectics with contemporary theoretical positions. This is ultimately true even for those interpreters who have called for a return to the 'true' Adorno, since their claim is made from a historical position clearly different from his. For the neo-Adornians, his writings serve as a platform to fend off as illegitimate later theoretical developments (such as poststructuralism) and, in particular, changes within Critical Theory. In other words, even orthodox neo-Adornians are no longer strict Adornians, for their use of his work is part of his *Nachgeschichte* (Benjamin). Efforts to refute Adorno – for instance from an orthodox Marxist or neoconservative position – become part of this logic as well. Any attempt at an unmediated confrontation with Adorno's position is likely to fail because it represses the historicity of his work – an element that Adorno himself repeatedly underscored.

The call for a faithful return to Adorno's theory as it was articulated and disseminated during his lifetime demands the impossible, for it turns the necessary task of reconstruction into a principle of dogmatic faith. This approach offers two arguments. One is that Adorno's thought is true and therefore relevant for the present, whatever historical changes have occurred in the meantime. But this argument not only removes Adorno's theory from its historical ground and makes of it a timeless theoretical construct but also contradicts a presupposition central to his theory: that all theory, as historically determined, communicates with its own time. In other words, this approach must eliminate an essential moment of Adorno's thought. The alternative argument assumes that the historical constellation that motivated Adorno's writings is, despite many empirical changes, basically identical to our own; thus, the structure of the historical process itself reconfirms Adorno's philosophy. The problematic nature of this perspective is more difficult to demonstrate, since it grounds Adorno's relevance for the present in our own historical conditions, which, according to this argument, can be adequately revealed through Adorno's theory. Yet it is possible to hold on dogmatically to Adorno's analysis of modern society and its culture only by repressing those elements that do not fit into his conceptual apparatus or by resolutely excluding alternative readings of the present constellation. Ultimately, either as a timeless philosophical construct or as the most significant response to the present, the truth content of Adorno's work is made an article of faith and a personal commitment – a development that would have troubled Adorno as a self-reflective critic and theorist.

Similar difficulties arise when we explore Adorno's work from within. It seems that his aesthetic theory, as well as his theory of history and his more implicit negative anthropology, cannot be upheld in a straightforward manner, because the dogmatic articulation of one part undercuts and is questioned by conflicting elements. The essence of his philosophy can be presented only in the form of paradoxes designed to expose the truth content of his writings by stressing the impossibility of resolving the contradictory moments of his thought. Furthermore, Adorno's presentation points to the social origin of these paradoxes. The structure of his thought undercuts any effort to reach a clean systematic solution that can postulate an unproblematic synthesis of reason and art, history and progress, function and meaning. For Adorno, resistance to a dialectical synthesis and rejection of systematic philosophy are the only ways to ensure the possibility of getting closer to the truth. His theory must rigorously question its own stability in order to preserve the utopian moment that makes theoretical articulation worthwhile.

Both the call for a return to Adorno and the emphatic rejection of his aesthetic theory have frequently been linked to the concept of aesthetic autonomy: that is, to the claim that the artwork is irreducible and cannot be communicated through extra-aesthetic means. In the course of such discussion, aesthetic autonomy becomes either a moment of social opposition or a sign of cultural elitism (for instance, in the popular culture debate). But Adorno's aesthetic theory is more ambivalent than either camp assumes. It contains two separate but related claims: autonomy and absolute truth. While the concept of autonomy can be grounded historically in the theory of social differentiation (according to which the aesthetic sphere was separated and 'set free' from social and moral functions during the eighteenth century), the concept of absolute aesthetic truth makes a more radical and exclusive claim: it interprets the autonomy of art as the negation of other (competing) discourses or, more specifically, as a fundamental critique of rationality. In the first instance, artistic production and aesthetic experience are compatible with rational discourses (economic, legal, moral). The concept of absolute aesthetic truth, however, creates an opposition between the artwork and rationality which has to be solved dialectically. For Adorno, as we have seen, aesthetic theory cannot be grounded simply in philosophy; he insists on the intertwinement of the two discourses and their need for reciprocal deconstruction. The concept of autonomy is compatible with a model of social differentiation, but the conception of absolute truth is grounded in the unique character of the aesthetic experience.

Because aesthetic experience needs both elements, Adorno conceives of them as the fundamental antinomy of his aesthetic theory.[1] The solution of this antinomy, which in Adorno's work is mostly retained as a paradox, requires a double strategy: on the one hand, it calls for a deconstruction of his category of negativity, particularly of its tendency to conflate aesthetic and social negativity; on the other hand, it requires a critique of the concept of absolute aesthetic truth, especially of its romantic versions but also of poststructuralist models, which share the romantic assumption that art itself should be the locus of the critique of reason.

Poststructuralist theory has reinforced and even deepened the paradoxical configuration presented in Adorno's texts and therefore tended to emphasize these moments in its effort to appropriate him; within Critical Theory, however, the reception and appropriation of Adorno has taken a different turn, placing the emphasis on the resolution of his paradoxes. The new paradigm developed in contemporary Critical Theory, mainly through a different linguistic model, has encouraged a restatement of Adorno's philosophy freed from its paradoxical structure.

One fruitful approach would be to argue in favor of a critical use of Adorno's theory, an appropriation that would make allowance for social and cultural changes after the 1960s and would also take into account the personal aspects of Adorno's response to the problems of his own time. One could not only acknowledge the marks that fascism and the Cold War left on his work but also recognize the determinants of the specific philosophical constellation that he found as a given for his own work. In fact, this approach has been a prevalent strategy within the second generation of the Frankfurt School – in the work of Jürgen Habermas, Oskar Negt, Alexander Kluge, Peter Bürger, and Albrecht Wellmer, for instance. To varying degrees (and not without internal conflicts and disagreements), these critics have defended the continued significance and relevance of Adorno's thought – once it has been reconstructed and modified in accordance with contemporary needs and the altered requirements of the present theoretical debate.

This strategy of adjustment through modifications can be pursued in various ways. One method is historicizing Adorno: that is, assigning him a specific but also limited place in the history of critical theory (Bürger, Jameson). Another method is emphasizing aspects of his work that are supposedly immediately relevant to the present by connecting certain elements of his theory with more recent theoretical developments such as poststructualism (Wellmer). A third mode is distancing, which recognizes Adorno's importance in the past but insists on the need for fundamental revisions (Habermas); this strategy sometimes comes close to a rejection of the more systematic claims of Adorno's philosophy.

The first method of preserving Adorno's philosophy delimits it historically through a phase model which, in one form or another, argues that his negative dialectics was the adequate theoretical articulation of its own time but is no longer fully appropriate for the altered parameters of the present historical situation. The now conventional distinction between modernism and postmodernism can be (and has been) easily applied to Adorno's work. This approach would place his writings squarely within the category of modernism in order to mark it as an older and no longer adequate model vis-à-vis rapidly changing historical conditions. More specifically, this argument would be linked to a new assessment of the economy, an assessment that underscores the transition from monopoly capitalism to global imperialist capitalism (Ernest Mandel), from Fordist capitalism to a decentered, post-Fordist structure (David Harvey). In this model, Adorno's obvious attachment to a theory of monopoly capitalism would also turn him into a defender of cultural modernism, reluctant to accept the legitimacy of the postmodern artwork because he is locked into a binary logic of high and low culture with its opposition of aesthetic autonomy and the culture industry.

The phase model has the advantage of demarcating Adorno's historical limits, enabling us to situate his work and thereby to measure the significance and relevance of his thought for the present debate. This clear and rigid historical definition also has its drawbacks, however, since it fails to allow for the possibility of locating Adorno's place on the map of contemporary theoretical discussion in a more complex way. A phase model tends to overlook the internal tensions within his writings, the fact that they point in more than one direction. Adorno clearly acknowledges the changes in the structure of aesthetic production during the twentieth century, changes that he describes as the aging process of modern art and music. For him, this process implies the loss of negativity in the transition from the early avant-garde to its later stages. But although his verdict underscores the loss of negativity and thereby a loss of authenticity, the shift itself is a moment of history that his theory does not thematize. One possible response might be to break down the rigid boundaries of the phase model in order to consider the opposition of the modern and the post-modern as two sides of a larger dialectic and thus to work out an alternative solution for the fate of art in the twentieth century. This might be done, for instance, within the context of systems theory (Niklas Luhmann)[2] but also in a modified form of Critical Theory as we find it in the theory of Habermas. In either case, Adorno's version of dialectics is replaced by a concept of social differentiation that allows for a broader conception of the aesthetic realm. As a result, the definition of the modern artwork becomes a special case within a larger context – a case that focuses on a specific historical moment and certain aspects of aesthetic production.

By replacing a dialectical approach (based on a logic of opposition) with a model of differentiation, more recent Critical Theory can resolve Adorno's aporetic position and reintegrate the legitimate but separate claims of art and philosophy – at the expense, however, of the extreme claim that Adorno makes for the truth content of the work of art. We find a similar move, although more radical in its thrust, in systems theory. Again, through the concept of differentiation, systems theory overcomes the need for a binary logic and the paradoxes – even in Adorno's version of negative dialectics – that result from it.

For Adorno's aesthetic theory, the link between art and social structure or, more broadly speaking, the dialectic of art and civilization is indispensable. Though he insists on the need for micro-analysis with respect to the artwork, he constructs the theoretical frame at the level of macroanalysis through a social and historical dialectic. By way of the concept of the monad, the exploration of the artwork is always at the same time an examination of larger social processes. For Adorno, social process is defined in terms of an internal logic that determines the process as necessary and irreversible. For this reason the decline of modernism appears as inevitable in Adorno's writings. Consequently, the postmodern artwork remains an illegitimate phenomenon.

One way of opening up this closure is to reconsider the link between social and aesthetic theory, to break up its rigid logic through the recognition of contingency. If we replace Adorno's determinate paradigm with an indeterminate one, we can read the development of modernist and postmodernist art along different lines, conceiving the artwork no longer as essence – whether negative or positive – but as virtuality.[3] Art is thus set free from the tragic logic of history prescribed by Adorno's theory. From the perspective of a sociological logic that stresses functional differentiation in modern societies, the literary system does not have to represent social totality. The emancipation of literature as a sub-system means the construction of virtual worlds that allow the pluralization of the empirical world and thereby also demonstrate its contingency. Thus, the artwork functions as the construction of an alternative possibility rather than as determinate negation. This solution would lead to parody and the possibility of a post-Adornian phase of art characterized by neither affirmation nor negation.

Breaking the spell of Adorno's aesthetic theory becomes feasible if we reinterpret the history of modern art from 1850 to the present in the light of a multifunctional concept of the work of art – as distinct from Adorno's exclusive concern with negativity. From the systems theory viewpoint the process of enlightenment is then read as a process of foregrounding latent structures to the point where they become manifest and thereby available to criticism. In this attempt to recast modernity, the concept of parody becomes important. In order to grasp the specific functions of parody in the present age, however, one has to distinguish between its traditional and modern forms: traditional parody ultimately confirms the pregiven hierarchical order even while manifestly subverting it; modern parody defines itself as a generalized mode of criticism that turns (for instance, through irony) against tradition per se and undermines the literary system in general.

249

A reformulation of Adorno's aesthetic theory would also call for a reassessment of his social theory. Here his concept of negative dialectics is bound up with a theory of social history that relies heavily on narrative devices. This is particularly evident in *Dialectic of Enlightenment,* where the critique of Western enlightenment presupposes that the history of Western civilization from Homer to the present can be narrated as a singular and linear dialectic development centered on the concept of rationality. In this respect, the study stays, as Herbert Schnädelbach has argued, within the context of a social myth.[4] What Adorno and Horkheimer narrate is the history of the subject itself: that is, its emancipation through the domination of nature, as well as its renewed submission to myth in the form of modern science. The philosophy of history presented in *Dialectic of Enlightenment,* insofar as it follows a narrative form, partakes of the very mythic structure it means to criticize. As a social myth (in the tradition of Rousseau and Hegel), it falls short of a theoretically grounded critique in which instrumental reason and rationality can be differentiated and analyzed as parts of separate and changing historical contexts. Instead, it insists on the possibility of exposing the essence of Western civilization and thought through a narrative that focuses on the transformation of a subject called 'Enlightenment.'

The question is whether Adorno's work remains completely bound up with this model or whether it can be recast in theoretical terms that would no longer conflate narrative history and a theory of history. To put it differently, one must ask whether negative dialectic can retreat from the presupposition of an absolute as the Archimedean point of the dialectic process. To do so, it has to withstand the temptation of asserting the totality of distinct historical narratives and make room for historical contingency. This means, for instance, that the dialectic of enlightenment has to be reconstructed as a complex process of specific tendencies, tensions, and contradictions, rather than as the unfolding of a preconceived (absolute) logic. While *Dialectic of Enlightenment* contains elements of such an understanding, its overall structures remain indebted to a narrative structure of history. Although it is only in *Negative Dialectics* that Adorno resolutely confronts

the problem of theoretical negativity – as distinct from a historical dialectic – a similar tendency can be detected in his later
essays, which undercut the totalizing perspective of *Dialectic of
Enlightenment.*

Thus his essays and *Negative Dialectics* might possess the actuality and relevance for the present that *Dialectic of Enlightenment*
cannot claim. From this perspective, one must stress the inevitable mutilation of Adorno's late theory in the post-Adornian shift
toward a linguistic paradigm. The shift has reshaped his position
in significant ways. The critique of Adorno's theory in Habermas's
theory of communicative action, as well as in Luhmann's systems
theory, although completely legitimate from the point of view
of the new paradigm, eliminates a crucial aspect of Adorno's
thought: namely, the idea of redemption (*Versöhnung*). Adorno
raises the possibility of happiness through a redemption of nature, but because this claim cannot be derived from formal principles, the substance of Adorno's thought cannot be grounded in a
form that would satisfy present standards of rationalist theory.
His philosophical paradigm is oriented toward substantial issues
that it means to explore, rather than toward procedural questions
(an orientation we find in Habermas's theory). Any defense of
Adorno will have to take this difference into account.

The enduring significance of Adorno's paradigm of negative
dialectics – beyond its specific importance for an aesthetic theory
in which art ultimately explicates the aporias of discursive language – depends on the concept of experience. Negative dialectics
can be redeemed as a form of immanent critique grounded in
experience (*Erfahrung*), but this concept of experience must not
be confused or conflated with empiricist notions in which a process of inductions is supposed to lead us to truth. Instead, Adorno
speaks of *Erfahrung* as an experience of aesthetic negativity that
claims a sovereign status for art.[5] Yet this mode of critique can be
separated from aesthetic forms; its dialectic procedure remains
discursive, although not bound by rigorous rules of rational argu-
mentation. Indeed, Adorno's advantage may be that his version of
dialectics does not exclude those forms of knowledge which do
not follow rigorous rules of epistemological grounding.

More important, one has to reconsider the aspect of materiality in Adorno's theory, which is articulated through the concept of nature. For him, the redemption of nature (inside and outside the individual) implies more than the possibility of rational consensus – or of a second-degree observer in systems theory, for that matter. Adorno's thought retains an idea of experience that brings together its material-corporeal and its cognitive aspects. In his model the concept of mimesis then becomes an index for the other side of experience – an element that later Critical Theory has either eliminated or marginalized.

Clearly, Adorno's integration into the present theoretical debate cannot be a smooth one. As we have seen, his writings resist easy and complete absorption or transformation into later paradigms. Whatever their deficits in theoretical articulation, they hold on to important moments that have remained unexplored in later models. In particular, Adorno's version of negative dialectics preserves the moment of the concrete that defies the conceptual apparatus: hence its willingness to be on the edge of rationality and to question the competence of the philosophical discourse to grasp the material experience of the concrete.

Adorno's more recent status as a classic should not be confused with a relegation of his work to a closed-off past. On the contrary, the increasing removal of his oeuvre from the immediate needs of the present can be an advantage rather than a disadvantage, as long as its historical distance is acknowledged and not concealed. For one thing, his 'outdated' theory can remind us of those significant moments within Critical Theory that need to be preserved despite their problematic articulation. Adorno's vigorous insistence on the impossibility of traditional philosophy, however much his own argument was couched in metaphysical terms, can act as a counterweight against a procedural or functional structure of theory. By questioning the competence of philosophy to describe and define the realm of the artwork, Adorno – far from seeking an aesthetic solution to his dilemma – redeems the moment of failure in the philosophical discourse and thereby articulates its limits. Through a paradoxical articulation of his theory he can hold together what for later Critical Theory has become a tension or gap between its normative and the descriptive level. Although it is correct that Adorno emphasized self-reflexivity as crucial to critical theory, this aspect – important as it is vis-à-vis objectivist definitions of theory – does not express completely his lasting contribution to the contemporary philosophical discourse; the concept of second-order observation in systems theory can claim similar accomplishments. What distinguishes Adorno's notion of theory from systems theory – apart from its structure – is its own acknowledgment of the overwhelming force of human suffering, a suffering that has defied traditional humanism.

Notes

❋

CHAPTER 1

1. See Robert Hullot-Kentor, 'Notes on *Dialectic of Enlightenment*: Translating the Odysseus Essay,' *New German Critique* 56 (spring–summer 1992): 101–8.

2. Examples are the feminist reading of *Dialectic of Enlightenment* by Andrew Hewitt, 'A Feminine Dialectic of the Enlightenment: Horkheimer and Adorno Revisited,' which challenges the traditional philosophical appropriation of the text; and Miriam Hansen's rereading of Adorno's theory of mass culture, 'Mass Culture as "Hieroglyphic Writing": The Alternative Adorno Revisited,' which critically responds to the postmodernist attack on Adorno's work, both in *New German Critique* 56 (spring–summer 1992): 143–70 and 43–75 respectively.

3. See, e.g., Eugene Lunn, *Marxism and Modernism: An Historical Study of Lukács, Brecht, and Adorno* (Berkeley: University of California Press, 1982).

4. For a comprehensive study of the reception of Critical Theory in North America, see Martin Jay, 'Adorno in America,' in *Permanent Exiles: Essays on the Intellectual Migration from Germany to America* (New York: Columbia University Press, 1985), 120–40.

5. Paul Piccone, General Introduction to *The Essential Frankfurt School Reader*, ed. Andrew Arato and Eike Gebhardt (New York: Urizen Books, 1977), xviii.

6. Fredric Jameson, *Marxism and Form: Twentieth Century Dialectical Theories of Literature* (Princeton: Princeton University Press, 1971), 58.

7. See, e.g., Rainer Nägele, ed., *Benjamin's Ground: New Readings of Walter Benjamin* (Detroit MI: Wayne State University Press, 1988).

8. Rainer Nägele, 'The Scene of the Other: Theodor W. Adorno's Negative Dialectic in the Context of Poststructuralism,' *Boundary Two* 11 (1983): 1–2, 67.

9. For an extensive discussion of Adorno's relationship to Heidegger, see Hermann Mörchen, *Adorno und Heidegger: Untersuchung einer philosophischen Kommunikationsverweigerung* (Stuttgart: Klett-Cotta, 1981). See also Fred Dallmayr's review of Mörchen's book in *Diacritics* 19, nos.3–4 (1989): 82–100.

10. See Martin Jay, *Marxism and Totality: The Adventures of a Concept from Lukács to Habermas* (Berkeley: University of California Press, 1982).

11. Nägele, 'The Scene of the Other,' 71.

12. Jim Collins, *Uncommon Cultures: Popular Culture and Post-Modernism* (New York: Routledge, 1987), 7.

13. Collins, *Uncommon Cultures,* 10.

14. Hansen's 'Mass Culture as "Hieroglyphic Writing"' can be understood as a response to and critique of the postmodernist position insofar as she explicitly uses Adorno's writings on mass culture to challenge the narrow reading of *Dialectic of Enlightenment* in the postmodernist culture debate. By focusing on the concept of the hieroglyph, Hansen underscores the masking of reification in the production of images by the culture industry, a masking that is coupled, however, with an element of authentic desire. Consequently, her reading emphasizes the critical moment in the silent film. She speaks of a 'double vision' where reified images are both vehicles of regressive consumption and means of articulating authentic moments of modernity. This argument implies an emphatic defense of Adorno against stereotypical charges of elitism. Yet by the same token, Hansen marks the difference between Adorno's use of the hieroglyph and its function in Derridian film theory – an unmistakable rejection of poststructuralist readings of Adorno's theory of mass culture.

15. Tania Modleski, Introduction to *Studies in Entertainment: Critical Approaches to Mass Culture,* ed. Tania Modleski (Bloomington: Indiana University Press, 1986).

16. Modleski, Introduction, xi.

17. Such a critical assessment of popular music, making use of Adorno's analysis, is offered in Bernard Gendron, 'Theodor Adorno Meets the Cadillacs,' in Modleski, *Studies in Entertainment,* 18–38. Gendron argues against the fashionable dismissal of Adorno's theory of mass culture and tries to show that it provides significant insights because Adorno's analysis of the musical material stresses its lack of innovation compared with avant-garde music. At the same time, Gendron convincingly demonstrates that Adorno, by foregrounding the question of tonality, misses the achievement of popular music in other areas, such as rhythm.

18. Fredric Jameson, 'Reification and Utopia in Mass Culture,' *Social Text* 1, no.1 (1979): 130–48.

19. Jameson, 'Reification,' 133.

20. Andreas Huyssen, *After the Great Divide: Modernism, Mass Culture,*

Postmodernism (Bloomington: Indiana University Press, 1986), 16–43.

21. Fredric Jameson, *Late Marxism: Adorno or the Persistence of the Dialectic* (London: Verso, 1990), 5.

22. The critical response to *Late Marxism* has made it quite clear that Jameson's construct of a postmodernist Marxism in the work of Adorno (which, of course, is Jameson's way of reformulating his own position) has met with more disapproval than acceptance. By and large, postmodernist critics are not inclined to rescue Adorno, and poststructuralist readings – which receive bad marks in Jameson's version – are usually not interested in a dialectical project that upholds the concept of totality.

23. Jameson, *Late Marxism,* 249.

24. See Peter Osborne's review essay 'A Marxism for the Postmodern? Jameson's Adorno,' *New German Critique* 56 (spring–summer 1992): 171–92; also Robert Hullot-Kentor's highly polemical commentary 'Suggested Reading: Jameson on Adorno,' and Eva Geulen's more balanced review, 'A Matter of Tradition,' both in *Telos* 89 (fall 1991): 155–60.

25. It is interesting to note, however, the Paul Piccone has not changed his critical position vis-à-vis Adorno. In his reply to Hullot-Kentor, 'Does Critical Theory Need Saints or Foundations?' *Telos* 87 (spring 1991): 146–57, he emphasizes the need for critical testing. See also the differentiated position of Russell A. Berman in *Modern Culture and Critical Theory* (Madison: University of Wisconsin Press, 1989).

26. Hullot-Kentor's review of Jameson's *Late Marxism* ('Suggested Reading') is an extreme example of this procedure. In the barrage of polemical criticism neither Jameson's position nor that of the reviewer emerges very clearly. To understand the direction of Hullot-Kentor's critique, one must return to his essay 'Back to Adorno,' *Telos* 81 (fall 1989): 5–29.

27. Hullot-Kentor, 'Back to Adorno.'

28. See also J. M. Bernstein, *The Fate of Art: Aesthetic Alienation from Kant to Derrida and Adorno* (State College: Pennsylvania State University Press, 1992). Bernstein argues that Adorno's work, like that of Derrida, has to be seen as a radical critique of idealism, carried out through a philosophy of negative dialectics and aesthetic theory. But unlike Hullot-Kentor, Bernstein validates the proximity to Heidegger and especially to Derrida, at least in his analysis of *Aesthetic Theory.* In his final evaluation, however, Bernstein tends to distance himself more carefully from an implicit affirmation of capitalism by post-

modernism and deconstruction. Thus, for him a politics of the aesthetic is necessary.

29. Michael Sullivan and John Lysaker, 'Between Impotence and Illusion: Adorno's Art of Theory and Practice,' *New German Critique* 57 (fall 1992): 87–122.

30. Among recent interpreters who mean to rescue Adorno's position, Lambert Zuidervaart (*Adorno's Aesthetic Theory: The Redemption of Illusion* [Cambridge: MIT Press, 1991]) has a special place insofar as he is considerably more conscious of the historical context of his own position within a post-Adornian configuration. Although he insists on the lasting importance of Adorno's work and clearly rejects a merely historicist approach, he is open to criticism of Adorno, especially the criticism coming from within Critical Theory (Albrecht Wellmer, Fredric Jameson). For Zuidervaart, the legacy of Adorno, esp. his aesthetic theory, has to be recaptured in view of the noticeable distance between the historical moment of his texts and the contemporary constellation. At precisely this point, however, Zuidervaart's own critique appears to break down. Although he gives a thorough and surprisingly sympathetic account (276–89) of Wellmer's critique, his own counterarguments simply reassert the lasting significance of Adorno's philosophy. In the end, he reinscribes Adorno's insistence on the centrality of human suffering for art and philosophy without paying much attention to the Habermasian argument that the specific historical conditions under which Adorno wrote are quite different from the present situation.

31. See chapter 2.

32. See Hewitt, 'A Feminine Dialectic of the Enlightenment'; Hansen, 'Mass Culture as "Hieroglyphic Writing." '

33. Martin Jay, *Adorno* (Cambridge: Harvard University Press, 1984); Rolf Wiggershaus, *Die Frankfurter Schule: Geschichte, Theoretische Entwicklung, Politische Bedeutung* (München: Carl Hanser, 1986); Helmut Dubiel, *Wissenschaftsorganisation und politische Erfahrung: Studien zur frühen kritischen Theorie* (Frankfurt am Main: Suhrkamp, 1978).

34. See Hewitt, 'A Feminine Dialectic of the Enlightenment.'

35. Osborne, e.g. ('A Marxism for the Postmodern?'), argues that there is a fundamental incompatibility between Jameson's method of reading and Adorno's philosophical position. Osborne is especially critical of Jameson's procedure of 'translating' Adorno's language into the idiom of the most recent postmodernist debate. Can one really, to give just one example, conflate Adorno's concept of the constellation with Althusser's concept of structural causality? What Osborne

tries to demonstrate is that Jameson's reluctance to perform an immanent reading (and critique) raises not just a minor philological question but a central issue for Jameson's and, by extension, our grasp of Adorno's position. If the emphasis is placed, as in the case of *Late Marxism,* on a strategy of 'rewriting' Marxism, the exact historical structure of Adorno's Marxist theory becomes a secondary problem. Consequently, Jameson's reading tends to move away from the text, sometimes to such a degree that it contradicts its textual basis.

CHAPTER 2

1. The most complete account of Adorno's life and reception in the United States is to be found in Jay, 'Adorno in America,' 120–40.
2. Andreas Huyssen, 'Adorno in Reverse: From Hollywood to Richard Wagner,' in *After the Great Divide,* 16–43.
3. For the reaction of Trotsky and his group, see Alan M. Wald, *The New York Intellectuals: The Rise and Decline of the Anti-Stalinist Left from the 1930s to the 1980s* (Chapel Hill: University of North Carolina Press, 1987), 128–38.
4. Richard H. Pells, *The Liberal Mind in a Conservative Age* (New York: Harper & Row, 1985), 76 f. Though Pells's assessment is generally correct, he tends to downplay the resistance of the radical anti-Stalinist left to mainstream liberalism and the Democrats. During the early 1940s it was not only James P. Cannon, Max Schachtman, and the Trotskyist radicals who defended a strictly revolutionary Marxist position, attacking the Stalinists from the left, but also intellectuals such as Sidney Hook, Irving Howe, and Dwight Macdonald, who later distanced themselves from their revolutionary past and insisted on a Marxist, antiliberal position during World War II. See Wald, *The New York Intellectuals,* 193–96, 199–210.
5. Helmut Dubiel, *Theory and Politics: Studies in the Development of Critical Theory,* trans. Benjamin Gregg (Cambridge: MIT Press, 1985). The exception was Herbert Marcuse, who, it seems, remained more faithful to the earlier program. See Douglas Kellner, *Herbert Marcuse and the Crisis of Marxism* (Berkeley: University of California Press, 1984).
6. Although Sidney Hook, stressing the imperialist character of the impending war, argued during the 1930s that it should not be defended in terms of an opposition between democratic and fascist regimes, during the 1940s the New York intellectuals came out in favor of the war against fascism. See Wald, *The New York Intellectuals,* 193–99.
7. Pells, *The Liberal Mind,* 18.
8. For this reason Macdonald, together with the editors of *Partisan*

Review, originally opposed the war. After the Hitler-Stalin Pact he joined the Socialist Workers Party and defended its pro-war stance, but he continued to define himself as an anti-Stalinist revolutionary struggling for socialism within the United States. See Wald, *The New York Intellectuals,* 199–207.

9. See Pells, *The Liberal Mind,* 21–23.

10. During the 1930s the position of Sidney Hook in *Towards the Understanding of Karl Marx* (1933) and of Max Eastman paralleled that of the early Lukács in *History and Class-Consciousness;* they used Lukácsian arguments to attack the Stalinist orthodoxy. See Wald, *The New York Intellectuals,* 118–27. The issue of the proletariat as the revolutionary agent was still alive during the early 1940s.

11. By and large, the editors of the liberal *New Republic* were pleased by developments in 1944–45. The journal gave public support to FDR's position in Yalta and Potsdam. The journal *Common Sense,* on the other hand, with its anti-Stalinist agenda, was disappointed to see a development in Europe that did not encourage radical democracy. See William O'Neill, *A Better World: Stalinism and the American Intellectuals* (New Brunswick NJ: Transaction, 1990), 110–15.

12. Hannah Arendt, *The Origins of Totalitarianism* (1951; New York: World, 1958).

13. See Wald, *The New York Intellectuals,* 268.

14. Pells, *The Liberal Mind,* 75. As Irving Howe points out in his memoirs, *Partisan Review* shifted its position after the war by moving away from Marxism altogether, becoming fascinated instead by French writers such as Sartre and Camus. Kafka replaced Trotsky. See Irving Howe, *A Margin of Hope: An Intellectual Autobiography* (San Diego: Harcourt Brace Jovanovich, 1982), 130–31, 143. The Waldorf Conference of 1949 was, in Howe's words, 'perhaps the last major effort of American Stalinism to reestablish itself as a cultural force in this country' (156). The anti-Stalinist intellectuals, though not effective in their opposition at that conference, had a much greater impact in later years. Also see O'Neill, *A Better World,* 143–68.

15. At the same time, James Burnham, in *The Managerial Revolution* (1941) and *The Machiavellians* (1943), undercut the conventional distinction between democratic and fascist states, insisting on the similarities between the New Deal in America, Nazi Germany, and the Soviet Union. After 1945 Burnham joined the left revisionists and focused his attack on Stalinist Russia as the embodiment of an antidemocratic system. It should be noted that Burnham's position was rather eccentric during the earlier 1940s, as Macdonald's and William Philipps's critiques make clear; Philipps, especially, denied the con-

tention that Stalinism was the logical extension of Marxism. See Wald, *The New York Intellectuals,* 280–82.

16. Another important line of criticism in the work of Adorno concerned psychological patterns and mental structures; see, e.g., the collective project of Theodor Adorno with Else Frenkel-Brunswick, Daniel J. Levinson, and R. Nevitt Sanford *The Authoritarian Personality* (New York: Harper & Row, 1950).

17. Seymour Martin Lipset, *Political Man: The Social Bases of Politics* (Garden City NY: Doubleday, 1960), 445. Under these conditions the work of the Frankfurt School could find a better reception among American left intellectuals. Thus Adorno claimed that Riesman failed to acknowledge the impact of Critical Theory in his work.

18. American critics such as Lewis Mumford, Gordon Allport, and Harold Lasswell had begun to examine the effects of the mass media during the 1930s. Pells allows that the Frankfurt School contributed to this effort but overlooks the difference in attitude. Adorno clearly rejected the neutral empirical method of the new radio research; he was closer to such critics as Macdonald and Clement Greenberg, who foregrounded the broader cultural and social ramifications of a culture based on mass media.

19. For the theory of state capitalism, see Friedrich Pollock, 'State Capitalism: Its Possibilities and Limitations,' in Arato and Gebhardt, *The Essential Frankfurt School Reader,* 71–94.

20. Dubiel, *Theory and Politics,* 79.

21. See also Moishe Postone and Barbara Brick, 'Critical Theory and Political Economy,' in *On Max Horkheimer: New Perspectives,* ed. Seyla Benhabib et al. (Cambridge: MIT Press, 1993), 215–96.

22. For an analysis of Mills's relationship to the Institute, see Martin Jay, 'The Jews and the Frankfurt School: Critical Theory's Analysis of Anti-Semitism,' in *Permanent Exiles,* 46.

23. C. Wright Mills, Introduction to *White Collar* (New York: Oxford University Press, 1956), xviii.

24. Pells, *The Liberal Mind,* 185. Also see O'Neill, *A Better World,* on the importance of the Henry Wallace campaign for the cause of the progressionists (142–60) and the Korean War as the final turning-point for the majority of American radicals (202–11).

25. For a more detailed account of this transition, see Wald, *The New York Intellectuals,* 226–63. Wald defines the transformation in terms of an ideological shift from an openly political understanding of literature to a more individual 'neoliberalist position' in writers such as Mary McCarthy and Edmund Wilson.

26. Dwight Macdonald, *Against the American Grain* (New York: Random

House, 1962), 7; Adorno, 'On Popular Music,' *Studies in Philosophy and Social Sciences* 9 (1941): 17–48.

27. Macdonald, *Against the American Grain*, 14; David Riesman, *The Lonely Crowd: A Study of the Changing American Character* (New Haven: Yale University Press, 1950).

28. Macdonald, *Against the American Grain*, 73.

29. Macdonald, *Against the American Grain*, xii.

30. In certain respects the position of Clement Greenberg, the influential modernist art critic, is even closer to Adorno's, since he does acknowledge the historical significance of the avant-garde for the evaluation of art. In 'Avant-Garde and Kitsch' (first published in *Partisan Review* 1946: rpt. in *Mass Culture*, ed. Bernard Rosenberg and David Manning White [New York: Free Press, 1957], 98–107). Greenberg uses a formalist and historical model to demonstrate the need for artistic change. The avant-garde appears as the historically needed opposition to bourgeois culture. Emphasizing the formal aspect of modern art, Greenberg insists, like Adorno, on the evolution of the aesthetic material: the absolute poem or painting is (historically) moving. Also, his definition of kitsch – i.e., mass culture – and its relationship to modern art is fairly close to Adorno's understanding of the culture industry: 'Kitsch is mechanical and operates by formulas .... Kitsch changes according to style, but remains always the same' (102). Greenberg argues that kitsch is part of a modern production system and relies on an already established cultural system whose traditions it exploits. Given the industrial character of kitsch, it is international and thereby inauthentic. Unlike Adorno and more in agreement with Macdonald, Greenberg assumes a stable cultural and artistic tradition that can serve as a foil to frame mass culture, but, more than Adorno does, he points to the close connection between high culture and political power when he discusses premodern art.

31. Clement Greenberg, 'The Plight of our Culture,' *Commentary* 15 (June 1953): 566.

32. Adorno, 'Scientific Experiences of a European Scholar in America,' in *The Intellectual Migration: Europe and America, 1930–1960*, ed. Donald Fleming and Bernard Bailyn (Cambridge: Harvard University Press, 1969), 339; GS 10 (2): 702–38.

33. Adorno et al., *The Authoritarian Personality*.

34. Adorno, 'Scientific Experiences of a European Scholar in America,' 358.

35. Wiggershaus, *Die Frankfurter Schule*, 452 f.

36. Wiggershaus, *Die Frankfurter Schule*, 450–51.

37. In this context it is crucial to distinguish an anti-Stalinist from an

anti-Communist stance. Whereas the former position allows for a variety of approaches to the issue of Marxist theory (one could agree with Marx against Stalin, or be critical of Stalinism as a strand of Marxist orthodoxy), the latter is predicated on a rigid opposition of two belief systems: Marxist theory as Communism takes on the role of a negative religion that has to be eradicated by the democratic forces in the name of Christian or at least humanist values. Although the Frankfurt School by and large was quite conscious of this distinction, its members did not always clarify their disagreement with vulgar forms of anti-Communism. Yet after its return to Germany the Frankfurt School, like the group around *Partisan Review,* could not sustain its belief in a third position and thus ended up in the liberal establishment of postwar West Germany. Unlike the editors of *Commentary,* however, Adorno did not tolerate the witch-hunts of Senator Joseph McCarthy. See Alexander Bloom, *Prodigal Sons: The New York Intellectuals and Their World* (New York: Oxford University Press, 1986), 209–15.

38. For this reason they disagreed with Herbert Marcuse's 1947 unpublished working paper in which he described the postwar situation in terms of two hostile camps: a neofascist camp led by the United States, and a Communist camp dominated by the Soviet Union. For Marcuse, both camps were antirevolutionary and therefore problematic. What Adorno and Horkheimer objected to was Marcuse's belief that one could rely on classical Marxist theory for an analysis of the postwar configuration. See Wiggershaus, *Die Frankfurter Schule,* 431–33. This disagreement parallels the split within the American left between the Trotskyist progressionists and the revisionists.

CHAPTER 3

1. Friedrich Nietzsche, 'Schopenhauer as Educator,' in *Untimely Meditations,* trans. R. J. Hollingdale (London: Cambridge University Press, 1983), 137.

2. Nietzsche, 'Schopenhauer as Educator,' 142.

3. Friedrich Nietzsche, *Werke,* ed. Karl Schlechta (Munich: Carl Hanser Verlag, 1966), 1:310.

4. See Peter Uwe Hohendahl, *Building a National Literature: The Case of Germany, 1830–1870* (Ithaca NY: Cornell University Press, 1989), 248–70.

5. See Ulrich Engelhardt, *'Bildungsbürgertum': Begriff-und Dogmengeschichte eines Etiketts* (Stuttgart: Klett, 1986); *Bildungsbürgertum im 19. Jahrhundert,* ed. Werner Conze and Jürgen Kocka (Stuttgart: Klett, 1985).

6. See Georg Jäger, *Schule und literarische Kultur* (Stuttgart: Metzler, 1981).

7. George L. Mosse, *German Jews beyond Judaism* (Bloomington: Indiana University Press, 1985).

8. See also David Sorkin, *The Transformation of German Jewry, 1780–1840* (New York: Oxford University Press, 1987), esp. 140–55.

9. For a brief biography of Adorno, see Wiggershaus, *Die Frankfurter Schule*, 82–112.

10. Wiggershaus, *Die Frankfurter Schule*, 479–565.

11. The equivalent rank in the American academy would be that of tenured associate professor.

12. This tension is exemplified in the exchange of letters between Thomas Mann, on the one hand, and Walter von Molo and Frank Thieß, on the other. See *Die große Kontroverse: Ein Briefwechsel um Deutschland*, ed. J. F. G. Grosser (Hamburg: Nagel, 1963), 18–36.

13. For an extensive account of the complex negotiations between Horkheimer and the University of Frankfurt, see Wiggershaus, *Die Frankfurter Schule*, 442–54, 473–84.

14. Even the appointment to the position of *Rektor* was seen as part of *Wiedergutmachung* by the city of Frankfurt. See Anson Rabinbach, 'The Jewish Question in the German Question,' *New German Critique* 44 (spring–summer 1988): 159–92.

15. With regard to Humboldt's reform, see Peter Uwe Hohendahl, 'Reform als Utopie: Die preußische Bildungspolitik, 1809–1817,' in *Utopieforschung: Interdisziplinäre Studien zur neuzeitlichen Utopie*, ed. Wilhelm Voßkamp (Stuttgart: Metzler, 1982), 3:250–72; also Karl Ernst Jeismann, *Das preußische Gymnasium in Staat und Gesellschaft: Die Entstehung des Gymnasiums als Schule des Staates und der Gebildeten, 1787–1817* (Stuttgart: Klett, 1974).

16. See Friedrich Meinecke, *Die deutsche Katastrophe* (Wiesbaden: Brockhaus, 1946).

17. See Michael P. Steinberg, 'The Musical Absolute,' *New German Critique* 56 (spring–summer 1992): 17–42.

18. See Jay, *The Dialectical Imagination*; also Wiggershaus, *Die Frankfurter Schule*, 224 ff.

19. Adorno's contributions to it, however, are now easily accessible in GS 9 (2): 121–324, under the title *Schuld und Abwehr: Eine qualitative Analyse zum Gruppenexperiment*; all quotations are translated from this edition. For the full study, see Friedrich Pollock, *Gruppenexperiment* (Frankfurt am Main: Europäische Verlagsaustelt, 1955).

20. Peter R. Hofstätter (1913–) retired from the University of Hamburg in 1979. He served in the army throughout the war, first as a psychol-

ogist and then in combat. From 1949 to 1956 he lived in the United States, where he held positions at the Massachusetts Institute of Technology and Catholic University in Washington DC; American social psychology had a strong and lasting influence on his work. In 1960 he joined the faculty at Hamburg, where he served as director of the university's Institute for Psychology. Hofstätter's review of the *Gruppenexperiment* appeared in *Kölner Zeitschrift für Soziologie und Sozialpsychologie 9* (1957): 97–105.

21. For a critical discussion of the West German restoration, see the important essay by Walter Dirks, 'Der restaurative Charakter der Epoche,' in *Frankfurter Hefte 5* (1950): 942–54; also Dietrich Tränhardt, *Geschichte der Bundesrepublik Deutschland* (Frankfurt am Main: Suhrkamp, 1986), 97–113.

22. In the writings of the historian and Heidegger disciple Ernst Nolte, this argument still plays an important role; see, e.g., his recent biography *Martin Heidegger: Politik und Geschichte im Leben und Denken* (Berlin: Propyläen, 1992).

23. For a study of the new Germany, see Ralf Dahrendorf, *Gesellschaft und Demokratie in Deutschland* (München: R. Piper, 1965), trans. as *Society and Democracy in Germany* (Garden City NY: Doubleday, 1967).

24. Adorno's 'Was bedeutet Aufarbeitung der Vergangenheit?' appears in English in *Bitburg in Moral and Political Perspective*, ed. Geoffrey Hartman (Bloomington: Indiana University Press, 1986).

25. There was, however, a strong movement for greater educational reform; a general overview may be found in the UNESCO report *Zur Bildungsreform in der Bundesrepublik Deutschland,* available in English as *Educational Reform in the Federal Republic of Germany* (Hamburg: UNESCO Institute for Education, 1970). See also Jürgen Habermas, *Technik und Wissenschaft als 'Ideologie'* (Frankfurt am Main: Suhrkamp, 1968), and *Protestbewegung und Hochschulreform* (Frankfurt am Main: Suhrkamp, 1969); portions of these have been collected and translated in Jeremy J. Shapiro, ed., *Toward a Rational Society: Student Protest, Science, and Politics* (Boston: Beacon Press, 1970).

26. It should be noted that Adorno's suspicion was probably caused by the very high degree of anti-Semitism expressed by the rural population in the *Gruppenexperiment.*

27. There is no empirical evidence for this claim; it must be seen as part of the topical opposition of town and country.

28. For an examination of the student movement, Heins Bude and Martin Kohli, eds., *Radikalisierte Aufklärung: Studentenbewegung und*

Soziologie in Berlin 1965 bis 1970 (Weinheim, Germany: Juventa, 1989); and Ulrich Schallwig, *Die Studentenbewegung der Sechziger Jahre in den USA und der BRD: Zur sozialwissenschaftlichen Perzeption jugendlichen Protestverhaltens* (Duisburg, Germany: Verlag der Sozialwissenschaftlichen Kooperative, 1983). Works in English include Ronald Fraser et al., *1968: A Student Generation in Revolt* (New York: Pantheon, 1988); and Cyril Levitt, *Children of Privilege: Student Revolt in the Sixties* (Toronto: University of Toronto Press, 1984).

29. Adorno, 'Resignation,' *Telos* 35 (spring 1978): 167 (GS 10 [2]: 784–99).

30. See Axel Honneth, *Kritik der Macht: Reflexionsstufen einer kritischen Gesellschaftstheorie* (Frankfurt am Main: Suhrkamp, 1985).

31. See Honneth, *Kritik der Macht,* 86.

32. See GS 8: 83. Adorno cites Freud's 'Über eine Weltanschauung' from the 'Neue Folge der Vorlesungen zur Einführung in die Psychoanalyse' (*Gesammelte Werke* [London: Imago, 1940], 15: 194): 'Sociology as well, dealing as it does with the behavior of men in society, can be nothing other than applied psychology.' The standard translation is 'The Question of a Weltanschauung,' in *The Standard Edition of the Complete Psychological Works of Sigmund Freud,* ed. James Strachey (London: Hogarth Press, 1953), 22: 179.

33. Adorno, 'Sociology and Psychology' (p.2), *New Left Review* 47 (1968): 96.

34. See Adorno, 'Sociology and Psychology' (p.1), *New Left Review* 46 (1967): 71.

35. See Adorno, 'Kritik,' GS 10 (2): 785–93.

CHAPTER 4

1. As a general assessment of Adorno's criticism with an emphasis on music, see Jameson, *Marxism and Form;* also, more recently, David Roberts, *Art and Enlightenment: Aesthetic Theory after Adorno* (Lincoln: University of Nebraska Press, 1991).

2. Samuel Weber in PR 11.

3. Samuel Weber in PR 15.

4. Georg Lukács, *Soul and Form,* trans. Anna Bostock (Cambridge: MIT Press, 1974).

5. Adorno, 'Reconciliation under Duress,' in *Aesthetics and Politics,* trans. and ed. Ronald Taylor (London: NLB, 1977), 151–76 (GS 11: 251–80).

6. Adorno, 'Commitment,' in Arato and Gebhardt, *The Essential Frankfurt School Reader,* 300–318; also NL 2: 177–95 (GS 11: 409–30).

7. See Bernd Witte, *Walter Benjamin, der Intellektuelle als Kritiker: Untersuchung zu seinem Frühwerk* (Stuttgart: Metzler, 1976).

8. See Susan Buck-Morss, *The Origin of Negative Dialectics: Theodor W. Adorno, Walter Benjamin, and the Frankfurt Institute* (New York: Free Press, 1977).

9. Adorno, 'Letters to Walter Benjamin,' and Benjamin, 'Reply,' in *Aesthetics and Politics*, 110–41.

10. Adorno, 'Rückblickend auf den Surrealismus,' GS 11: 101–5 ('Looking Back on Surrealism,' NL 1: 86–90).

11. See Terry Eagleton, *Walter Benjamin, or, Towards a Revolutionary Criticism* (London: Verso, 1981); Michael W. Jennings, *Dialectical Images: Walter Benjamin's Theory of Literary Criticism* (Ithaca NY: Cornell University Press, 1987).

12. Adorno, 'Bach Defended against His Devotees,' P 133–46 (GS 10 [1]: 138–51).

13. Adorno, 'Zu einem Porträt Thomas Manns,' GS 11: 335–44.

14. Adorno, 'Der Artist als Statthalter,' GS 11:114–26; 'Valérys Abweichungen,' GS 11:158–202.

15. Adorno, 'Notes on Kafka,' PR 243–71 (GS 10 [1]: 254–87).

16. Walter Benjamin, *Reflections: Essays, Aphorisms, Autobiographical Writings*, trans. Edmund Jephcott, ed. Peter Demetz (New York: Harcourt Brace Jovanovich, 1978).

17. Adorno, 'On the Fetish Character in Music and the Regression of Listening,' in Arato and Gebhardt, *The Essential Frankfurt School Reader*, 270–99; 'Über den Fetischcharakter in der Musik und die Regression des Hörers,' GS 14: 14–50.

18. Georg Lukács, *Deutsche Realisten des 19. Jahrhunderts* (Berlin: Aufbau-Verlag, 1953), 49–65.

19. Freiherr Joseph von Eichendorff, 'Erlebtes: I. Der Adel und die Revolution,' in *Gesammelte Schriften*, vol.10, *Historische, politische und biographische Schriften* (Regensburg: Verlag von J. Habbel, n.d.), 383–406.

20. See Karl Immermann, *Die Epigonen* (Düsseldorf, 1836).

21. Adorno, 'Voraussetzung: Aus Anlaß einer Lesung von Hans G. Helms,' GS 11: 431–46.

CHAPTER 5

1. For background, see the comprehensive study by Jost Hermand, *Kultur im Wiederaufbau: Die Bundesrepublik, 1945–1965* (München: Nymphenburger Verlagshandlung, 1986).

2. Karl Kraus, *Heine und die Folgen* (München: Langen, 1910).

3. In his essay 'On the Question: "What Is German?"' Adorno underscored that the German language was special, since it was more able 'to express something about the phenomena which does not exhaust

itself in their mere this-ness, their positivity and given-ness' (*New German Critique* 36 [fall 1985]: 129; GS 10 [2]: 691–701). For Adorno, Heine's prose style was a threat to this potential.

4. Heinrich Heine, *Sämtliche Schriften*, vol. 1, ed. Klaus Briegleb (München: Hanser, 1968), 108.

5. The English translation is taken from *The Complete Poems of Heinrich Heine: A Modern English Version*, trans. H. Draper (Cambridge MA: Suhrkamp/Insel, 1982), 77.

6. For the historical context, see Sander L. Gilman, *Jewish Self-Hatred, Anti-Semitism, and the Hidden Language of the Jews* (Baltimore: Johns Hopkins University Press, 1986), 167–87.

7. See Ludwig Rosenthal, *Heinrich Heine als Jude* (Frankfurt: Ullstein, 1973); Hartmut Kircher, *Heinrich Heine und das Judentum* (Bonn: Bouvier, 1973); Ruth L. Jacobi, *Heinrich Heines jüdisches Erbe* (Bonn: Bouvier, 1978).

8. See Jeffrey L. Sammons, *Heinrich Heine: A Modern Biography* (Princeton: Princeton University Press, 1979), 35–42.

9. Hannah Arendt, *Die verborgene Tradition* (Frankfurt am Main: Suhrkamp, 1976), 52.

10. See the extensive treatment in S. S. Prawer, *Heine's Jewish Comedy: A Study of His Portraits of Jews and Judaism* (Oxford: Clarendon Press, 1983).

11. Gerhard Sauder, 'Blasphemisch-religiöse Körperwelt: Heinrich Heines "Hebräische Melodien," ' in *Heinrich Heine: Artistik und Engagement*, ed. Wolfgang Kuttenkeuler (Tübingen: Metzler, 1977), 140.

12. Jay, 'The Jews and the Frankfurt School,' 90–100. See also Dan Diner, 'Reason and the "Other": Horkheimer on Anti-Semitism and Mass-Annihilation,' in Benhabib et al., *On Max Horkheimer*, 335–63.

13. GS 10: 555–72; trans. in Hartman, *Bitburg in Moral and Political Perspective*.

14. See Eric A. Blackall, *The Emergence of German as a Literary Language, 1700–1775* (London: Cambridge University Press, 1959).

15. After his American exile Adorno enriched his vocabulary by integrating English words. See Stuart Hughes, *The Sea Change: The Migration of Social Thought, 1930–1965* (New York: Harper & Row, 1975), 166.

CHAPTER 6

1. Collins, *Uncommon Cultures*.

2. For the relationship between Critical Theory and the contemporary American discourse on popular culture, see chapter 2.

3. For a good summary of the German discussion of the 1960s and 1970s, see Jochen Schulte-Sasse, *Literarische Wertung*, 2d rev. ed. (Stuttgart: Metzler, 1976).

4. See Hans Magnus Enzensberger, 'The Aporias of the Avant Garde,' in *The Consciousness Industry* (New York: Seabury Press, 1974), 16–41.

5. Christa Bürger, *Textanalyse als Ideologiekritik: Zur Rezeption zeitgenössischer Unterhaltungsliteratur* (Frankfurt am Main: Athenäum/ Fischer, 1973).

6. Peter Bürger, *The Theory of the Avant-Garde* (Minneapolis: University of Minnesota Press, 1984).

7. Typical is the work of Hans Robert Jauss: e.g., *Toward an Aesthetic of Reception*, trans. Timothy Bahti (Minneapolis: University of Minnesota Press, 1982).

8. Helmut Kreuzer, 'Trivialliteratur als Forschungsproblem,' in *Veränderungen des Literaturbegriffs* (Göttingen: Vandenhoeck & Ruprecht, 1975), 7–26.

9. The exception was the research on working-class literature, which at least in part challenged the aesthetic theory of bourgeois high culture, arguing that in making generalized validity claims it blocked the development of a genuine working-class literature.

10. Umberto Eco, *Travels in Hyperreality* (1983; San Diego: Harcourt Brace Jovanovich, 1986), 154.

11. Modleski, *Studies in Entertainment*, x.

12. Collins, *Uncommon Cultures*, 8, 10.

13. See also Adorno, 'Fetish Character in Music.'

14. Jameson, *Late Marxism*. For a more detailed discussion of Jameson's position, see below.

15. For detailed discussion of the American film industry, see Douglas Gomery, *The Hollywood Studio System* (New York: St. Martin's Press, 1986).

16. Still, Adorno kept a critical distance from Huxley's kind of culture critique, which struck him as ultimately nostalgic. See his 'Aldous Huxley and Utopia' (P 95–118; GS 10 [1]: 97–122).

17. David Harvey, *The Condition of Postmodernity: An Enquiry into the Origins of Cultural Change* (Cambridge: Basil Blackwell, 1989), 135–36.

18. See also (with a decidedly different emphasis) Siegfried Kracauer, 'The Mass Ornament,' *New German Critique* 5 (spring 1975): 67–76; and Martin Jay's critical comparison in 'Mass Culture and Aesthetic Redemption: The Debate between Max Horkheimer and Siegfried Kracauer,' in Benhabib et al., *On Max Horkheimer*, 365–86.

19. Harvey, *The Condition of Postmodernity,* 134.
20. Ibid., 129.
21. A similar point of view was expressed by Herbert Marcuse in 'Some Social Implications of Modern Technology' (1941), in Arato and Gebhardt, *The Essential Frankfurt School Reader,* 138–62.
22. Adorno, 'Culture Industry Reconsidered,' *New German Critique* 6 (fall 1975): 12–19 (GS 10 [1]: 337–45).
23. For a more extensive discussion of the concepts of the artwork and aesthetic autonomy, see chapter 8.
24. Adorno, 'Culture Industry Reconsidered,' 17.
25. Adorno, 'Transparencies on Film,' *New German Critique* 24–25 (fall–winter 1981–82): 199–205 (GS 10 [1]: 353–61).
26. Miriam Hansen, 'Introduction to Adorno's "Transparencies on Film,"' *New German Critique* 24–25 (fall–winter 1981–82): 186–98.
27. Hansen, Introduction, 190.
28. See Hanns Eisler, *Composing for the Films* (New York: Oxford University Press, 1947). There are two versions of the German text, first, Eisler's version, published in East Germany in 1948 without the mention of Adorno's name; second, Adorno's version in GS 15. According to Adorno's postscript, he wrote about 90 percent of the text. The two versions differ significantly; the common *Urfassung* (original version) of Adorno and Eisler has not yet been reconstructed.
29. Adorno, 'Transparencies,' 200.
30. Adorno, 'Transparencies,' 203–4.
31. See also Thomas V. Levin, 'For the Record: Adorno on Music in the Age of Its Technological Reproducibility,' *October* 55 (winter 1990): 23–64. This thorough and highly suggestive essay calls attention to Adorno's early involvement with technical recording: the young Adorno hailed the record (*Platte*) as a new form of language, an indexical form superior to arbitrary language systems; this interpretation of the record as a form of writing allowed him to praise technological innovation. In fact, he suggested that the production of a record should proceed analogously to the production of film: it should employ the principle of montage. Levin rightly underscores the importance of this argument for Adorno's position on mass culture. His findings make it clear that Adorno was not the foe of technology as which he is frequently portrayed in the debate on mass culture.
32. It is interesting to see that Eisler remained very skeptical, objecting to the use of twelve-tone music, for example, on the grounds that formalist techniques would not enhance the true function of music within a film (GS 16:49).

33. Adorno, 'Fetish Character in Music,' 278.
34. For a detailed analysis of Adorno's problem with popular music, see Gendron, 'Theodor Adorno Meets the Cadillacs,' 18–36.
35. Adorno, 'On Popular Music,' 19.
36. Adorno, 'On Popular Music,' 19.
37. Huyssen, 'Adorno in Reverse,' 16–43.
38. In this respect, Richard Strauss's oeuvre comes to mind. For Adorno, the composer continued and radicalized Wagner's style up to *Salomé*; beginning with *Der Rosenkavalier* he returned to a more traditional style and thus regained his public prestige as Germany's foremost composer but did so, in Adorno's eyes, at the expense of a consistent working-through of the aesthetic material. See Adorno, 'Richard Strauss,' GS 16:565–606. For an excellent discussion of Adorno's *Philosophy of Modern Music* (New York, 1973) and its historical position, see Roberts, *Art and Enlightenment*.
39. See Hansen, 'Mass Culture as "Hieroglyphic Writing," ' 43–73; Hansen also underlines the need for a reassessment of Adorno's position on mass culture and calls attention to his use of the concept of writing (hieroglyph) for the analysis of film. Drawing on *Dialectic of Enlightenment*, esp. the section 'The Schema of Mass Culture,' Hansen argues that for Adorno, film production in a monopolistic culture entails a return to the origins of language (in the form of hieroglyphs) that predates phonological language; that the production and reception of film (images) participates in the dialectic of enlightenment as a dialectic that turns on itself. As Adorno notes: 'Dialectic, on the contrary, interprets every image as writing. It shows how the admission of its falsity is to be read in the lines of its features – a confession that deprives it of its own power and appropriates it for truth' (GS 3:41; DE 24).
40. Hansen, 'Mass Culture as "Hieroglyphic Writing," ' 54, emphasizes two kinds of readings, which she defines as a literal deciphering (economic and social), and a figurative decoding that stresses the enigmatic character of art as *écriture*.
41. Jameson, 'Reification,' 130–48.
42. Jameson, 'Reification,' 137.
43. See Scott Lash and John Urry, *The End of Organized Capitalism* (Madison: University of Wisconsin Press, 1987).
44. E. Swyngedouw, 'The Socio-Spatial Implications of Innovations in Industrial Organization,' working paper no.20, Johns Hopkins European Center for Regional Planning and Research, Lille, 1986.
45. See Collins, *Uncommon Cultures*, n.1.

46. See esp. Pollock, 'State Capitalism,' 71–94.

47. For a critique of this position, see Hohendahl, *Building a National Literature*, 307–51.

48. Jameson, *Late Marxism*, 144.

49. See Raymond Williams, *Marxism and Literature* (Oxford: Oxford University Press, 1977).

CHAPTER 7

1. See Lucien Goldmann, *Pour une sociologie du roman* (Paris: Gallimard, 1964); and Goldmann, *Recherches dialectiques* (Paris: Gallimard, 1959).

2. See Jauss, *Toward an Aesthetic of Reception.*

3. In his later work, in open contrast to Adorno, Jauss emphasizes the elements of pleasure and communication in the artwork; see Jauss, *Aesthetic Experience and Literary Hermeneutics,* trans. Michael Shaw (Minneapolis: University of Minnesota Press, 1982).

4. See Emil Staiger's famous interpretation of Mörike's poem 'Auf eine Lampe,' in Emil Staiger, Martin Heidegger, and Leo Spitzer, 'A 1951 Dialogue on Interpretation,' PMLA 105 (May 1990):409–35.

5. Adorno, 'Theses on the Sociology of Art,' *Working Papers in Cultural Studies* 2 (spring 1972):121–28 (GS 10 [1]: 367–74).

6. See Dubiel, *Wissenschaftsorganisation.*

7. Adorno, 'Society,' in *The Legacy of the German Refugee Intellectuals,* ed. Robert Beyers (New York: Schocken Books, 1972), 147 (GS 8:12).

8. Ibid., 151 (GS 8:17).

9. See Alfons Silbermann, 'Kunst,' in *Soziologie,* ed. René König (Frankfurt am Main: S. Fischer, 1958).

10. See Norbert Fügen, *Die Hauptrichtungen der Literatursoziologie* (Bonn: Bouvier, 1966).

11. See Jay, *Marxism and Totality,* 241–75.

12. The English translation goes far beyond the German edition in its attempt to give readers the impression of a 'normal' book that follows the logic of chapters and paragraphs. This impression is misleading.

13. See Adorno, 'Commitment,' 300–318 (NL 2:177–95; GS 11:409–430).

14. See Goldmann, *Pour une sociologie du roman.*

15. See Piccone, General Introduction to Arato and Gebhardt, *The Essential Frankfurt School Reader,* esp. xvii.

16. Fredric Jameson, *The Political Unconscious: Narrative as a Socially Symbolic Act* (Ithaca NY: Cornell University Press, 1981); see also, more recently, Jameson, *Late Marxism.*

17. See Eagleton, *Walter Benjamin.*

18. For this critique, see Louis Althusser, *For Marx* (London: Verso, 1979).

19. Jameson, *The Political Unconscious,* 39.

20. This line of argument pushes into the background the aspect of mimesis; for a more detailed discussion, see Josef Früchtle, *Mimesis: Konstellation eines Zentralbegriffs bei Adorno* (Würzburg: Königshausen & Neumann, 1986).

21. See Jameson, *The Political Unconscious,* 42.

22. Terry Eagleton, *Criticism and Ideology: A Study in Marxist Literary Theory* (London: Verso, 1978), 45.

23. Eagleton, *Criticism and Ideology,* 49.

24. Eagleton, *Criticism and Ideology,* 47.

25. Eagleton, *Criticism and Ideology,* 48.

CHAPTER 8

1. For an analogous situation in the United States, where deconstruction took over the institutional position of New Criticism, see Frank Lentricchia, *After the New Criticism* (Chicago: University of Chicago Press, 1990).

2. See Jameson, *Late Marxism,* 3–12.

3. With respect to Heine's modernity, see Albrecht Betz, *Ästhetik und Politik: Heinrich Heines Prosa* (München: Hanser, 1971); Peter Uwe Hohendahl, *The Institution of Criticism* (Ithaca NY: Cornell University Press, 1982), 83–125.

4. See Bürger, *Theory of the Avant-Garde.*

5. For this reason, Bürger concludes that Adorno's aesthetic theory remained basically a theory of modernism; he describes accordingly its concept of the artwork as *organizistisch* (organic) and represents the avant-garde by fragmentary artworks and the principle of montage. In this context, Bürger reads Adorno's hostility toward Igor Stravinsky as a polemic against the avant-garde (*Theory of the Avant-Garde,* 83–94). Yet Bürger's attempt to link Adorno exclusively with the project of modernism overlooks the emphasis on contradictions and tensions within the modern artwork, its fragmentary nature and its lack of permanent closure. Thus, in the case of *Aesthetic Theory,* a principal distinction between modernism and the avant-garde remains unsatisfactory.

6. See Harvey, *The Condition of Postmodernity,* 338–42.

7. 'The most external form in which the notion of an enigmatic quality of art can be conceived is in terms of whether or not there is meaning. There is no work of art that does not address, in one way or

273

another, the problem of the complex of meaning. Complex of meaning (*Sinnzusammenhang*), however, presupposes the objectivity of meaning as such, because art objectifies itself in works' (GS 7:193; AT 185).

8. 'Preceding these prehistorical pictures must have been an evolution of a mimetic mode of behavior, which is the assimilation of the self to another. Mimesis is not the same as the superstitious belief in the ability to have a direct impact on things. In fact, had there not been, over a long period of time, a considerable differentiation between mimesis and magic, the striking features of autonomous elaboration in the cave drawings would be inexplicable' (GS 7:487; AT 453).

9. Adorno's reading of Goethe's play *Iphigenie* exemplifies such a reception. In 'Zum Klassizismus von Goethes Iphigenie' he emphasizes the tensions between the mythical level and the dimension of enlightenment (NL 2:153–70; GS 11:495–514).

10. See Jameson, *Late Marxism*, esp. 1–14.

11. Jameson, *Late Marxism*, 246.

12. See Peter Bürger, 'Adorno's Anti-Avantgardism,' *Telos* 86 (winter 1990–91), 49–60.

13. For Adorno's critique of Benjamin on aura and technology montage and the avant-garde, see Walter Benjamin, *Gesammelte Schriften*, ed. Rolf Tiedemann and Hermann Schweppenhäuser (Frankfurt am Main: Suhrkamp, 1974), 1 (3):1000–1006.

14. See, e.g., Peter Uwe Hohendahl, 'The Autonomy of Art: Looking Back at Adorno's *Ästhetische Theorie*,' in *Reappraisals: Shifting Alignments in Postwar Critical Theory* (Ithaca NY: Cornell University Press, 1991), 75–98.

15. See Harvey, *The Condition of Postmodernity*, 327–42.

16. Nägele, 'The Scene of the Other,' 59–79.

17. See Jochen Hörisch, 'Herrscherwort, Geld und geltende Sätze: Adornos Aktualisierung der Frühromantik und ihre Affinität zur poststrukturalistischen Kritik des Subjekts,' in *Materialien zur ästhetischen Theorie Th. W. Adornos Konstruktion der Moderne*, ed. Burghardt Lindner and W. Martin Lüdtke (Frankfurt am Main: Suhrkamp, 1980), 397–414.

CHAPTER 9

1. See Benjamin, *Reflections*; Richard Wolin, *Walter Benjamin: An Aesthetic of Redemption* (Berkeley: University of California Press, 1994), 31–47; Michael W. Jennings, *Dialectical Images: Walter Benjamin's Theory of Literary Criticism* (Ithaca NY: Cornell University Press, 1987), 82–120.

2. Adorno, 'Why Philosophy?' in *Man and Philosophy*, ed. Walter Leifer (München, 1964), 15 (GS 10 [2]: 463).

3. Adorno, 'Why Philosophy?' 17 (GS 10 [2]: 465–66).

4. Adorno, 'Why Philosophy?' 18 (GS 10 [2]: 466).

5. Adorno, 'Why Philosophy?' 23 (GS 10 [2]: 471).

6. Adorno, 'The Actuality of Philosophy,' *Telos* 31 (spring 1977):131.

7. See Buck-Morss, *The Origin of Negative Dialectics*.

8. 'Certainly the immanent critique of epistemology itself is not exempt from the dialectic. While philosophy of immanence – the equivocation between logical and epistemological immanence indicates a central structure – can only be ruptured immanently, i.e., in confrontation with its own untruth, its immanence itself is untruth' (AE 25; GS 5:32).

9. See Buck-Morss, *The Origin of Negative Dialectics*.

10. Walter Benjamin, 'On Language as Such and on the Language of Man,' in *Reflections*. For a rigorous reading of Benjamin's theory of language, see also Winfried Menninghaus, *Benjamins Theorie der Sprechmagie* (Frankfurt am Main: Suhrkamp, 1980), esp. 9–11.

11. Benjamin, 'On Language,' 316.

12. In the writings of Benjamin, mimesis plays an equally important role. In more general terms, he defines mimesis as *unsinnliche Ähnlichkeit* (nonsensual similarity); more specifically, he understands mimetic language as the capability of approximating nature, ultimately becoming one with nature. In 'On the Mimetic Faculty' (*Reflections*, 333–36), Benjamin argues that writing (*Schrift*) consists of an archive of nonsensual correlations between sign and nature. Therefore, he also suggests the possibility of reading nature as a configuration of hieroglyphs. See also Früchtl, *Mimesis*, 17–29.

CHAPTER 10

1. See Christoph Menke, *Die Souveränität der Kunst: Ästhetische Erfahrung nach Adorno und Derrida* (Frankfurt am Main: Suhrkamp, 1991).

2. See Niklas Luhmann, *Soziale Systeme: Grundriß einer allgemeinen Theorie* (Frankfurt am Main: Suhrkamp, 1984).

3. See Roberts, *Art and Enlightenment*, esp. 154–73.

4. Herbert Schnädelbach, 'Die Aktualität der *Dialektik der Aufklärung*,' in *Die Aktualität der Dialektik der Aufklärung*, ed. Harry Kunneman and Went de Vries (Frankfurt am Main: Campus Verlag, 1989).

5. See Menke, *Die Souveränität der Kunst*, 189–91, 260–66.

Index

✳